D1522107

"I'd Give My Life"

From Washington Square to Carnegie Hall

A Journey by Folk Music

Erik Darling

*To my BEST FRIEND, CHRIS
HAPPY 65TH BIRTHDAY!
LOTS OK GOOD MILES BEHIND YOU —
AND LOTS OF GOOD MILES TO GO.*

Of the Tarriers, Weavers, and Rooftop Singers
("The Banana Boat Song," "Goodnight, Irene," "Walk Right In")

Science and Behavior Books, Inc.
Palo Alto, California

Copyright © 2008 by Erik Darling

All rights reserved. No part of this book may be reproduced
without permission from the publisher.

Printed in the United States of America

Library of Congress Control Number 2008924076

ISBN 978-0-8314-0093-4 (hardcover)

Editing by Rain Blockley
Interior design by BookMasters, Inc.
Cover design by Jim Marin
Typesetting by BookMasters, Inc.
Printing by BookMasters, Inc.

To Joni & Bill

Thank you for sharing the struggle,
and renewing my cars.

Contents

Gratitude   vii

Introductory Notes   ix

Book   I.   Washington Square   1
        II.   The Tarriers   73
        III.   The Weavers   125
        IV.   The Rooftop Singers   179
        V.   Political Quagmire   247
        VI.   Reflection and Triumph   255

Afterword   279

About the C.D.   281

Discography of Erik Darling   287

Index   289

Gratitude

I am grateful to those without whom these pages could not have the detail, depth, or reconstruction of time and events that they have: to Dave Samuelson, who suggested I write them in the first place; and then to Joan Darling, Pat Street, Alan Arkin, Pete Seeger, Bill Svanøe, Bess Lomax Hawes, Frank Hamilton, Allan Shaw, Nick Reynolds, Ada Brown, Tony Price, Billy Faier, Dick Rosmini, Don McLean, Heidi Wilson, Roger Sprung, Tommy Geraci, Susan Holt, Susan Warner, Bob Spitzer, Richard McCord, Steve Rada, Jennifer Reasoner, old Uncle Tom Cobley, and all.

Introductory Notes

Emerging from Greenwich Village's burgeoning folk scene of the mid-fifties, Erik Darling pulled off the impossible. During an era when Elvis Presley, Little Richard, Chuck Berry and the Platters dominated A.M. radio, his folk trio, the Tarriers, scored a Top-4 hit in 1956 with "The Banana Boat Song." Besides fueling a brief national mania for calypso, the Tarriers laid the foundation for the Kingston Trio and the many folk groups that followed. After four years with the Weavers, Darling formed the Rooftop Singers, an innovative folk/jazz trio that topped the charts with "Walk Right In" and introduced twelve-string guitars to popular music. More suited to introspection than self-promotion, Darling maintained a deep-seated integrity and restless curiosity that stands in sharp contrast to the usual *modus operandi* of the American entertainment business. Looking beyond the hit records, concert performances and colorful personalities, this book documents Darling's journey towards self-discovery.
—Dave Samuelson
   Music Historian/producer

Erik and I schlepped halfway around the world together for a couple of years when we were both twenty-two—singing, laughing, analyzing everything and everyone in sight—and every single moment of that time was filled with joy and generosity, humor, and a great sense of discovery. His passion is always about the work. You never see a hint of ego in the process. Ever. He'll change anything and everything to make the work better.
—Alan Arkin
   Actor

You might find it hard to believe, but I don't like "folk music" all that much. At best, it was a transitional musical form in its commercial context, and the records made by its practitioners are all but unlistenable, sadly. I can still listen to Josh White, The Weavers, and Erik Darling. Erik has a special talent. He is a group singer, a soloist, and an instrumentalist. This doesn't tell you much about him, really, so let me attempt to clarify.

Erik was the first white person whom I thought of as a guitar gunslinger. If you listen to the song "True Religion," you can hear a white blues that has the intensity of something by Son House. All these years later, Erik's performances hold up. They are "timeless." This is a plateau we, as musicians, seek.

Erik never dressed like a folk singer—that is, like a "bean picker," as Woody Guthrie did, or Pete Seeger. He looked more like a beat poet or an actor. Listen to the song "Train Time." This is not folk music, this is a French movie or a beat poem set to music. I realized only recently how much this track influenced me to try new guitar approaches and philosophical layers. The song is a recitation about moments in time: a depot man is speaking, and when the train roars by him, he says, "There's one thing that I know. I'm alive!" Being completely alive in the moment has been Erik's way of life through music.
—Don McLean
    Singer/songwriter

I know of no better first-hand account of the onset of a panic disorder in the psychiatric literature than the account written in this book. What we can all learn is how to use such adversity and grow from it. Darling's description of treatment with Dr. Leonard is fascinating and hilarious.

Bob Dylan's autobiography shows us some of the same people and times. Washington Square was where folk singers found each other and learned their trade. I don't know how Erik Darling and Bob Dylan learned to write so well. They each strive for authenticity. These people, who are so creative and productive in many areas, have a remarkable ability to maintain and focus our attention. They are the self-actualizing people that humanist psychologist Abraham Maslow wrote about. But they are also ordinary folk and have much to share.
—Robert S. Spitzer, M.D.
    Psychiatrist

Book I

Washington Square

These recollections are of overlapping experience, much like an impressionist painting: the colors make sense only when seen from afar, as they all come together behind the last words. And although the account is about time (the middle 1950s to now) and places (New York, London, Milan, Greenwich Village, Israel, Paris, Mexico, and upstate New York), it is more about the distance between conscious and unconscious awareness. It is the story, as well, of others who traveled a similar path, and I've given them space in these pages.

1

"In Scarlet Town, where I was born . . ."

In the House of My Father

David Thurston Darling, my father, I knew as an artist, a man, an apostle, if you will, although he didn't sermonize, preach, or give lectures. His religion had no heaven or hell, and its reward came from the day-to-day living it out; some of its virtues were held in the drawing of a line that had life, or the creation of work that compelled in some way, told a truth, or reminded him of why it was good to be human.

I never thought to ask what attracted my father to art, why it had become a life force, or what made him think as an artist. More to the point, I didn't comprehend that it was anything other than how we lived life at the time, that it had any validity, or that he was passing that sort of thing over to me. He unwittingly taught by the way of his being, stuff I could feel by living nearby, sleeping in the same room, watching him rise every morning, or the way he liked coffee or looked out at the lake. The temple he lived in and painted from was nature. He wasn't a Sunday-church-goer, he went to his church every day. His world passed over to mine in an endless flow of such things as spotting a tree toad the size of the end of your pinkie, watching a hawk, making note of the wind late at night.

We lived in a house he had built out of studding, covered with a thick, gray, cardboard-like material called Homasote, which came in four-by-eight–foot sheets. Built ten feet from the shore of Canandaigua Lake in upstate New York, the house was cold and damp in the winter, hot and damp in the summer. Medaglia d'Oro coffee, bacon fat, turpentine, gin, DDT, and nicotine flowed through my father's veins, along with his blood. Once DDT came on the market, we sprayed each other's backs in hot summers to keep away flies.

I called him Dave, like he was a man with a name, instead of that generic, impersonal "Father" or "Daddy" or "Dad." I've not the vaguest idea how that started. His hands would smell of old sailboat ropes, garlic, sawdust from woodcarvings, or fish scales, depending on what he'd been doing. The deodorant that pervaded the house was the clean smell of turpentine. To this day, turpentine brings up a feeling of comfort and home.

He painted everything from vulvas and flowers and pine trees and horse skulls to clouds flying over the lake. He looked at the human condition unclothed and up close to where authentic decency gathers. This drew him close to the skin of life, for he knew well the lines in the face of a charlatan, a braggart, a kind person, or a trustworthy one. An understanding of the human condition evolved far more, I think, than if he had studied sociology, scripture, or politics. I'm not sure I ever saw what he saw, as he saw it, but his style would keep me on this side of death, later on.

My school friends in upstate New York were the sons and daughters of farmers, and I occasionally slept over at the farm of one of my buddies, rode hay balers, and played in their haymows and bittersweet-smelling silos. A safety exists in growing miles of potatoes and corn, manufacturing shoelaces, or becoming a fanatic that is absent from being an artist, per se. The empty canvas or theater requires that you put something there that wasn't before. The one salient rule is: don't bore the audience.

Dave sometimes took me into the hills overlooking the lake to paint pictures. He would look at some tree and then back to the pad on his lap, rinse out a brush in a jar of water, flick it out, pull it to a point in his mouth, pick up a color he'd mixed, and then draw a quick line on the paper, while unwittingly shooing a bug from his head. In those moments, the broken-down car, the leak in the roof, and the bills that were due no longer had currency. Nor did he have to tell me to be quiet. That was an axiom of what he and I did as a family sometimes.

I think the rebel in me was born of these times, a commitment to personal values, moment to moment. This awareness was there when we walked along hedgerows with shotguns, waiting for pheasants to flush or rabbits to jump. This commitment was there as we sat at our breakfast on cold winter mornings looking at five miles of ice on the lake. It wasn't a rebellion of tantrum, of blowing things up, of adolescent angst or complaint, but rather a rebellion of painting the sky as you saw it, a rebellion of following your heart and not someone else's. You couldn't possibly dream of painting a painting to match someone's sofa or dining table. It was a belonging to God, perhaps, but not to The Church.

"My Brother"

Only a photo remains of my brother, bundled up in his carriage in the middle of winter on Canandaigua Lake, like an outtake from *Dr. Zhivago*. In his fifth year of life, he was caught in a motorboat fire on the boat of a friend of the family. Who the friend was, where the child was buried—such details were never discussed. Of his marriage to my mother, Dave said only that nothing was ever the same after my brother's death. There remained a child-sized space between my mother and father, and between them and me, I suspect. My father lived with an aura of sadness around him. As a kid, I picked up on his sense of the sad and the lonely. This may well have drawn me to folk music, among other things.

2

"Oh, I don't want to be a gambler,
And I'll tell you the reason why . . ."

Cripscule

Dave would take a piece of raw, week-old beef out of the refrigerator, cut off the greenish, rotted part, and fry it with butter and garlic in a thin, hot pan, filling the entire house with its smoke. As we didn't have closets with doors, all our clothes smelled of steak smoke. And I don't think he ever noticed. In France, they aged pheasants by hanging them from porch roofs by their necks, he told me, until they had fallen. Thank God he didn't do that. When he first took that meat out of the refrigerator, the stench and the look of that stuff made me want to throw up. The rule was, I didn't have to eat anything I didn't like, but I had to taste it, at least. I don't remember a thing I didn't like eating.

A black nun showed up at our back door asking for donations one time. Rare for upstate New York. He thought she was wonderful and gave her some money. One thing about Dave was that he didn't have a prejudiced bone in his body. Most of his acquaintances in upstate New York, however, used the word *nigger* as a regular term. Never, not once, did he ever use it. One day, a starched couple stopped their car on the West Lake road, next to our house, and asked where the religious retreat was.

"Oh, that. It's where the statue of old man Christ is, up on the hill," he shouted, pointing back down the road. His family's church had been Episcopalian, and he had found religion hypocritical, mean-spirited, and centered around exclusivity. The self-righteous, he thought, were a slap in the face of God, if there was one.

Lying in bed aware of the rustle of leaves when a storm blew up and both of us getting up to be sure that we had pulled up the canoe and turned it over, or we had moored the sailboat properly—these sorts of things drew us together. Dave had grown up on a farm and had known work horses, cow barns, pickaxes, chicken coops, crowbars, and ditch digging. He knew the names of the trees, which birds of the woods made which calls, and which mushrooms were edible. He was an earth person and took me with him out there.

When he swung his feet out of bed in the morning, he'd put on his glasses, then take an Old Gold cigarette butt from an art deco ashtray, light up, and inhale. Never did I see him without a cigarette. The last paying job he had before dying of lung cancer on October 21, 1958 (one of the few dates I will never forget), he was working at a fishing-tackle company, running a machine that coated fine cable-leader with plastic. Fred McKechnie, owner of the company, showed up at our house now and again when having trouble with his wife. Dave's house was a haven for disparate people who needed to get away from whatever it was. The huge windows that looked down the lake, the flycatchers and seagulls, the gin and bitters, and the calming effect of the water brought relaxation and peace to the place.

As we sat on the porch at twilight one summer, a slow outboard motor droned as it pulled a deep trolling line out on the lake, and that made it more quiet. After having been silent awhile, Dave said something odd. "Thousands of bugs get born, live their entire lives, and then die just in this time before dark. The French call it *crepuscule*." He pronounced it *cripscule*. It could have been the idleness with which he pondered this moment, or that I'd never heard of that word, or maybe he was just thinking of France, but it struck me that each of our lives in relation to the universe was unique, and that our experience had an immensity to it, a magic of some kind that mattered. A stillness crept over my heart. I don't know how else to put it. My relationship to living a life shifted, somehow. It was what mattered that counted, and not what people said mattered. Maybe this was why he loved the music of Beethoven.

My father at work
Paris, France

"Paris Rooftops"
Oil on canvas

Dave as a young man,
at the inlet of Canandaigua
Lake, New York

My father and me in a canoe
Canandaigua, New York

3

*"Goin' down to Lynchburg Town
To carry my tobacco down . . ."*

City of the Night

The phone rang in our house on a Sunday. I thought Volney Mosier might be coming up the lake with his Chris-Craft, and we would go water skiing or go up to the inlet where the great blue herons lived. Or, it might be my Aunt Laura calling, and we'd be going to town for a Sunday dinner, with biscuits and jelly, and pie. Later, maybe a movie.

This particular day, I knew by the tone of Dave's voice, it was Mollie, my mother, calling from New York. As their conversation went on, I could tell they were talking again about whether I should go live with her in New York. She felt I would get a better education in a prep school there than in the upstate public elementary school of Cheshire, New York.

I felt alone in the house, aware of the smell and the grain of our soft wood floors under my bare feet. Part of me wanted to stay with my father and be with our life by the lake, and part of me wanted New York. When I visited my mother, at night, before sleep, with the covers pulled up to my chin, I'd hear the car horns, the buses, the sirens, hundreds of sounds that suggested adventure. The clatter of the subways, the Fifth Avenue shop windows, Rockefeller Plaza with its statue of Atlas, the museum of Modern Art. I had eaten in Little Italy, Chinatown, and the Seafare Restaurant on Eighth Street, with Dave. Even though I'd always had difficulty getting along with my mother, I knew I would have my own room in my mother's apartment. But I didn't want my father to think that I didn't love him.

"Dave, how I love you. Yet I want a room of my own, and the city. I want an adventure, whatever it turns out to be, and that doesn't mean I don't love you. Is that okay? Can I come home when I need to?"

I didn't know how to say that. I would eventually be asked if I wanted to go, and I said, "Yes, I guess so," shrugging my shoulders, not sounding too eager. As well, I had learned a few chords on the guitar by this time, and I'd heard from a friend of my father's who lived in New York that there was a group of young people who sang folk songs in Washington Square.

At sixteen, I found myself living in my mother's apartment, 60 West 68th Street, apartment 2D, between Columbus and Central Park West. The apartment had two bedrooms, each with full bath, a living room, and a five-by-five New York kitchen. I had my own room with a window that opened on to the airshaft that came down through the building from ten stories up. If I opened the window, I could hear people's arguments echoing there.

My mother had remarried. She thought that would make us a "family," I think. However, her new husband, a self-proclaimed philosopher, didn't know if cabbages grew on trees or not. I thought this was ridiculous for a middle-aged man not to know. I mean, who ever heard of a cabbage tree? And one of the first things he said was that I was too young to understand his philosophy. At that point, I began noticing how stiff his neck was, how beads of sweat formed on his upper lip, and how his round, vacuous face didn't register much, except for a silent pasty-like arrogance. Whatever train we might have been on, I got off, and the city's complexity beckoned me into its world of tall buildings, museums, and singers at Washington Square.

4

*"I had no money to pay my fine, no one to go my bail.
So I got stuck for ninety days in the Portland County jail."*

On Trial

Mollie thought I should join my five uncles, go into her family's paint-manufacturing business (the Baltimore Paint and Color Works), have a house next to similar houses, with a tenth of an acre of lawn, separated by white picket fences, with a dog, a wife, and the kids. The American dream. One problem with that was, I had grown up in the woods, and grass didn't mean shit. My uncles' new cars, their suits, and their homes, however, made becoming a businessman seem like a good thing to do, an adult thing to do. My father had always complained about how our second-hand cars "nickeled you to death," and he thought my uncles were wonderful people.

Living the life of an artist had brought my mother nothing but pain and the death of a child. She often said, "We don't need another artist in the family." She said it as a half-joke, but it didn't feel funny. So the one agreement we might have shared became a contentiousness. On the other hand, to complicate things, I took it for granted that human survival depended more on house and road paint, among other responsible things in the world, than it did on art (or any purely creative activity). I didn't see the connection between creative thinking, per se, and all that's created, everywhere, anywhere. I was at odds with myself in the world, as well as with Mollie.

Meanwhile, when my mother took me to Baltimore to visit my uncles, one of them always took me on a tour of the paint plant. Workers poured cement-sized bags of pigment into the top of huge vats that extended to the floor below, and my eyes stung in these rooms. I saw where they stored paint, shipped paint, and tested and invented paint. Boxes and cans, wire handles, and packaging labels. In the bowels of the factory, lit by bare light bulbs, were dank, sodden, paint-spattered caverns—perfect places, I thought, for a murder by paint. I worked in the lab one summer, testing the viscosities of stored cans of paint to record how aging or heat changed their consistency.

There was always a day, however, every damned summer, when all five uncles gathered in my uncle Al's office to take a deposition on how I was getting along with my mother. She had asked them to see if they could get me to get along with her better. Being nine, ten, and eleven years old, I hadn't the vaguest idea where my mother or I was at. In my mind, these men were like gods, and I have to believe that they had not the slightest idea how distressing and painful those sessions were. It was like being on trial—only I had no lawyer.

"Look, fellows," I might have said, "I can't prove this to you, you'd have to be there. But I'm innocent. I'm the kid. You wanna know why it ain't going so well with my mother? Ask her. She's the adult. What is *she* doing?"

That sort of answer wasn't within five thousand miles of my brain. And I looked up to these guys and their view of the world, even though there was no way I couldn't live from my own point of view. I just didn't quite know what it was. Nonetheless, I had shot and skinned rabbits, plucked feathers off partridge we'd hunted, put worms on hooks, and gutted fish, so I knew there was a truth of things beyond all the stories. If you deal with a fishhook the wrong way, it ends up stuck in your hand, and it bleeds, and it hurts, and it must be pulled out, barb and all. Or, if you find yourself on a ridge in a gully and feel you can't move without slipping two hundred feet to your death, you can't complain about that; you know it's your fault. You get to know what's yours and what isn't, what you've earned, what you haven't. And I knew that I wasn't guilty.

Uncle Al, the president of the company, never said much in these meetings, and outside of these meetings, he was hard-edged, emotionally volatile, and critical of everyone, including me. He was an equal-opportunity critic. One time, I was sitting in his office, reading a book about all the laws that were still on the books (e.g., it's against the law to shoot rabbits off the back of the Third Avenue el) when he began berating my mother about something. They were at the far end of the office and I was at the other end of a long conference table, but I listened while pretending to be engrossed in the reading. "Don't say those things in front of Erik," she said. But he had. He may not have been a particularly kind person, as the term is generally meant, but he inadvertently gave me a sense of sanity that day, a sense of equality, in that he treated her just like he did me or anyone else. Suddenly, I was an equal.

If I were to be truly successful, however, it struck me that I would do well to become part of the family paint business, my mother being essentially right about that. And it was right there for the taking. I thought about having an office, a big desk; I'd be smoking a pipe, sitting back with my feet up, signing papers, and talking on the phone, like in the movies. My uncles had the nice cars, the new houses, the new dogs, the new lawns, the new children, and everyone's eyes blinked open and shut. Then one day I took the wrong bus.

5

The Breadth of Humanity

It was a double-decker open-air bus, which I caught at 65th and Fifth Avenue, running all the way down, past the Plaza Hotel, Tiffany's, Rockefeller Center, Lord and Taylor, and the Empire State Building. Its run ended at the arch at Washington Square, one block below Eighth Street. I took my guitar to the top of the bus and got the front seat—wind in my hair all the way down.

The fountain at the Square looked to be about fifty feet across, with deep, wide, low-profile steps leading down to its floor. At the center was a brass waterspout, which wasn't turned on. When my parents had lived over on Charles Street, before their divorce, the fountain was filled with water, and children sailed toy boats and splashed in the spray. Now, it was one-quarter filled with singers of folk songs, surrounded by onlookers. George Sprung sat on the top step of the fountain, three typewritten books of words on his lap. His brother, Roger, was playing a longneck, five-string banjo, and a few others strummed guitars, everyone singing full out.

I was mesmerized. One time, as I stood on the end of my father's dock in upstate New York, watching seagulls through a pair of new binoculars, I was entranced by the way they turned on invisible currents of air. They would come in by the dozens for bread we sailed out on the water. Caught up in my contemplation, I stepped off the end of the dock and plunged into the lake. The shock was astounding. As much as anything else, I was afraid I had screwed up the binoculars.

Hearing those folk songs was like watching the gulls, only when I walked off the end of the dock, I found this water warm and caressing. And I kept going back. These folk-song enthusiasts were a family I swore I would forever come back to. Some people talked of how when people "made it," they stopped coming down to the Square. I couldn't imagine what could possibly draw me or push me away.

People drifted into the Square from all over the country. You never knew who might turn up. Harry Belafonte (before he was known), Woody Guthrie, Oscar Brand, and Pete Seeger could show at the Square. No way on earth would I take out my guitar in front of these people, I thought. On subsequent Sundays, I discovered that people who didn't know the chord changes or songs sat on the outside of the circle and played quietly, until they caught on. Then, over time, they might move toward the center.

The singers of folk songs were New Yorkers, all ages, all colors, all sizes. No one can nail down what a New Yorker is, as no two people are truly the same. A Macy's saleswoman who had been at the store fifteen years, dealing with the breadth of humanity, didn't take any shit. Or an old New York waiter, twenty years at the same place—you would do well if you knew what you wanted before calling him over. After you've lived there a while and ride the subways in the middle of rush hour, packed in like a sardine, you become a New Yorker. You learn to spot con artists and to accept human weirdness and let it go by. When I ran across someone who was nuts, I usually knew it. Not so in L.A.

By late afternoon in the Square, the sun and the grime of New York seeped into my pores, while I seldom took time to eat or go pee. I might go a quarter block down Sullivan Street to a dark-green stand for an Italian lemon ice, spoon-packed into a small paper cup. The best Italian ice in the world. It got hot on the pavement, my hands got sticky and cramped, and the ends of my fingers were lined from corroding instrument strings. Honorable markings.

When it rained, someone usually invited various people to an apartment nearby, or, at the end of a day, we'd sift down to Sam Wo's in Chinatown, have curry lo mein, crab, or sweet-and-sour whole fish. Or, we'd try getting to someone's apartment by six to hear Oscar Brand's "Folk Song Festival" on WNYC. There were folk music parties, concerts at Town Hall, and the nightclub The Village Vanguard, where the Weavers had performed, as well as Josh White, Ed McCurdy, Burl Ives, and others. At the Palladium, you could hear great mambo bands, and at Birdland, I heard Freddie Green, the great rhythm guitarist, with Basie. The pawnshops and junk stores on lower Third Avenue, as well as on the Bowery, had five-string banjos and guitars that dated back to before the turn of the century. This was New York as I found it, as it surrounded Washington Square.

6

"Did you ever hear the story 'bout Willie the Weeper?"

Squirrely Levels of the Real and Unreal

Folk music came to New York through Library of Congress recordings, Folkways Records, John and Alan Lomax's field recordings, and people like Carl Sandburg and Pete Seeger, whose father was a well-known folklorist. Compared to the pop music of the time, folksongs struck me as music without a persona. The word *persona* comes from Latin and it referred to the masks worn by Etruscan mimes. In modern times, Carl Jung described *persona* as the artificial or masked personality complex developed by a person in contrast to his innate personality. Folk music was, for me, without something put on. When I heard the recording of a chain gang or somebody singing a ballad who had never set foot out of the mountains except to get sorghum or flour, I heard an honesty, an authenticity that was chilling. It resonated to the marrow of my bones. There was no over-emoting, nothing where someone was trying to be hip, be somebody they weren't, put on an act, or sell me on something.

A prime example, for me, was Leadbelly. His name caught my attention, as did the photo on the front of his album: a black man who looked like a piece of dark granite. In those days, we could play records before buying them, and when I first put on his record in the store, I understood why his name was Leadbelly. There was an unvarnished truth to the guy, and the sound of his twelve-string guitar was outside anything else I had heard. If there's a vibration, a musical sense to the seat of one's soul, an essence that is there, if the right tone is struck, Leadbelly struck mine. His music personified authenticity, as I heard it. I spent all my money on that record.

Coming into my mother's apartment, I intuitively kept the record hidden as much as I could. It was too private a thing. But before I could get into my room, she saw the L.P. and asked what it was. When it came out that I'd spent all my allowance plus all I'd saved up, she went into a rage: "You don't spend all your allowance on a phonograph record, that's not how to handle your money." In the row, somehow, the L.P. fell out of its jacket. Miraculously, it didn't get scratched, but the idea that it might have filled me with horror.

Was it because he was a black man that made her so mad? I didn't think she was prejudiced. But her reaction was a betrayal. It betrayed the innocence of me, the inner response I had found to the justice of Leadbelly's voice. I was shamed, and the child of me would never forget the pain of that treachery. And reality, later, would prove I was right.

Burl Ives, Josh White, Pete Seeger, Richard Dyer-Bennett, Woody Guthrie, and Leadbelly were the big names in New York. These were the show-folk, as it were, who had recorded or given performances that brought this music alive in the city. Some of these fellows sang closer to the bone than did others, but these were the kings.

Then, there were those at the Square who would construct personas based on one of these showmen. One fellow had Seeger down cold. With my eyes closed, I could not tell the difference between them. When he wasn't doing Seeger, however, this guy was articulate and well-spoken, thought about things outside of the music, and didn't sound like Seeger at all. Jack Elliott, on the other hand, imitated Woody Guthrie but never came out of that role. When he had me out for dinner at his parents' place in Brooklyn one night, the entire family was there, and the aura at dinner was formal: white tablecloth, special glasses for water, lit candles, and decorated china. I was growing a beard at the time, and Jack's brown-suited father got into the subject of beards. He went on and on, plucking at his chin, saying, "It's okay to grow a beard, but you've got to do something else with your life while you're growing it."

It was all aimed at Jack, to be sure, and I was embarrassed for him, yet he just seemed to wear his usual enigmatic smile, along with his cowboy shirt, jeans, and boots, unbothered, perhaps, by this usual scene. The way his father got into it, though, was like a streak of pulsating resentment flashing up. It didn't fit with his being a brown-suited doctor. He treated people out of their five-story brownstone, which had intercoms all over the place. His specialty was people's assholes, as Jack put it. Jack opened the intercoms one time, he told me, while a patient was there, and started making up verses to a song about his father working on people's assholes. That was a work of art, I thought. I could understand the beauty of that, given the family's rigidity, as well as how his father had not taken the time to understand Jack. It began to make perfect sense that Jack would be drawn to folk music, as well as take on a safer persona than being the person he actually was. And he did it so thoroughly well.

One night in the street, just as I thought Jack would be straight out and open (this once), he jumped up on one of those huge round-topped mailboxes and pretended he was riding a bronco. Although he could write wonderful verses to some melody right off the top of his head, he didn't seem to be into the music, per se, it wasn't his passion. His passion seemed to be playing this character, and the music was only a prop. The character he played was fun to be with, and I was having a ball until the fact sank in that it wasn't quite him.

There were others, as well, who took on roles they imagined came with the folk music scene: wearing the right belt, the right hat, the right shirt, the right shoes, the right pants. Some carried a banjo or guitar slung over their backs, as if that's all they had in the world, the clothes they had on and their music. Wandering waifs of the road, singing their songs of a wandering life, they were clear imitations of the Guthrie persona. An ex-boxer I knew, who lived way over in the East Village on Fourth, played only Leadbelly stuff, but it sounded nothing like Leadbelly.

Some people played more uniquely than anyone else, and I wanted to hear them whenever I could. One was Tom Paley. One afternoon in someone's apartment off Sixth Avenue, just up from Bleecker, Paley took out his 00–42 Martin and played "Woman Lover Blues" and "Tom Cat" in the style of Merle Travis.

"If only I could play like that," I thought, "all of life's problems would be totally solved." I went home with one picking pattern and stayed up all night learning it in the echoey bathroom next to my room in my mother's apartment. Every time it would gel, I went into a small state of nirvana.

We were constantly picking up new kinds of songs: calypso, blues, Elizabethan ballads, old mountain tunes. Some were songs to crawl into, like novels. Some would hold you and remind you of honor, bravery, love, anger, frustration, curiosity, humor. Singing a song was like falling in love with some aspect of life. It was beyond philosophy, politics, theater, and yet was an essential part of it all. It was like getting to experience different parts of the person I was going to be.

7

"And I shivered where the cold winds blew . . ."

Rosmini & Carbone's Beard

In the Village, south of Eighth Street, and west, the streets take on names, such as MacDougal, Waverly Place, Bleecker, Christopher, Jane, Charles, Cornelia—a labyrinth of twisted one-way passages that no cab driver was happy at entering. The spine of the Village, Mac-Dougal Street, runs southward from Eighth. After one block is Washington Square. Three more blocks past the New York University law buildings (which bordered the south side of the Square), was the Café Wha, the Rienzi, the Caricature, and a couple of small places to eat.

Then came Peter Carbone's guitar shop, on the southeast corner of MacDougal and Bleecker. Its grimy windows were filled with such things as a wooden slave banjo, odd kinds of flutes, an old fiddle, and a gourd thing from Africa. West of MacDougal, on Bleecker, between Cornelia and Seventh, Italian sausages hung in the butcher shop windows, a sidewalk market displayed fresh fish, and a coffee-bean shop with huge red-and-gold grinders spread its aroma out on to the street. Bleecker hosted, as well, typical Italian bakeries, and an old Catholic church.

On the north side of Bleecker, east of Carbone's and past La-Guardia Place, was an eight-story building with wide office windows, designed by Louis Henri Sullivan, the father of skyscrapers. An intense Art Nouveau ornamentation framed its windows and ran the entire height of the building, nonstop. Later, as folk became a branch of pop music, Art D'Lugoff's Village Gate and The Bitter End settled on Bleecker, near Thompson, two blocks over from Carbone's. The Bitter End started the careers of Bill Cosby and Woody Allen, the Gate featured jazz, and both featured folk.

All this was the landscape within which we sang songs out of Ireland, Great Britain, the West Indies, and the agricultural southland of the United States.

Carbone had the beard of all beards. It was flowing and coarse, as if carved out of ebony with streaks of silver pine, and his resonant voice went along with it. His shop was jam-packed with instruments hung from the ceiling. He lived in the back of the shop with some woman to whom he never referred, but I'd hear her back there, on occasion, and smell cooking sometimes. The only problem with Peter was that a two-day repair could take him a year to finish, and then it might not be right. It was worth having something in his shop, though, just to have a reason to go in there and hear what he had to say.

I heard about a talented banjoist, Billy Faier, coming to town from New Orleans; Frank Hamilton, a singer, from L.A.; and so on. The first professional job I ever got came through Carbone. How the grapevine was tied into his store was a mystery, because his shop was not a hangout, he sold nothing, and he never came to the Square. Later, a shop even smaller than Peter's went in on MacDougal: The Folklore Center—it was more of a hangout, perhaps, but the owner, Izzy Young, eventually got fed up with people coming in and playing for hours, and taking up space.

When Bob Dylan first came to town, a year or so before he was known, I met him at Izzy's doorstep. He had come to our immigrant city to join the disparate singers of folk songs. We didn't talk a whole lot, but he seemed like a loner, as most of us were. Not like the type that let people in or let himself fully out easily. He looked down or to the side, essentially shy. That resonated with how I was constructed. I could tell he had inner purpose, but I just didn't know whether or not he would develop a persona.

Riding a bicycle down MacDougal one evening, this fellow turned into the park where Mike Steig and I were quietly playing our guitars on one of the benches, not far from the checkerboard tables where Italians were still at their checkers. It was as if this guy had been looking for someone to play the guitar with for most of his life. He skidded his bike to a stop, almost fell over, introduced himself as Dick Rosmini, and then would not let us be. The last time I spoke to Rosmini was in December 1991, forty-some years after that night in the park.

"When I was fourteen or fifteen," he said, "I remember going to one of the White Tower hamburger joints late in the evening, and singing with you and Billy Faier. We actually managed to make a couple of dollars. We did songs most of us knew, like 'Tom Dooley.' 'In the Pines,' and 'Only a Tramp.' There was a guy who was drunk and offered us his entire paycheck, just for the singing we did. We wouldn't take it."

All I remembered of that night was being embarrassed about forcing our music on people who were eating in relative peace, and who hadn't asked us to be there. Rosmini's take was quite different: "Singing with Billy and you wasn't any different than singing at any of the community churches or settlement houses. A stage was a stage, it didn't make any difference how it got arranged, or how big it was. My perception of an audience was that it was familial, not social. A performance was always for my mother. The fact that I might be performing in front of five hundred people or a million didn't matter. Once you bite the bullet and put yourself at risk in that game, the stage is the same. I learned to play, though, to impress you and Mike Steig. I wanted to be accepted. I had no family to speak of. Felton's Lounge, 125th Street and Lenox Avenue, Harlem, is ingrained in my mind. Brownie McGhee was up there. I remember you and Mike Steig getting up on the stage, singing and playing. Older Negro men and women thinking it rather odd, sort of a smile they had, 'What are these white boys doing up here?' That took more courage than I thought existed on the planet."

It had nothing to do with courage, however, from my point of view; it had to do with a foolhardy desperation and wanting to be part of this music because of how it had grabbed us. We hoped that Brownie would give us a nod of some sort.

"My mother became terrified," Rosmini told me, "thinking I'd never be able to make a living. Her viewpoint of the world was distorted by the Depression and her inability to get work in the forties. She was pathological about it. From the time I was thirteen and a half 'til the time I was seventeen, she would beat me to get me to go get a job. I couldn't get anybody to hire me, even to carry a paper bag at Gristede's Market. I stood on the corner offering to carry people's groceries for a quarter, but I looked too old. I learned to play the guitar partly because I didn't think I had a prayer at anything else."

But the fragile connections of putting this music together brought us a sense of existence, of being worthwhile, no matter how thin those connections to the heart of the matter. We felt it was okay to be; it felt like it was worth every risk we could take. It remained to be seen if it would keep us alive, or if we could hang in there, or how we would change. All we knew at the time was that little else mattered. It was nearly a religion, the songs, the ritual of gathering together, and our worship and prayers were found in the singing we did. No alcohol, no drugs, and no money.

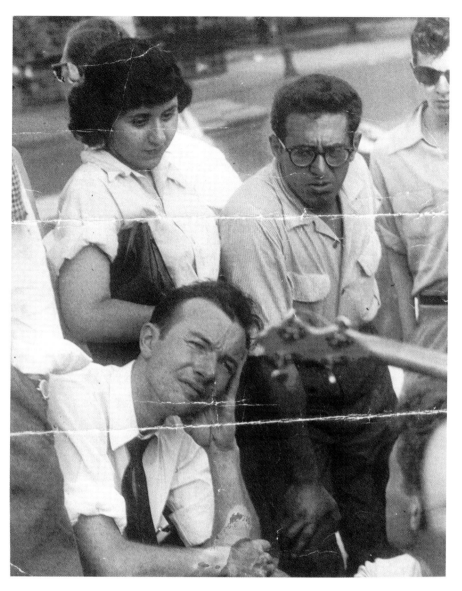

At Washington Square
(*L to R:*) Mickey Geraci, Pete Seeger, Tommy Geraci, and my banjo neck

Typical Sing
(*L to R:*) Jimmy Gavin, (unknown), David McAdams, me,
Tommy Geraci, and Al Meyers

Sonny Terry and Brownie McGhee

8

"I went to the animal fair,
The birds and the beasts were there. . . ."

The Folk Singer Who
Came to Dinner

The vagabond life was part of the romance that went with the singing of folk songs, at least for big-city kids who had never seen the Depression. As inspiration, Woody Guthrie's lifestyle personified this. People drifted in and out of New York, and stayed with whomever they could. The idea was to hang in and hang out, and hope that the music would carry you through. There's always the difference, of course, between the romance of things and what's going on when you get there. It's the difference between the surface and what lies beneath, between the idea and the truth.

"Billy Faier would do anything to make a quarter," Rosmini said. "Even so small an amount as ten cents was significant. He was the cheapest, stingiest, most concerned-with-money human being I'd ever met. He was staying at my mother's and my apartment because it was the cheapest rent—namely, zip. But he didn't think we were real people."

"Those were beautiful times," Billy said, when I asked him what he might remember. "I was trying to save all the money I could in order to join the woman I loved in Naples, Italy. I was living in New Orleans where I had met this woman, Barbara, but she was going to Italy. I intended to join her, but I couldn't get a passport. The guy at the passport office said you have to show that you have a thousand dollars. A lot of Americans had been going over and had been running out of money, throwing themselves on the mercy of the state department, who then had to send them back, and they never gave them the money back. I wasn't able to make money in New Orleans, so I went to New York and made a deal with Rosmini's mother, that I would help her clean house if she'd feed me and let me stay there. I did that for about five months. And then Barbara came back from Italy; she was pregnant with our son, Nicco."

Frank Hamilton hitchhiked from Los Angeles and showed up at the Henry Street Settlement house in the lower Village, where I happened to be singing one night. I was impressed that someone would hitch-hike from L.A. to New York just to sing folk songs. We became fast friends.

In the early 1950s, Frank took a trip to the South with Jack Elliott and Guy Carawan, and invited me to go with them. This is what Carl Sandburg, Alan Lomax, Burl Ives, and Pete Seeger had done in the 1930s and '40s, traveling around collecting folk songs. Such a trip was a dream a lot of us had.

At that moment in life, however, I was searching for a sense of my own inner purpose—an emotional grounding, if you will—and I didn't feel the trip would serve that endeavor. I also didn't feel I was remotely good enough to play on street corners where this music had come from. And then there were the police. In New York, if somebody didn't have a permit to sing at the Square, the cops chased us away. Four Yankees singing their way through the South? I didn't think so. I stayed behind, and the three of them left. Frank related the story like this:

> We played on street corners to raise money for gas, visited folk lu-
> minaries in places like East Virginia, North Carolina, Newport News. All
> kinds of people took us in. We went into the black sections of towns,
> met blues guitarists. We were looking for John Ball, who was a black
> poet living in Virginia. This was pre–civil rights. We met a black labor
> leader there, and he told us we had better get out of town because the
> sheriff and the Ku Klux Klan had been at his doorstep, and they were
> looking to bust our asses. We would have been locked up in one of
> those southern jails, and nobody to get us out. Some company had
> burned their own warehouse down for the insurance and figured they
> would pin it on us. You know, agitators from the North. We took off.
>
> In Maggie Valley Gap, we met Ted Sutton, who claimed to have
> written the song "Little Maggie." He took us up to his home in the
> mountains. Early in the morning, he got into an argument with his
> brother, overturned a gallon of milk, and one of them started to pull a
> gun on the other. We figured it was time to leave there, as well.

At Bascom Lamar Lunsford's Asheville Folk Song Festival, we found his tent and we knocked on it. Guy said something like, "Mr. Lunsford, we're three young folk singers right down from New York. We know Pete Seeger, and we'd like to be on your————."

We heard this groan coming out of the tent, then this big booming voice said, "You boys communists?" Guy gasped and stammered something; I don't recall what it was.

Mr. Lunsford let us be in the festival and introduced us as "Three Communists from New York"—something outrageous like that. Dick Greenhouse, Arnold Feldman, Bob Rachlis, and Diana Pinkus were down there the year before, and he introduced them as "Four Jews from New York." He just assumed every one of us from New York was a Jew or in the left-wing movement. Of course, I had been around it a lot, we had all been around it. It was something that was going on with a lot of people. I had sung some of the political songs, I guess, but I never really liked them, they were poorly written songs. I was more interested in the traditional stuff than I was in the singer-songwriter-left-wing-movement-type writing. I was interested in Afro-American music, Appalachian music. Bess Hawes [Alan Lomax's sister] had a lot of influence on me. And a lot of it did grab your heart because it was beautiful music. It couldn't help but grab you, if you heard the real stuff.

The day Frank got back from the South, he had no place to stay. It was okay with my mother that he stayed in my room for the night. It had a carpeted floor, so I figured it would be more comfortable than a lot of floors Frank had slept on. My mother made us both food. His socks had to be moved into the bathroom that night, as they hadn't been changed in a month.

My mother didn't seem to mind that he stayed a couple more nights. Before long, a week had slipped by. Then a month. Every day, it seemed, I would learn something new. "Swannanoa Tunnel" was a song he'd brought back from the South:

Asheville Junction, Swannanoa Tunnel,
All caved in, baby, all caved in.

When you hear that hoot-owl squall, baby,
Somebody's dyin', baby, somebody's dyin'.

If I could gamble like Tom Dooley,
I'd leave my home, baby; I'd leave my home.

When you hear that pistol growl, baby.
Another man's gone, another man's gone.

I'm goin' back to Asheville Junction,
That's my home, baby, that's my home.

No pistol growled and no hoot-owl squalled in my mother's apartment, but the distance between Frank and my mother began to expand. The apartment seemed to get smaller with each passing day. Frank recalled:

> Your mother had a boyfriend, and they watched the Milton Berle Show religiously, week after week, the Texaco Theater. I hated Milton Berle, and when she asked me what I thought of him, I told her the truth. I must have been a thorn in her side, after two months in that apartment. She had cast me in this mold, as if somewhere in her thoughts, I'd be a degenerate influence on you. I assured her that I was not the kind of person she thought, and that I maintained a moral standard that she should respect. I always thought of myself as naive compared to the people around me, like Mary Travers, Bob Gibson, and people who I saw as practically junkies. I felt it was amusing that I would be cast in the role of your corrupter. People, because of their class system, find they are put into roles of trying to play out other people's lives in ways that simply don't fit.

My mother went nearly berserk, and that was the end of Frank's stay. Frank let her have it, however, without being vindictive or angry or intentionally hurtful. I could hear in the air of the room that he was doing no more and no less than rebuking her error. Although that may have been the end of our completing an album of sea shanties we'd been putting together, it was a moment of sanity.

I think we hang on to threads in this life that keep us from losing it. They can come from a moment like this, or from something we read, or a teacher who gives us a positive sense of ourselves. You can't add them up as they happen, saying, "Now I've got that one to save me, when the chips are all down," because they slip by in the night, as it were, and you never imagine the chips will be down, or how far down they can get.

9

The Ecstasy and the Agony

Carrying an instrument in the streets of New York was a way of defining myself. It gave me something to be, in lieu of an actual self. Sometimes a stranger in an elevator would say, "What's in there, a machine gun?" It was fiddle cases that gangsters had used for machine guns (at least in the movies), but I didn't quibble. I liked the attention.

Getting off the subway at Eighth Street and Sixth Avenue, walking the block east to MacDougal, then down to the Square and over to the fountain, and waiting for people to gather—this was an ecstasy. It spread to small gatherings at someone's apartment, with a bottle of Chianti, some cheese, and a few candles, perhaps. At some of the larger apartments, there could be bluegrass in one room, blues in another, and the general music we sang, in another. We had to close doors so one music didn't drift into the spell of another. Drugs hadn't happened as yet, and people didn't do booze; the turn-on was the music.

At the same time, however, we shared a critical elitism, like a tribal resistance to change or to difference. It had to do with the idea of being authentic, who was or who wasn't. Were you doing some song the "right" way, as the original people had done it back in the Ozarks, or off of some record? This flew in the face of the fact that we were New Yorkers singing this music that had been created by people who had a tradition of making their own music as part of their culture: "Daddy sang bass, mamma sang tenor," that sort of thing. I'd never met anyone's mother in all of New York who played any music whatever, except Sandy Bull's. She played the jazz harp, and I don't mean the harmonica. One of those big suckers with strings and push pedals. Maybe somebody else's mother played the piano, but not in a band with her children.

There was no possible way a New-York-City–raised person could sing white southern music, or blues for that matter, with the musical nuance and mindset of a white southern person or a black man or woman. For the people whose music this was, black or white, it was part of how they had lived life, body and soul, birth until death. In many cases, music was all they had beyond just getting by. This makes a difference. No white man has ever played the blues, for example, with the feel of a black man whose life it was about. No Anglo-American can play flamenco in the way a gypsy can play it. You can't drink enough booze or smoke enough pot to learn that sort of thing. Even young blacks can't touch old-timers like Son House, Blind Boy Fuller, Mississippi John Hurt, Robert Johnson, or Leadbelly. Sneakers and television have shifted the landscape. People can learn the math, but the odd nuance of timing and touch is a whole different story. And that's what folk music is about.

Blues are a construct of minor riffs against a major chord structure, so the music goes from minor (sad) to major (happy). It gives you permission to feel sad, and then happy, again and again, over and over; and that always feels good. It's a nonlethal drug that works at some level, no matter who's playing the math of the stuff. The old guys did it in a way that had a visceral magic, however. In lieu of that magic, people in the Square often played lots of notes, or growled, or mugged their way forward, seeking to imitate the masters instead of seeking what they sought. And some got away with it. Flamenco refers to this magic as *duende;* in blues, they don't have a name for it. You could call it swing, I suppose, but that belongs more to the feel of a jazzman. Really good blues is a heart-love-and-gut sort of thing, I suppose you could call it, that comes from a place in this life you can't fake; it isn't a head-trip, the hours you keep, or the clothes you got on.

As a child, I was raised on the music of Beethoven, Mozart, and Dvorak, and I couldn't help but be influenced by that, at one level or other, unless I were to deny who I was. And I loved all that stuff. As well, jazz was a part of the New York experience. It came out of cafes you walked by at night; and from some open window, a saxophone played in mid-afternoon, part of the breath of New York. Folk music asked that you do it from where you were standing, kind of like a chameleon, soaking up some of the culture around it.

Bess Lomax Hawes, the sister of the late Alan Lomax, had grown up under the tutelage of their folklorist father, John Lomax. When I got the chance to interview her, the first thing I asked was about folk music, as she'd come to know it. She said:

> You've got to distinguish between a folk song and the perfor-
> mance; the song is the thing, and then the singer or the performer is
> the artist. When Marian Anderson sang a spiritual, it was a beautiful
> song, but it had been taken completely out of its original style and
> moved into the concert style. And so it's not the same thing anymore.
> The song can be picked up, the tune replicated, and the words repli-
> cated, but when you hear someone of a truly different artistic and cul-
> tural experience attempt to sing it, a part of its essence is changed.
>
> But authenticity, per se, isn't the only criterion. A good example
> is Maxine Sullivan, who bopped up a lot of children's game songs. She
> had a beautiful voice, and she did those songs exquisitely. They
> weren't authentic children's game songs any more, however, they
> were authentic Maxine Sullivan jazz tunes. For me, though, over
> time, the most moving performances have always been by the people
> whose original cultural property the music was. People tend to feel
> there's only one kind of thing that's any good, and I don't think that's
> true. I think there are lots of things that are any good. They vary,
> sometimes, in their degree of goodness. I use to go with Father on
> some of his collecting trips, and, boy, it was a bore, sometimes. As
> Alan says, "One of the reasons I started thinking about style was that
> I had to have something to think about as I was hearing the nine-
> thousandth version of 'Barbary Allen' that I recorded in my life."

Around the time Elektra released my first record, someone invited me to a woman's apartment for one of the usual parties. The woman seemed rather nice when she first came to the door and bid me in, but the first thing she said as she walked idly toward the kitchen was, "By the way, I hate your L.P." This wasn't joke-like. It was as if she didn't want me there under false pretenses. I wasn't sure what pretenses she did want me there under, in that case, except to be nasty. I hadn't learned, by that time in life, that some people thrive on that sort of thing. In any event, I didn't leave, as I should have. I went into a process of philosophical damage control, telling myself, "Well, I should be grown up about this, she's just being truthful. I can be big-ger than to let that bring me down." I wasn't, however.

Ethnic, my music was not, and some people did not like it on that count alone. I knew that, but the bigger part of my angst was that I knew the L.P. hadn't reached what I'd hoped to achieve. Two or three songs were okay, but I couldn't listen to the rest without cringing over one thing or another, not the least of which was the sound of my voice. I just hadn't been nearly as prepared as I should have been, a lesson I'd never forget. This woman had only rubbed salt into a wound that was already there.

In the end, the reason I didn't give it all up at that point, although it did cross my mind, was that when I was doing the thing—making up the arrangements, standing in front of a mike on the seventeenth take of some song, or singing at Washington Square—those were the times I felt most alive and secure in myself, and I wasn't about to give up on that.

10

"Give me three grains of corn, mother,
Only three grains of corn . . ."

Mouse on a String

Nicky Thatcher stood between five-seven and five-nine, slight of build, with high cheekbones, thinnish blond hair, and blue eyes. Except for his sarcasm, there was an aristocratic sense to Nicky that, no matter how crumpled his clothes were, or how sad his life, he still looked like the duke's nephew. Nicky knew exactly who everyone was and the numbers they were running. Above all, he was a no-bullshit musician. He never sang with any sort of accent or affectation, as if he were pretending to be some kind of folk person. We had one of those connections wherein we tracked words in a similar way, got the same jokes, and felt understood even though we may not have agreed. There was always a smile between us.

When Nicky sang, he grasped the guitar from the middle of his back, his eyelids closed, and he gave all he had. Every single time. I can still see the tendons on the insides of his wrists as he held on to those strings, as if his life depended on it. My feeling was that it didn't have to be that much of a life-and-death issue. It made sense, though, in the person of Nicky. It crossed my mind, also, however, that one's way of singing is a metaphor for the importance one places on life. Nicky's commitment said: "Life is important!" After he sang, he always had to take a moment to come out of it, come back to the world we usually live in. He was one of the most original people around, and that may have been why he never showed up at the Square, except to walk by now and then, a wry smile on his face. Whenever I saw this, I'd find myself asking, "What am I actually doing?"

Out of the blue, I got a call from a dean at Bard College, uptown, a college for women. The caller wanted a folksinging group. "An

audience of women?!" I was eager. One of the many reasons for playing the guitar and singing was to attract to women. Where she got my
name, I didn't ask.

"What do you mean by a group?" I said, right away. Tommy
Geraci, one of my buddies, and I had a duo thing going, and this would
be perfect for us.

It had to be three or more people, she said.

Nicky came to mind immediately. "Oh!" I said quickly, "I've got
a group." I figured Tommy and Nicky and I could put something together that they would believe was a group. This was folk music, after
all, not choral singing, and we knew the same songs.

The first time the three of us got together, however, in the process
of making this real, I saw that Nicky and Tommy were different kinds
of people, having their own musical habits and ways of relating to others, and that their manners didn't mesh easily. There was no way
Nicky could just sing on the songs Tommy and I did, for example; and
Tommy, who didn't play an instrument, had limitations in terms of
what he was able to hear. At the Square, as many as thirty-five people could be singing: someone would start, the rest would fall in, but
there were no intros, no endings, no subtle nuances, no need for stage
presence, and no formal audience. In this case, the college was expecting a group, a performance, people who had worked some things
out—we would be paid fifty dollars apiece! This was a professional gig.

Tommy was Sicilian, from a working-class background, built like
a tank, and straightforward—you got what you saw. If he did something odd with the time, I could follow; there were only the two of us.
Nicky was more intellectual, lived life in his head, wrote his own versions of songs, and never sang anything the same way twice. Because
I loved how he played, that made me think we could do this.

After we ran a few songs, it could not have been clearer that we
were as far from a group as it got. What made it worse was that I could
not have been more enthusiastic with each of these guys, in getting
them to sign on to this job. I did not have the heart to say, "Fellows,
this doesn't work, we have no sense of each other's time—or of each
other's awareness, for that matter."

We had three weeks before the big night to pull this together. I
thought maybe, somehow, if we spent enough time, we might manage to get the job done. But, I had to decide, one way or another, right
then, and not string these guys along. I let the ball roll. Then Nicky
didn't want to rehearse more than two or three times! Welcome to
show business.

Before the three weeks were up, we managed (more or less) to work up five or six songs. We'd fill in with duos from Tommy and me; Nicky would sing his best songs; I would sing two or three. We had to sing for only an hour, and I had a rough program worked out.

We took a big Checker cab up to the college that night. Sitting in the back seat, the three of us didn't have a whole lot to say. An uncomfortable silence took over. As I watched the city glide by, knowing the moment of truth would soon be upon us, I could not help but think: "What if, under the pressure of being in front of these women, if it all falls apart, stops in its tracks?" It had at times, in rehearsal. Could I say: "Ladies, I'm sorry. I had this idea————" and then apologize to them and leave? Not take their money. A hell of a thing to go through, yet an honest way out. But how was it going to feel, putting our instruments back in their cases, putting on our overcoats, turning our backs on those women, and then leaving?

The bars and cafes we went by were beacons of safety, even if seen from a cab that was running uptown. Soon enough, we were there, with our instrument cases stacked in a corner, along with our coats, and then we were standing in front of a room full of women and singing. And it did fall apart.

Only, out of our deepest convictions, and out of having to keep up with Nicky, we fell back together. It became something different and beyond what we could have imagined. Sam Hinton, a folklorist, once said, "Recording a folk song is like catching a bird in flight." It was like that on this night. Something creatively fleeting took place. A thing live. In the darkness of the unknowns, in the back seat if that cab, I'm sure each of us had similar feelings of doubt, but over forty years later, Tommy remembered it this way:

> We played well over an hour. We did "The Midnight Special," "Ain't No More Cane on the Brazos," "Whoa Back, Buck," "How Long Blues," Geraci–Darling stuff, Leadbelly stuff. Nicky was with us in his way, we were with him in ours. We were together, somehow.
>
> There was one song we did, "The Rock Island Line," the three of us on that one particular song. I never heard "Rock Island Line" sung by anybody, including the Weavers, the way we sang it that night. We never rehearsed it. We said, at the end, let's do "Rock Island Line." We did it, and it brought down the house.

As Tommy related the events of that night, I remembered that after a solo Nicky had done, the women applauded, nearly gave him a standing ovation. He looked back at the two of us, grinning his face off, as if he'd never known life could be quite like this. I remembered, as well, how sad Nicky's life had turned out in the end.

By the time I met Nicky, although I didn't know it, he was a heroin addict. One of the few people in the folk scene in those days who had anything to do with drugs, and he did the big one. Nicky's lady, at the time, was a beautiful, dark-haired French girl, Nicole, and they never got along very well but were always together. I got the feeling that Nicky wasn't at home enough in himself to be with a woman. Some years later, I remember hearing that Nicole had committed suicide.

On a crisp, clear day, small winds now and then, a clear bite of cold in the air, I ran into Nicky in the Village. This was fourteen years after that concert. He was wearing a threadbare camel's-hair coat over a white shirt and black pants held up by a careless black belt. He looked chilly. We were both glad to see each other and it was as if only some weeks had gone by. He said he would call, that he wanted to see me right away. I was looking forward to this, but I couldn't imagine what his urgency was, after fourteen years. It turned out he had some guitars he'd acquired and wanted to know if I could sell them. He knew I was teaching guitar, as I had an ad in *The Voice,* and he figured I'd be an outlet. We agreed he would come over that weekend.

He arrived with four flimsy, cardboard guitar-shipping boxes with the remains of a guitar in each one, three of them damaged beyond reasonable repair. Against the typical white walls of my New York apartment, Nicky's fine bones, wrinkled white shirt, and bloodshot blue eyes seemed out of place. I offered him tea. He asked if I had a beer, said he no longer did drugs, that all he did now was drink beer, and he chuckled. In a rumpled navy-blue suit, he sat on my couch as if someone had told him, and he'd never forgotten, "Nicky! Don't ever sit back on a couch!" I'd never noticed these sorts of things when I was over at his place, when Nicole was alive.

About the guitars, he explained, now and then the Mafia union gangs on the docks of Staten Island (where Nicky lived with his mother and stepfather) would "accidentally" drop a big crate. The contents were declared damaged and then sold as salvage. Somehow, Nicky had gotten these guitars from the Mafia, and he mentioned that they were angry at him. I found this bizarre. I mean, over these use-less guitars, and angry at this waif of a person? There was no chance of selling any of the guitars for more than ten dollars. They were the cheapest Japanese imports I'd ever seen and would be of value only to an absolute beginner, and only after the insanity of repairs. They weren't worth the cost of the wood they were made of. In the inter-est of avoiding the issue of the guitars, I asked what he did for a liv-ing these days.

"I'm a thief," he said, and he chuckled again. He always had this chuckle he ran, sort of as if he were above it all, amused at himself as well as at the rest of the world.

"You're kidding," I said.

Nicky explained how he would steal someone's credit card—say, a Bloomingdale's card—take it out of a purse, or from where it might have been laid for a second, then charge just enough on one floor so that he could turn in the item for cash on another, without raising sus-picion. As well, he knew about rare etchings and would go into an art dealer and ask for an etching he knew the dealer would probably not have but would know about, such as a Rembrandt with a broken line, thus setting himself up as an expert. Then he'd ask the dealer if he could look through some of the portfolio racks. When the guy wasn't looking, he would slip a rare etching under his coat, slip out of the store, take it down the street to another dealer, and attempt selling it there. One time, he said, he got caught in the act and had to duck into a subway to escape.

After a few other stories like that, he told me about living in the south of France for a while. Nicole, at that time, had a job at an orphan-age supported and run by people with money, and so she always knew when people were leaving their villas for vacations. Nicky and some friends broke into an unoccupied villa, stole a Monet, and took it to Paris to sell. The Monet turned out to be a fake. On the way back, they ran out of gas, broke into a gasoline station to turn on the pumps, and got caught. Nicky ended up in a jail where all they fed prisoners was wine, bread, and cheese. He chuckled some more about that one. In the cell with him was a guy with huge scars on his chest, who had once been a lion tamer. He had tamed a mouse in the cell to walk on a string.

I had never met anyone who saw the world so completely against him as Nicky. I tried talking to him about the value of therapy. He told me he went to a psychiatrist once, a guy with a beard and a big photo of Freud behind his desk. The first thing the guy said was, "How often do you masturbate?" At that, Nicky got up and walked out.

It seemed as if Nicky figured things down to an endless tightrope that only ended him up where he'd started. But I didn't think that, for one moment of his life, from the day of his birth, he was ever given an idea of how gifted he was, and that he should fulfill his life's journey in his own unique way. Maybe that one time, in that concert at Bard, when he had that ear-to-ear grin, that may have been it. Someone heard who he was, and he'd understood that. That one time.

I got this idea that I wanted to interview Nicky and write his life story, calling it "Mouse on a String." Something resonated about Nicky's life that I felt was important, the essence of something worth writing about. I hesitated a week, because I didn't know if I wanted to get involved with someone who was playing games with the Mafia. For all I knew, he'd borrowed money from them and had not paid it back. Having learned from reliable sources that they had thrown people off roofs down on Mott Street, I had to ponder the question.

I got to the point where I knew I had to do this, no matter what. The minute I'd made up my mind, I gave him a call. No answer. Now, I was impatient.

Early the following morning, his mother picked up the phone. She said that Nicky had had too many beers the night before, had fallen down the basement steps on the way to his room, and was killed. It was matter of fact, the way she said it.

I'd been out to his place, I'd met her as well as his stepfather. She had fine, short, reddish-blond hair and a rounded white face with blue faded eyes, and she wore a faded print dress. His stepfather had sat in a corner and looked out a window. The house had a feeling of having been closed. No dust in the air. She was a low-key, matter-of-fact human being, one thing no more important than the next: a steamship, a watermelon seed, her son's death, grains of sand, bugs during crepuscule. No doubt he had been a difficult child. What child isn't? As I thought of his thin, crumpled body at the base of those steps, I wondered if he'd had one final chuckle. I was one week too late.

11

*"Where have you been all the day,
Randal, my son . . . ?"*

The Quest

Nicky personified the quest, however. From my father, I'd learned to spot the unstudied but "perfect" line, the line that had a compelling sense of life to it. Commercial artists have the skill to draw anything—a set of suitcases, a bulldozer, a woman ironing shirts—and the perspective and relative sizes of things are always right on. You see these kinds of drawings in newspaper ads all the time. But these accurate lines don't often have the kind of life that a single strand of hair or a line in a face drawn by Leonardo Da Vinci has. And it was that sort of spontaneous effort within someone's intention that always gave me a kick. Not repetition or ego, but the expression of creative life. Nicky had that.

The question I had, although not held in words, was how do I get there, find out who I am through the music, without being like Nicky, exactly, or Leadbelly, or Josh White? I hadn't lived enough life on my own to have a sense of its cost, but folk songs seemed to be moving me closer to that. What drew me to them, in the first place, was that I felt you could trust them, they had been there and back, and they spoke of the cost.

Onlookers would throng at the Square if we sang a song we could grab on to. In turn, that raised the excitement, and we gave even more of ourselves. But, if we followed that song with a dud, they would all disappear before the song ended. It became clear that the songs to which we had the deepest connection resonated with the most people. A universal attraction seemed to accompany being deeply connected, and this educated part of the quest.

Somewhere in the Ozarks, a woman was murdered and thrown into a river, and somebody wrote a song about that, because it was shocking and real.

> He stabbed her in the heart,
> And her heart's blood did flow.
> He stabbed her in the heart,
> And her heart's blood did flow.
> Down into her grave Pretty Polly did go.

Or:

> Stagolee, Stagolee,
> Meanest man around.
> Stagolee is dealin', boy,
> Better lay your money down.
> Way down in New Orleans,
> Got that lion's club.
> And every step you step, you steppin'
> In Billy D'Lion's blood.

Singing songs that had been inspired by actual events and places in somebody's life inspired this reach for a personal identity. Yet, when I first auditioned for Oscar Brand's Folksong Festival, a 6 p.m. Sunday-night radio show on WNYC, Oscar let me sing quite a few songs before he finally said: "When you sing a Burl Ives song, you sound like Burl; a Josh White song, you sound like Josh; a Woody Guthrie song, like Woody," and so on. He told me, "Go find your own voice and come back."

I didn't have the vaguest idea how to do that. I mean, what the hell do I do? Look at myself in the mirror more often? Before I recorded my first solo L.P., I managed to get there, somehow, without thinking a whole lot about it, time being the teacher. At the same time, I never ceased finding places to snap a chord like Josh White, or add a sweet feel to a love song like Ives. Meanwhile, I knew I had so far to go. I wish I had known at the time that the quest for your truth never ends, that you just keep on going wherever it takes you, and that a whole lot of stuff gets revised over time.

12

"I'm looking rather seedy, now, holding down my claim . . ."

Mott Street

MacDougal was in a haze on this night, with the pavements smelling damp; all of the city huddled under its mist. There's no drizzle like a New York one; it isn't quite rain, yet it's beyond the comfort of fog, and the air is just miserably wet. The short hairs on the back of my neck felt like they were gathering droplets of mist. I hunkered down in my jacket, hoping the tuning pegs on my banjo wouldn't corrode. I'd had the banjo elongated so it would play in a lower register, as well as look as heroic as Seeger's. This necessitated cutting a hole in the end of the case to let the end of the neck stick out. In those days, no one made longneck banjos commercially, let alone appropriate cases.

I was hoping to find a late-night coffeehouse scene, some people to sing with, or a cup of coffee and a piece of dark chocolate cake with a walnut on top. I knew where that cake was, at least.

I was sliding along on the surface, trying to hang on to the beginnings of some sort of life, and putting this music together with someone was usually an emotional fix.

The few people around were tourists, uptowners, or nonmusical macrame types. Having been raised by an artist, having seen Brancusi's "Bird in Space," I broke out in hives whenever I came across macrame stuff. It seemed like the sort of make-work given to halfwits in asylums for occupational therapy. As soon as I found the place that had the cake with the walnut, I went in and sat down. I knew you couldn't play music in there and that a huge fern hung in a huge macrame holder, but the chocolate cake always worked as an antidote, and I liked the huge fern.

After I'd made the coffee and cake last as long as I could, I pondered the pastel drawing of a woman's face that hung on the wall.

There was a yearning I liked in that face. I finally got up and walked into the mist, which was turning to rain.

As I stepped onto the sidewalk, a black guy pulled up to the curb in a car and asked if I wanted to go to a party. I figured he'd seen me at some gathering and knew who was throwing a party that night. I got into his car, and he headed south and east of the Village. I tried placing the guy but I couldn't. He seemed less familiar the more that I watched him, and he dressed a little too neatly for one of the folk crowd. Goodly worn dungarees were the basic uniform then. Girls wore long hair and full-circle skirts. I liked those; they seemed easy to get under. This guy wore slacks and a new leather jacket. At one point, he put his hand on my leg. "We can really have a good time," he said. The guy's fingers were like a vise. I was naive enough not to know, instantly, what he was after, but by the next stoplight, I'd figured it out. I jumped out of the car.

This had me downtown at the Bowery, the heart of Skid Row, where the more recognizably lost of the city lived in the street. A sudden fatigue had me not wanting to wend my way all the way back across town to the west side subways and home. I knew that down here, you could find a flophouse with a white-tiled hallway that led up a steep flight of stairs. I figured these places exist, how bad could they be? They had to be dry, and I could always walk out.

The marquee of the first one I saw advertised beds for fifty cents a night. The next one said seventy-five. I figured I'd stay at the Ritz. I had always been curious about these places, anyway: stark-white tiles in the night, easy to clean, seemingly sterile.

The place was a warren of rooms whose walls were gray plywood partitions that didn't go all the way to the ceiling. A wire-spring cot left little space in the five-by-eight room that was mine for the night. A bare light bulb hung from the ceiling, and there was a coat hook. No table. No chair. The sheets were grayish and rough, smelling of disinfectant.

When I finally got under the sheets, I felt out of place. Until then, I had felt how great it would be to get out of the rain and into a clean, dry bed. The adventure of seeing the inside of a flophouse, as well, had drawn me into its beacon of white. But it didn't seem like much of an adventure now, under the sheets, in its disinfected night.

If someone were industrious enough, I wondered, could they make it over the partitions in the middle of the night looking for more money than they had in their pocket? All the songs I knew on the banjo didn't mean shit. The banjo itself seemed rather useless. I thought about the manufacture of road paint; Baltimore, Maryland; upstate New York, my father, the lake, my mother's apartment. Who I was or was not, or who I was becoming, I hadn't a clue.

I knew I had finally slept, only because I awoke from some dream. After a bit, I slipped off again. The next time I awoke, it was time.

I washed in the white-tiled communal bathroom next to a guy who never looked in the mirror, then got the hell out of the place. As I walked out into the Bowery, into the long shadows of a morning sun, I was glad for the sun and the shadows, glad for the city, glad for the weight of the banjo. I walked by store windows filled with big pots and pans, butcher knives, butcher blocks, piles of coffee cups, saucers and plates, stainless industrial sinks, the commercial restaurant stuff of New York. Only a few people were sleeping in doorways as I walked up to Canal Street, the border between Chinatown and Little Italy. I went west on Canal until I found the subway and clattered my way back uptown to my mother's apartment.

I was glad that she wasn't at home. Having her bring me to New York was a blessing, for sure. I probably loved her in some way, don't know in which way, but no understanding existed between us, no way to evolve. And love of whatever sort, without understanding, has not much to go on. At that point, I felt I had to find my own place.

After living for a while in a loft on Green Street, a block east of the Square, forty-five dollars a month, I sublet a place down on Mott Street from a banjo-playing photographer. Thirty-five dollars a month. This was in the heart of Little Italy. The place had one room and a huge laundry sink with a white metal top, so it worked as a table as well as a bath. You went through a hallway from Mott Street, then through a courtyard to the building in back, and the apartment was the first one on the left. Now and then, the sweet smell of sautéing tomatoes and garlic wafted down through the clotheslines that went from one side of the courtyard to the other, up several stories.

It felt quiet and protected in there, and I tended to leave the apartment door unlocked, if not open, as did the guy from whom I'd sublet the apartment. Seemed like a hip, folk-like thing to do. You know, bond with all of humanity, even though you did not need to stress that in New York. You bonded enough in the subways.

Walking down Mott Street from the Village, toward this apartment and Chinatown, was like being in a movie, except it was real: women resting their arms on pillows as they looked out their windows through fire-escape railings; kids playing stickball; and at night, odd-looking men in dark doorways, with wide-brimmed hats and dark suits. One thing you learned in New York was to mind your own business and look straight ahead. I always gave furtive glances, however, so I wouldn't miss any cool scenes.

One morning, while brewing Medaglia d'Oro coffee, the stuff my father had lived on, I began hearing a strange whistling off in the distance, as you hear all sorts of things in New York: somebody playing a drum set, an opera singer practicing scales, a couple getting ready to beat each other to death, all muffled in with the car horns, sirens, bus engines, and somebody yelling for someone to do something. New York.

But this whistle was eerie. There was no melody to it, yet it had a mindless intention, like atonal music, and it kept getting closer. It would start and then stop. It made the hair on the back of my neck stand on end. Okay, I thought, this is Little Italy. I went back to feeling grown up in my own little place, in control and on track. It's all about putting things into perspective.

Then the apartment door, slightly ajar, slammed all the way open, like the sound of a shot. A thickly built man stormed into the room. About five foot six inches tall, he barely fit through the door, though there was no fat on this guy. He was wearing a typical white, skintight T-shirt, and there was no smell to the man. He seemed to be looking for something, his eyes darting around the edges of the floor, while constantly whistling those long, drawn-out, meaningless notes. He had dull bluish eyes, a crew cut, and a visceral force like I'd never felt.

I would have been willing to give him whatever he wanted, except for my banjo, of course—and I had to think hard about that. Was my banjo worth risking my life for? What could I offer this person instead? My camera? A half-empty box of spaghetti? I felt I needed to do something, because he wasn't leaving. I didn't dare blink. Without any question whatsoever, he could have broken my neck in an instant.

Then, there was my guitar. I figured I'd rather lose that than the banjo. I stood at the side of the room, trying to fade into the wall. I was as quiet and watchful as I'd been when hunting in the woods with my father. Only, this time, I was the hunted.

As suddenly as he walked in, he walked out, through the courtyard and out onto Mott Street. He didn't close the door when he left. But I sure as hell did. The whistling continued until it gradually faded into the din of the city, leaving only a shiver in the front of my chest and under my chin. I never left the door open or unlocked again. Any door. Ever.

13

"I ride an old paint, I lead an old dan,
I'm goin' to Montana to throw the hoolihan. . . ."

"Musical Americana"

Word came through the Square that Carbone wanted to see me. I was surprised. As indicated earlier, I went into his shop once a month, maybe, and, other than liking the man as a character, I had no relationship with him. He wasn't part of the folk crowd that I knew. Billy Faier had known him in earlier times as the center of it all, but these times were different. I went right over, however. It turned out that a Mary Hunter of the Theater Guild was looking for people to be in a road-show production of American folk music. Carbone didn't make a big deal of it, hadn't the slightest idea what the scene was, just gave me the info and told me who to call. I thanked him and left.

A dozen or so professional singers, actors, and dancers, most with music folios in hand, gathered for auditions at the Theater Guild on 56th Street, between Sixth and Seventh avenues. They were sight-reading melodies under their breaths. This was the Broadway show scene, known as a cattle call, and was out of my league. Not only was my vocal range no more than five or six notes, give or take, but I couldn't read music. I learned folk songs from people I knew or heard, not simply singing them from pages or making them more clear with arm gestures and facial gyrations. Show tunes they are not.

I sat for a while, taking in the whole scene, and began thinking I ought to leave. But by the time I'd heard some of the auditions through the closed door, I figured I'd stay. Maybe I had an edge. I could hear that this was my music, not theirs. I took my turn and was asked to come back. The third time, it was "Don't call us, we'll call you." By the end of that week, however, they had called, and I was on board.

I would be part of a show, "Musical Americana," that would travel the country on a Greyhound-sized bus, sponsored and booked by Columbia Concerts Management. Regardless of whether these people could sing folk songs, they were professionals, they would show up on time, and everyone would be giving their all. Two of us would play instruments and sing onstage: one being Keith Chalmers, who played the guitar as well as the flute; the other, me. Offstage would be a pianist, a violinist, and a jazz guitar player. The company would crisscross the country: Pennsylvania, Ohio, Michigan, North Dakota, Iowa, Texas, California, and Nebraska. In short, I would be going out west! I'd never been. I'd get a salary of $110 per week, all hotels would be paid, and I'd be playing the banjo and the twelve-string guitar.

I signed on to the crew, as it were, at age twenty-one. We would set sail at the end of three weeks and reach Pueblo, Colorado, by January 22, 1954, to play the City Auditorium. From then on, we would be doing one-night stands until May. I'd come home a professional, I thought. But I hadn't the slightest idea what I'd gotten into.

14

"Fare you well, old Joe Clark.
Fare you well, I'm gone . . ."

Sam Herman

Rehearsals began at 8 a.m. and went eight hours a day, Monday through Sunday. They were held in upstairs dance studios over on Third Avenue, below 57th. Three weeks of rehearsal were for the stage movements, songs, choreography, lighting, and dress rehearsals. I'd never learned a song in my life in less than a month, and even then I'd have trouble. This time, I'd have to. And some were songs I'd never have chosen to sing in 8,500 years.

There were songs out of early America, some of them folk, some of them not. We were to act out each song, as it were, with dance movements, costumed tableaus against minimal stage sets, lighting and scrims, dramatic productions. For example, I played a version of a banjo tune, "Old Joe Clark," at the beginning of a campfire scene. Sam Herman, the jazz guy, accompanied a Martha Graham dancer doing a tortured death sequence, the theme being death on the prairie when crossing the continent. All the male performers, myself included, sang "Haul Away Joe," an insipid sea shanty, while wearing sailor outfits and pulling imaginary ropes. I loved doing that one, right? A saloon number had cowboys and dance-hall girls. Broad kick'-em-up-hoedown-like stuff. Our closing number was "Fireball Mail," choreographed by Jerome Robbins. He was a big name in the musical Broadway show scene.

Whether you liked it or not, you were obliged to bring the material to life. An audience would be paying money, out of which we were getting paid, and in that agreement, you owed them a good show. As a professional, you had to reach down and find the resources to make the material work, the best that you could.

Twenty-one of us made up the troupe. What we could stow in the overhead racks was all we were allowed to take on the bus. The lights, cables, light board, and sets were stowed in the compartments below decks. Other than the performers, the bus carried an electrician; the stage manager, Tom Skelton; and then the bus driver, a vacuous-eyed maniac who literally ran cars off the road on occasion when passing. After a particularly harrowing trip on some twisted road coming out of a pass, Skelton had the bus company send out a new driver. Tom Skelton was tough and kept the show running, insisting on rehearsals when the show got sloppy.

In mid January, a six-day section of our itinerary looked like this:

Toledo, Ohio Jan. 11 Peristyle Aud.
La Porte, Indiana Jan. 12 Civic Aud.
Ludington, Mich. Jan. 13 Lyric Theater
Midland, Mich. Jan. 14 Midland H.S.
Hillsdale, Mich. Jan. 15 High School
Chicago, Ill. Jan 17 Civic Opera House

The stage at the Chicago Civic Opera House was big enough to build a small town on. A massive backdrop was lowered for us, cutting the depth of the stage by two-thirds. It was also raked, as in built sloping down toward the footlights, so the audience could see actors in the back, over the heads of the actors downstage. Even with the backdrop, it still was too big, and our dancers still had to dance on a slope. When I played the first notes of "Old Joe Clark," they managed to carry over the gulf of the orchestra pit to about the eighth row and sank into oblivion. It was like doing the show for people who were in the next valley.

After a show, we often had to jump on the bus and be driven deep into the night to make the next date. I'd often sit in the front seat, mesmerized by horizontal streaks of snow and the fact that a blizzard seemed to have no effect on the bus. Wisconsin, North Dakota: flat, frozen, snow-blown.

Fargo, N.D. Mar. 28 STOPOVER
Eau Claire, Wisc. Mar. 29 STOPOVER
Kohler, Wisc. Mar. 30 Kohler Recreational Hall

People asked us, on occasion, to a reception or dinner after a show, where the big shots who were responsible for bringing this culture to town would get a chance to "meet the artists." One of these dinners was at the home of Mr. Kohler, of Kohler & Kohler, which makes toilets, bathtubs, and sinks all over the country. He was the biggest man I'd ever seen, or had seen since. He had a huge, roundish face dominated by huge, bushy eyebrows and was perfect Hollywood casting for the head of a giant midwestern family-owned corporation.

He sat alone at one end of a long, narrow rectangle of tables under tablecloths, with a space in the middle. Five men sat on each side of him, facing each other, all wearing dark suits and ties, darker than his. Some of the men's wives were there, farther down, not sitting with their husbands. Mr. Kohler introduced us to everyone and said we were free to ask any questions we wanted.

It took a bit of a while for someone to come up with a question. I mean, what would you ask? How do you make sure a toilet flushes well? I think Keith Chalmers came up with the first question, and that broke the ice. Any question anyone asked, however, Kohler gave to one of the ten men below him to answer, saying: "Robert, I think you know a lot about that." Then Robert would speak. Not one question did he handle directly, and I wondered if his entire life was held in the minds of these men. All he had to know was which one to ask. And if one day he was alone, and if they weren't around, would he know who he was?

In the look of his eye, however, in the turn of his head, and in every other respect, Mr. Kohler seemed in possession of his part of the world. And although he was quiet, even gentle, he looked—as well as felt—bigger than anyone else in the room. It was a passive but powerful aura he had. I don't think he was even at our performance that night, but I wondered what he would have thought. Could be he had no frame of reference for it, any more than I had.

Sam Herman, a heavy-footed man with a bald head, whose life had been playing rhythm guitar in sixteen-piece jazz bands, was my roommate. He had played with Tommy Dorsey, Les Algart, and Buddy Rich, and had filled in for Freddie Green in the Count Basie band. Sam was the most unpretentious and wrinkly-clothed guy imaginable. He just didn't care how he looked, except when he showed up to play the guitar. Then, he was clean-shaven, had just washed his hands, and wore a neat beige suit, huge, brown-laced shoes, and some sort of cologne.

When we hit the southwest, Sam bought a pair of deer-hide Indian moccasins that tied with a thong. He wore those damned things everywhere and anywhere, no matter what the inclement weather or where we might go after the show. His hulk sort of hung over itself and down through those moccasins and into the ground. All of this fit with the way he folded himself around his guitar when he played. He played a big Stromberg acoustic F-hole guitar. I learned about rhythm from him, the African-American core that was driving American music. He taught me to play the sort of three-note chords Freddie Green played with the Count Basie band. We would play blues for hours on end, trading off on playing rhythm for each other.

Whenever we'd get to a big enough town, he would find out where the big bands were, and after the show we would go down and hang out. He would point out who was dragging or pushing in a rhythm section. Some bands would swing; others would not. When a sixteen-piece jazz band gets it together, however, it's one of the heights of human experience, and like no other music on earth. It may be the ultimate American sound. Born here, for sure, and so far, it hasn't migrated.

This was the world of swing, that had become Sam's reason for being. It was the world of getting one's body, as well as one's soul, into the music, and the world of playing *with* someone, not *along* with them. A lot of the folk musicians I'd known were more interested in running an image, side-by-side playing, perhaps, but not listening, not ever listening. Jazz was about people listening to each other and getting it together; and that was its visceral metaphor. What I learned from Sam Herman affected the whole rest of my musical life.

Sam Herman

Me with Banjo
(Photo: Larry Shustack)

15

"Por la luna doy un peso,
Por el sol que doy un tostón . . ."

Journey to Mexico

Dallas, Texas Jan. 30 McFarlin Aud.
San Antonio, Texas Jan. 31 STOPOVER
Edinburg, Texas Feb. 1 STOPOVER
Brownsville, Texas Feb. 2 Civic Center
Fort Brown, Texas Feb. 3 STOPOVER

After our show in Brownsville, Texas, Sam and I crossed the border to Matamoras, looking for Mexican music. Matamoras was dead. In broken English, someone told us that all the music was over in Boy's Town. Father Flanagan? In Mexico? We took a taxi to Boy's Town, a couple of miles into the desert, where out of the dark came a dim glow hovering close to the earth.

Every building in this town, all set within a grid of dirt roads, was for ladies of the night. Among bars and juke joints and surrounding patios were hundreds of one-room abodes, where women stood at their doors and beckoned. Others worked out of bars or nightclub-like places, and the music was here.

One group after another, trumpets, *guitarróns*, fiddles, *requintos*, and singers who sang at the top of their lungs like nowhere else in the world made up the night-sounds of the *mariachi* bands. Every culture's folk music is completely unique, idiosyncratic, except for its honesty, its inner perfection of difference. That is what gets to you. The musicians wore huge bandit hats, *concho* belts, pants lined with *conchos,* and sharp-pointed boots. Some wore revolvers. I had never heard this music before, but the boots with their deep-angled heels, the hats, and the blaring trumpets supported by polyrhythmic contrasting guitars had me feeling: Oh God, if I could only do this! If only some part of it, even.

I had my first taco that night, and could not get enough of those things. Before I started wolfing them down, however, Sam said, "Do you wanna get high?" This was 1954 and "reefers," or "joints," as they were called, were things I'd only read about. I knew that, in the States, pot was illegal, and I didn't know what it meant to get high, but I figured Sam had been there and back, and why not be initiated into the world of hipness? We bought two fat ones from a weird guy on a street corner. From then on, it was tacos, *mariachi* bands, being stoned out of my gourd, and the choice of as many women out of 300 as I thought I could handle.

We had learned from some soldier at a bar that these women were allegedly clean of disease, having been checked out every week at a United States air force base, not far away. I had always been particular about who I even kissed, so it took a long while before I found someone with whom I could imagine it would be worth getting naked and into bed with. She had an olive complexion, dark around the eyes; her hair was dark brown. Attractive in a natural way, she wore little makeup for that town and place. She and I left the juke joint and walked through the dirt streets to her room, which was cozy, clean, and nicely appointed, with a little shaded lamp on a night table. This didn't match the neon-lit sense of the town. A silver-framed photograph of her husband or boyfriend, I guessed, stood on the night table. She lit a candle and turned out the light, and then began taking off her clothes.

I hadn't seen many women by that time in life—my father's photographs of art models, a girlfriend I'd had back in New York—but this was a woman. She had a difference in style, a way of filling out her skin without thinking about it, a comfort with nudity. Her waist was narrow and her pubic hair was a thick, dark V in the soft candlelight. Her nipples were dark, matching the color that surrounded her eyelids. It was all rather simple, direct, natural and, from an artist's point of view, I thought she was a woman to draw. A woman of women.

It was the photo of her man on the night table, though, that stuck in my craw. I picked up on the idea that this was her job and had nothing to do with her heart, nor with mine. So what was the point of this dance? I didn't have the slightest idea who this person was. The whole situation was not making sense. In fact, it had made less and less sense as I'd walked with her through the dirt streets. I was following a primitive blueprint that life's options made possible, here, in this town, but it wasn't my blueprint. I had no reason to kiss her, to say nothing of anything else.

Later on, I'd make up my own blueprint for this sort of thing: love, or something like it, while you're hoping to find it. Otherwise, if it doesn't already exist, you ain't gonna get it in bed (but you try). Not a lot better than this situation, perhaps, but maybe less meaningless. Then again, maybe not. I don't remember what happened, how it went down, but it could not have been great or I would have remembered.

The pot was so good that Sam wanted to find out where we could get a supply of the same exact stuff to take back to the bus. I didn't think it was possible, not speaking Spanish, and having to rely on the haphazard connections to be made in this town. But we did find the street corner as well as the guy who had sold us the joints. I was amazed we'd done that, but I wasn't encouraged. Sam tried to make clear that he wanted to buy stuff that was exactly like the stuff in those joints; only, he didn't speak Spanish at all. He was just insistent and repetitive. I had taken Spanish III in high school, three times in a row without passing, so it wasn't my language, either. "*No habla Español.*"

The guy told us to wait on that corner and he would be back. But, I'd had enough for one night. We had to be on the bus early the next morning, and I had discovered that I hated waiting on street corners in Mexican boy's towns. "I think we should head back," I said finally. Right then, the guy showed. He took us to a taxi that would take us back to Matamoras, and there, we would transfer to a second taxi, which would take us to a place where we could buy pot. Half a pound for twenty-five dollars.

The second cab driver was short, stocky, and mean looking, and he could barely speak English. He headed out into the country. We finally got to a cluster of adobe one-story houses, lit with kerosene lamps. The potholes in the road seemed as deep as the wheels on the cab. The driver pulled to a stop in front of a house that was some distance behind a barbed-wire fence, barely visible behind huge *chemisa* and cactus. The driver left the motor running with the heater on, went in, and stayed there for what seemed like forever. The cab was getting unbearably hot. When he came back, he handed Sam a brown paper bag filled with pot. Sam turned on the dome light and looked into the bag. It was pot, but not clean, lots of twigs, stalks and seeds, certainly not like the stuff we had smoked. "This is not like what we had before," complained Sam.

The guy went ballistic, noisily slammed opened the glove compartment, reached in, took out a Colt forty-five, and slapped it down on the seat. I remember the gun had a cheap silver finish and reddish-brown crosshatching pistol grips. Sam didn't say anything. I was struck cold. "You want eet or not?!" shouted the cab driver, sweat pouring down the sides of his pock-marked face.

Here we were in the middle of nowhere, this wasn't our country, and there was no question in my mind that we should keep our mouths shut, pay for the pot and get the hell gone. "TWO GRINGOS FOUND DEAD" was the headline I pictured. I was frantically signaling Sam to let this thing go. Sam finally took out the twenty-five dollars and handed the cash to the driver, while grudgingly saying, "This isn't what we asked for!" As if that was going to make the driver feel guilty or noble or do the thing over.

I gritted my teeth.

The guy took the money, did a U-turn from hell, and drove off. It was the worst ride in a car I ever experienced. Every pothole we hit, the car bottomed out, and I think he was searching to hit every one he could find. He finally pulled to a stop in Matamoras on a paved street behind the first taxi and told us we had to get out and into that cab. We made the transfer and the new driver said he had to take us to yet another cab, which had the right sort of registration to take us back across the border.

When we saw the lights of the checkpoint, it felt like a miracle, and I couldn't wait to get back to the States, to our room, and tomorrow, back on the bus. In that moment, I realized that the Broadway lighting of our show was lovely, the show's intentions were good, and I couldn't wait to get back on the road. As we were coming up to the crossing, less than minutes from being back on U.S. soil, I could feel the tension dropping out of every cell in my body. Until I realized we had this huge bag of pot on the seat.

We couldn't throw the bag out the window; we were too close to the checkpoint. I saw us in jail, the show ending up in the newspapers. The only reasonable place to put the bag was in my right-hand coat pocket, next to the door, where the border guard would be looking into the car but the bulging pocket would be in shadow and out of his sight line. Sam didn't have pockets to speak of in his wrinkly cotton sports jacket. I had a suede jacket I'd picked up in Colorado. Only seconds before the cab pulled to a stop, I shoved the bag into my pocket. The border guard motioned me to roll down the window.

"Did you buy anything in Mexico?" he said.

"Yeah," I said, looking him straight in the eye with as much sincerity as possible. "A couple pieces of jewelry." And I started to take them out of my other coat pocket.

"Okay," he said, and before I could show what I'd purchased, he waved us back into the States. Strictly speaking, we were still outlaws, of course, but not dead ones or caught.

The next night, the bus was too hot, but I was just glad to be in the U.S. Some of us slept while others, having gotten tired of word games, got involved in the trading of old on-the-road war stories. I listened. We'd been driving for hours, everyone wanting to get to Fort Brown already.

After a lull, somebody quipped, "Well, it's better than a day job"— as if to say a day job was real and this wasn't; as if being a musician, an actor, a dancer, a painter, an artist, wasn't as valid as growing potatoes or manufacturing road paint. This resonated with the fears I had had all along about what I was beginning to do with my life. Somewhere inside, I knew they were wrong. I knew what it had felt like to sing as I had with Nicky Thatcher, and what hearing the Weavers had meant. What hearing Toscanini conducting Beethoven over the radio in my father's house had meant. I knew that without music, the church would be dead, for one thing, but so would the rest of the world. What would life be without music? But, I had no words to explain it, to them or to me. I just knew that an answer was there, and that I needed to find it in order to find out who I was. I needed the words that would go farther than feelings alone.

16

"When the curtains of night are pinned back . . ."

Assemblage Point

Do you not think it is true that we experience events from the point of view of how we're assembled at any given moment in time? You know, out of what we have learned or not learned? Take the assemblage point of a baby, for instance, whose only response to the world is crawling. That assemblage point moves once that child can walk, and moves yet again when he or she comes to know language.

The writer Carlos Castaneda talked about an assemblage point being moved. I'm not sure what he was talking about, it never got clear in my mind, but I think there's a point within us where our resources gather instantly, or a way that they gather, given some need that confronts us. Some of us go into our heads, for example, while others come more from the gut. But we come together for ourselves, one way or other, when need be, as best we are able.

The nature of that gathering point can be shifted because of some fundamental change in our understanding of life. The shift may come quickly or slowly, be a lot or a little, but when something big enough happens, I think how we gather together can change, and from that time forward we are never the same. I find this the best way to explain how I got drawn into the final vortex of committing to music, body and soul.

When I sang with Nicky, the experience resonated with stuff I already had, and it gave me something to remember about the value of being alive and doing this music. When I heard the *mariachi* bands, it was like that. But when I first heard the Weavers, at seventeen, in a Town Hall concert, that was a different story.

Although Burl Ives, Josh White, and the lesser-known icons of the time—Leadbelly, Woody Guthrie, Richard Dyer-Bennett—differed dramatically from one another, they fit into a spectrum. All were individuals who played their own instruments, made their own kind of music, and had been recorded in New York, just as the Weavers had. But the Weavers had become world famous as pop music stars because of humongous hit singles with Gordon Jenkins' orchestra: "Goodnight, Irene," and "On Top of Old Smoky." But, there was more to their art than hit singles.

This first time I saw them, the minute they came out on stage, they looked rather misplaced. I wondered how these folks could possibly pull off this concert. No matter how they might have dressed, they simply were not of the same cloth, as if they didn't belong with each other or on a stage. They looked almost goofy.

In every popular group I'd ever seen, the members looked like they grew up in the same neighborhood, or went to the same high school, and a lot of them had. They were much the same size and shape, the same skin tone. Their stage presentations were slick. Not these guys. Lee Hays was portly and dour. Fred Hellerman, thinnish and bony, stood flatfooted and looked down a pointed nose at his fingers. He could have passed for a Turk. Pete Seeger, gangly and tall, with his longneck banjo, seemed to tilt his head back and sing out of the top of his mouth, looking down at the audience from somewhere beyond. And then Ronnie Gilbert, full-cheeked, well bosomed, and radiant, sang as if she were rooted to the center of the earth. She had a voice somewhat like Kate Smith's, the national anthem singer of the time, but next to Ronnie Gilbert, Kate Smith sounded like a cyborg.

The group's blend wasn't slick, either. Their voices were as different as their personalities seemed. They didn't actually blend like the Mills Brothers, say, or the Ink Spots, or the Crew Cuts. And they didn't run out on the stage as a unit, showbiz-ta-daaa, either. They ambled onstage as if they weren't quite sure they had found the right room.

When they first started singing, I still wasn't sure they could pull this thing off. The magic began with the fact that they did sing together. What made that compelling was that they were still far enough apart so that you could hear all the parts working together, like a magician exposing how a trick is done. Yet they ended up sounding like more than they were. They had worked carefully on the banjo and guitar parts; it wasn't just two people strumming along, like down at the Square. Their metaphor stood for the idea that people, quite different, could get along, after all, and that when they did, they became superlatively human.

They were doing folk songs from traditions that were not their own, but their respect for the material, and the level of art that they brought to it all, made it so that they were more than the sum of their parts.

Then, there's the issue of size. I don't mean as in number, eighty musicians in a symphony orchestra, or as in the idea of loud. It's an issue of emotional substance, somehow, a spiritual aura, if you will, a form of not being cute. There's nothing cute about the composition that makes a great symphony. It's an aura, not volume, that lights up the sound, and the style of passion. No fidgeting, wiggling, dancing, or hysterical frenzy can do this sort of thing. They lifted the folk song to the level of a Beethoven symphony, while keeping a sense of its roots.

One song they sang that first night wiped out the others, for me. It was their original version of the African chant "Wimoweh," which later got bastardized into "The Lion Sleeps Tonight." The Weavers' version had only the one African word. No English. Just music. No limitations. It left one's mind free to bring to it whatever one needed to bring.

It began with Ronnie, Freddie, and Lee in a tight spotlight, close to the mike. (Groups sang to one mike in those days and had to make room when the lead singer came in to the mike.) Pete stood in the back of the group, in the dark. The song began with Freddie, Ronnie and Lee starting the repetitive chant:

"Hey up boy, Wimoweh . . . Wimoweh . . . Wimoweh."

Freddie filled the spaces between the repeated word *wimoweh* with guitar strums, echoing the word's syllables. Ronnie added a repetition of *wimoweh* that filled out the chant's filigree. And at that moment, the group made way for Pete Seeger, who threaded his way to the mike and began a high, yearning, mixed falsetto, which floated out over the chant. The course of this melody ended with hollers of resistance, frustration, or anger, only to be followed by the gentle relief of a lullaby sound.

I was astonished.

The original theme came in once again, and the song ended with hollers and one final "Wimowaaaay," moving from one octave down to another. The ending paid off the journey with a determination that was the essence of something resolved.

The drama, pathos, valor, and life affirmation of this performance shifted my sense of myself. From that moment on, I knew that I understood something about the value and ecstasy of this kind of art. It had something to do with the essence of life. It was a knowing that happened without any words, a form of existence, of not being miserable, defeated, or negatively alone. It was not a definition but rather a celebration of life, which included its fear, yearning, and ultimate joy—but a serious one, more exquisite than pain, so that pain didn't matter as much.

My assemblage point had been moved. From then on, I would be trying to form my own group, modeled after the Weavers, with whomever I could find at the Square or anywhere else.

The WEAVERS

JOE GLASER, President
NEW YORK, CHICAGO, HOLLYWOOD

The Weavers
(*L to R:*) Pete Seeger, Ronnie Gilbert, Fred Hellerman, and Lee Hays
(Photo: J. J. Kriegsmann)

The Weavers
Pete, Lee, Ronnie, and Fred
(Photo: Joe Alper)

17

"When cockle shells turn silver bells,
Then will my love return to me . . ."

Julia

I met Julia one day when she invited a few of us up to her place near Washington Square after it began raining. She was married to a big bear of a guy named Dryden, a gentle but powerful man, intelligent, forthright, easy to laugh, a psychologist. She played the guitar a bit and cooked very well. They weren't a part of the folk crowd, but she loved the music and she got my sense of humor, as few people did. I remember her as catlike, unafraid of the dark, living within her own world— a deeply hurt world. I learned later that she dealt with her pain by sleeping around. I suspect sometimes she liked who she slept with and other times not. Sexual encounter seems to be one of the universal attempts people make to find wholeness when wholeness is missing. She had a talent for writing, and you couldn't put anything over on Julia.

I'm not sure why it happened to us, exactly, except for our similar process of thought as well as the style in which we were impoverished souls. That also could have been why we were drawn to this music. There was a huge loneliness in a lot of it. I drank on occasion, like most everyone else, and smoked pot now and then, when I didn't feel right with the world. Any mind-altering substance is a great way to blur the rough edges. Then, in your hipness, if you can find some other person to cling to, you've got it made. At least for the night, if not the month.

She had come over to my apartment at 29 Cornelia Street, a one-block street between Bleecker and West Fourth. I'd rented the place from an old friend of my father's who had an upholstery store there, in the front of the building; I had worked there for a time. Julia and I had become friends, although there was a way in which she kept to herself or at home, so I was surprised that she showed up at my door. I'd never known her to be out and about, so to speak, and the etiquette of the city was that you called before showing up at somebody's door. She smiled and said she just wanted to talk. It didn't seem to be about anything in particular, however. We smoked some of the pot she had brought, drank a few beers, the usual deal. It was nice to have company, as I usually didn't. But, it doesn't take a whole lot, if two people are needy, to almost mistakenly touch while crossing a room, and then kiss. She wanted to be touched and retouched more than anyone I'd ever met. Shamelessly. She awakened a desperation of this need in myself.

After a bit, when it could not have been clearer that this was not going to stop where it should, I asked about Dryden. "You're not going to give me a hard time about that, are you?" she asked. I couldn't tell if she was angry or not. "We have an arrangement," she said.

She wasn't wearing underwear. That became clear when she moved my hand there. She wanted me to go down on her. It all seemed to go on forever, one thing after another, as we faded away from the rest of our lives. She wasn't ashamed of her body or how it found pleasure in itself. She had no inhibitions whatever about it. In a way, she seemed like a totally innocent child, wanting to be loved, and to love. It was as if she understood, at some level, that this was the kind of pleasure that bodies were designed to experience. Not a big deal.

But, when it was over and we sat on the bed, her intensity went in a different direction. "Do you really want to be my friend?" she said.

I didn't know how I could be more of a friend. I always liked talking to Julia, and to very few others. If we hadn't been friends, she wouldn't have been there, as far as I knew. I didn't know how to add the word "really" to that. You like someone a lot or you don't. Nonetheless, I said, "Sure."

"Then make a blood pact with me," she said.

This would be done by cutting our wrists and then holding them together for our bloods to exchange. At first this appealed because of those scenes from old swashbuckling movies. I was for it, except for figuring out how deeply to cut. It dawned on me that the wrist was a delicate place to be cutting. I knew I didn't want to use one of my kitchen knives, as I kept them razor-sharp, as my father had done, and Julia was definitely intense about this. The reality of Julia began to get scary, and I wasn't sure how to come off it.

I got her to settle for a beer-can opener. A lot harder to cut with, but a hell of a lot safer. This didn't work very well, there wasn't a flow of much blood, but this made us blood brother and sister for life, even though, in the end, I wasn't quite sure what that meant. By the time this was done, she had stayed way too late. The phone rang. It was

Dryden. They had some words, she hung up the phone with the coy look of a teenager caught, and dutifully left for home, saying, "I'm in trouble now." This sure didn't jibe with "We have an arrangement."

Dryden called the next morning and wanted to come over and see me. I waited in dismay. What in God's name was I doing in life? I felt out of place in my skin once again, like finding myself on the Bowery under uncomfortable sheets.

Dryden wasn't upset, this was an old story, I gathered, but I was someone he knew, and he felt he might help her in some way by talking to me. He wanted to know what had gone on, and I told him the story, blood pact and all. He was grateful. We remained friends.

Dryden finally gave up, I suppose, as they ended up with a divorce. Julia and I got together many years later, and this time, without any games and without getting stoned. We seemed to have a deeper connection. She had no problems teaching me what she liked most, and asked what I liked. She would say simple things like: "I like telling you just what I want. Few men ever listen." I took her upstate to visit my father, as it seemed like this one could last for a while. I'd never told her I loved her, and she'd never said that to me. I didn't want to upset any delicate balance by my need for commitment; I figured she was too catlike. I let the commitment thing go. Then she didn't call, and her phone didn't answer. I knew she was gone. Back to where she had come from, Los Angeles, maybe. Never saw her again, until one night at the Rienzi, down on MacDougal, many years later. For a brief second, she came over and spoke, as if we'd never parted. Under her breath, of the guy she was with, she proudly said, "He just got out of prison." In looking at him, and there was no doubt in my mind that he had. That was it. She went off to have coffee in the back of the place.

November 2007

Dear Julia:

I wish I could see you again. I hope you read this. Did you ever know that I loved you? I thank you for being my friend, for the things you taught me. I hope you are well.

Love,
Erik

Book II

The Tarriers

18

"Every morning at seven o'clock,
There were twenty Tarriers workin' on the rock . . ."

The Right Song

In her midtown brownstone apartment with twelve-foot ceilings, Cynthia Gooding threw dinner parties with her boyfriend, Leonard Ripley, the engineer and half-owner of Elektra Records.

There were candles and wine, *hors d'oeuvres,* then *paella* or steak, French bread, a big, fresh salad with olive oil, vinegar, and garlic. Cynthia and Ripley had spent time in Europe, and they did these evenings with respect. They were like music salons for the level of people who had performed at Town Hall, such as Hillel and Aviva, from Israel; or the Flamenco guitarist, Sabicas from Spain; or Gene and Francesca, older more eloquent artists than I. Hillel played the shepherd's pipe and could make people weep with that thing.

It was at one of Cynthia's big Christmas parties that my friend Lee Haring introduced me to a young Shakespearean actress, Joan Kugell, who would one day end up as Joan Darling, keep death from my door, and then, later on, become the best friend I'd ever have.

It wasn't so much that the people who came to Cynthia's parties were professionals and well known at the time, it was that when anyone performed, everyone listened! You could hear a pin drop. Nobody played along with you unless you had asked. That was a shock. The silence of that respect left you out there, exposed with whoever you were.

It was through Leonard Ripley that I began making recordings as a banjo and guitar accompanist, first for Elektra, with people like Cynthia and Ed McCurdy. Then it was Oscar Brand, Judy Collins, Jack

Elliott, the Chad Mitchell Trio, and so on. Ripley was responsible for my first solo L.P. (on Elektra), recorded in his apartment. But none of those things were getting me closer to making a living.

I might have liked singing alone, going it that way, except for two things: I didn't have much of a voice, and there wasn't a general market for folk music. No circuit of coffeehouse clubs, no college concerts wherein you could work up a following—all that would come later. Many coffeehouse owners did not let us play. The folk crowd was notorious for singing all night, not spending money, and taking up seats.

More than that, however, singing with others, in harmony, created a process, a feeling, a sense of aliveness that could not be experienced alone. And I found that my voice added a compelling element when mixed with a group. This was why I had sung with Tommy Geraci, and why I felt putting a group together was my way to go. And it couldn't have been clearer that popular groups in America—of which the Weavers were one—made their living as a result of hit records. And for that, I needed a song that could capture the imagination of the entire country, as "Goodnight, Irene" or "On Top of Old Smoky" had done.

I ran into Bob Gibson, a Chicago folksinger, one day at the Square. He had come back from the West Indies and had two fragments of songs, among others he'd collected. One went "Hill-and-gully rider, hill-and-gullee," having to do with fishing boats riding the waves. The other was merely a chorus: "Day-O, day-O, day de light and I wanna go home." It was apparently sung among banana-boat workers. There were no verses to make a full song, but the melody yearned, and who doesn't want to find daylight and go home? "That's a hit!," I thought.

I'd hung out with Gibson, busking at bars in upstate New York and Connecticut, when he'd first come to town. I thought we could easily work up this "day-O" thing, write some verses, add somebody else, and we'd have a career. Bob didn't think the song had it. Many times, he told me he did not like to sing unless it was for money, so I found it hard to believe he did not want to give this a try. He shrugged and took himself back to Chicago, which was where he'd been headed.

But I was convinced. And I'd make a group one way or other. The Tunetellers.

What a godawful name, I thought at the time, but when we were about to audition for a big New York D.J., Al "Jazzbo" Collins, we had to call ourselves something.

Not only was Collins excited when he heard us audition at his studio, but he wanted to bring people to see us perform on a stage. We rented Jose Quintero's Circle in the Square Theater, on West Fourth, between Barrow and Seventh. By putting flyers all over the Village, we nearly filled the place for the night of the concert.

At the time, I didn't think it made any difference how many people we had in the group as long as we managed to get it together, somehow. It was the song that would make us. I had started the group on MacDougal one night, when I'd asked Bob Carey if he wanted to make a hit record. He and I had recorded with Roger Sprung on an obscure label called Stinson, a year or two earlier, as the Folksay Trio, so I knew that Bob had a good baritone voice and a good sense of time. Bob had a friend, Carl Carlton, who was a fan of Lee Hays and the Weavers. Somewhere, I found a great gospel singer, who was with us awhile, and from the Square, a guitar-playing lawyer. This one and that one.

Nobody, however, except Bobby and Carl, showed up on time for rehearsals. I don't know how many people we went through. We were a quintet when we performed at the Circle in the Square. "The Banana Boat Song" had a full set of verses by then, it worked as a closer, and the audience liked us. But Jazzbo had never shown up. As far as we know, neither did any of his people. Perhaps they were there and chose to say nothing. It would not have surprised me; once we

The Folksay Trio at Washington Square
(*L to R:*) Bob Carey, Roger Sprung, and me

got on that stage, everyone vied for himself. Any cohesiveness we might have found in rehearsal was gone. As I walked down the street after that show, I was incredulous, frustrated, and filled with self-doubt. Five people were one person too many, for one thing. At least in this case.

Bobby and Carl were willing to keep hanging on, but we needed a fourth, as Carl didn't have much of a voice, he barely sang bass. What he did have was a friend in L.A., one Alan Arkin, a young actor whom he thought would come to New York and be in the group. Fly from L.A.? In the middle of his life as an actor? To become part of a nonentity group? I didn't think so. Not if he was any good.

Alan flew to New York with his pregnant wife, Jeremy, signed on with the group, and turned out to be better than the rest of us.

After a month of rehearsal, we went to Pete Kameron, one of the Weavers' old managers, who now managed the Modern Jazz Quartet. He said he would set up auditions for Decca, Columbia, RCA Victor, United Artists, and Epic—the top labels in the country—but he said he didn't have time to manage us. He told us to get a new name (bravo to that). We came up with "The Tarriers," taken from a song about the Irish workers who set blasts in the building of railroads:

Drill, Ye Tarriers, Drill

Every morning at seven o'clock,
There were twenty Tarriers a-workin' on the rock.
The boss comes around and he says, "Keep still!
And come down heavy on your cast-iron drill."

CHORUS:
And drill, ye Tarriers, drill.
Drill, ye Tarriers, drill.
For it's work all day for the sugar in your tay,
Down behind the railway.
And drill, ye Tarriers, drill,
And blast. And fire.
And blast. And fire.

Meanwhile, we auditioned for an agent who booked resorts in the Catskill Mountains. He said he would call us.

The auditions began for the labels. One after another, they recorded our sound, including "The Banana Boat Song," on which Alan sang lead. Week after week, it went on. Nobody wanted us.

No-bo-dy.

I thought we were fresh and unique, and the folk sound had already proven itself.

All these dreams, all the work, the finding of songs, being guys on a quest, and the delicate process of writing arrangements. No interest whatever? Only we had begun sensing that something was wrong within us. It was an issue I did not want to face because of the bonding we had.

But if one person in a group doesn't feel the music quite as the others, the group doesn't work. Period. It can be close, but that's not enough. Carl was not on the same musical wavelength as Alan, or Bobby or I. He had brought Alan into the group, he'd hung in there and toughed the thing out, putting off what he might have done elsewhere in life. Unfortunately, art doesn't work on intentions, it has to be right, unto itself. In truth, you can't fake it.

We went through an awkward process of disbanding the group, and then Bobby, Alan, and I found ourselves out there, as it were, not knowing for sure if the three of us wanted to keep pushing this forward, or even if we actually could. The Catskills agent had booked us three gigs. We decided to take them, even though the entire effort was now anchored in doubt.

The next time we met, we chitchatted for as long as we possibly could, avoiding the unavoidable. We pulled out our instruments, tuned to each other as long as we could, and sang the first lines of some song.

The lid simply blew off the pot and flew against the wall. We couldn't stop laughing. We were swinging like we should have swung all along! Not one note had been changed, the arrangements were exactly the same, but the feel was on fire in every respect. No other feeling like that on this earth, and the promise of what we had dreamed came fully alive. We went back to Pete Kameron, who told us he could not set up new auditions for those labels, that once they think they know who you are, that's it. It was almost like finding the meaning of life only to find that it's over. But now that we knew, we had to keep going.

Ed McCurdy and me
(Photo: Joe Alper)

Oscar Brand and me
(Photo: Larry Shustack)

19

The Moveable Magic

The Catskill Mountain resorts were places where performers got to be known or discovered. What we could not have imagined was that when we would perform on a stage the first time, we would have morphed into a pancake that had been left overnight in a pan of dishwater. And that what we had found in rehearsals, since we'd come alive, had closed down, disappeared, vanished into thin air. Adios. *Sayonara.* Go home.

It was like we were in a *Twilight Zone* show and someone had pulled the plug on our brainstems. The audience all but sat on their hands, for good reason. "If only they could hear us rehearse," Bobby said at the break. We doubted that the audience would even come back for the second half of the show, except for the fact that they had no other place they could go, stuck in a Catskill resort for the weekend. Does it ever end?, I thought.

"I got an idea!," Alan said, in his usual way, as if lightning had struck him. Back in the dressing room, in our first intermission of life, he had us go over some song as we usually did, sitting and facing each other. Before we had gone very far, he stopped us and put his fist at the center of the circle we sat in, where our eyes would have met. "Here's where we usually sing to," he said. Then he moved his fist to the left several inches, and said, "Let's see if we can't move our focus to there." We sang once again and were able to do that! Interesting thing. Then he said, "Let's move it to just outside the door." We did it. The next job was to move it all the way out to the audience, once we got back to the stage.

Wine, women, and song, with the emphasis, women, was the story I would have written to explain Bobby; Alan was somewhat like

Hamlet, a furrow-browed "to be or not to be" sort of person who oftentimes brooded, then came up with ideas. Me? I was hoping to find feelings of personal hope and ways to express them. We were not the same sort of people, but when we moved the intimate musical connection we had all the way out to that audience, we became one. Another explosion occurred, as we joined with these people. Their applause came back as explosive, as well. And once we got that, we found we could share even more of ourselves. After the performance, people were asking, did we have any records? Were we coming back? Were we performing anywhere in New York?

One roly-poly, good-natured fellow told us we were terrific, said his name was Art D'Lugoff, and that he knew a fellow who owned a record company, Glory Records. (Who had ever heard of Glory Records?) Well, there was no point in not giving Glory a try, since we had exhausted all other options.

The Tarriers
Me, Alan, and Bobby
(Photo: Larry Shustack)

Rehearsal in Brooklyn
Alan, Jeremy, me, and Adam (*lying down*)

20

"Come all you bold sailors that follow the Lakes
On an iron ore vessel your living to make."

Glory Records

Forty-seventh Street, between Fifth and Madison, middle of the diamond district, is a great block in which to look for a diamond, but no place you would ever expect to find a record company. In fact, the only time I had ever been in that block was when I was stuck in midtown, trying to get over to Grand Central Station on foot, wanting to connect with the shuttle to Times Square, or with an empty cab coming out of the station. Glory was on the south side of the block, up one flight, in a barren, nondescript office, walls painted green, at the top of a long flight of stairs. The elevator was so small and rinky-dink, the three of us couldn't get in there along with our instruments; we chose to walk up the stairs.

Scotch-taped to the left wall as you came into the office was a Glory L.P. of Sidney Poitier reading poetry. This was before the great man was part of the American psyche. I don't know if the company had any other releases at that time, but if so, they weren't Scotch-taped to a wall. Waist-high gray partitions stood with a swinging gate through the middle. Behind them were two typical gray metal desks, and behind one sat the owner of Glory, Phil Rose.

He wasn't short, or tall, or particularly narrow—I guess he was average. He wore a nondescript suit, a striped tie, had a high forehead, and thin, balding hair. He seemed to hold his head down and looked up with a hint of derisiveness, maybe. His brown eyes peered out the top edge of black-rimmed glasses. With a handshake, he pleasantly welcomed each of us into the office.

With no carpeting and no curtains, the office was live: nothing soaked up the sound as we sang. And our sound was the size of the

Weavers in that little place. Before the end of our first song, we could see a thin little smile reluctantly pulling at the corners of Phil Rose's mouth. We had a cash-register sound, and Phil knew it. Within two weeks, we had set a deal and signed contracts. When it happens, it oftentimes happens that fast.

We didn't care about lawyers and working out deals relating to the future, or even the present. Somebody finally wanted us! All we wanted was to make music. No matter how small or unknown Glory was, singles and an album would be cut and released, and we would be recorded in a top New York studio!

The catch? There isn't always a catch, but this time there was. Glory had signed another artist, Vince Martin, a six-foot-tall, curly-haired, blue-eyed, Brooklyn-born "balladeer," as he would be called. That's what they called singers in Tudor England in the sixteenth century, when songs had as many as twenty-five verses. People like Burl Ives and Richard Dyer-Bennett may have been called balladeers, but they sang those old songs.

"Cindy, Oh Cindy" was the song they had for Vince Martin. Only they had no idea what sort of band to put behind him. That is, until now. As a favor, they asked us to write arrangements and give him a musical context within which to exist. Small price to pay, we thought, for being finally wanted.

Sixty years before Vince was born, someone had recorded African-American Georgia Sea Island dockworkers singing a song called "Pay Me My Money Down." Pete Seeger made it popular around New York.

> Pay me, oh pay me,
> Pay me my money down.
> Pay me or go to jail,
> Pay me my money down.
>
> I thought I heard the captain say,
> Pay me my money down,
> "Tomorrow is our sailing day."
> Pay me my money down.
>
> Pay me, oh pay me,
> Pay me my money down.
> Pay me or go to jail,
> Pay me my money down.

The very next day we cleared the bar,
Pay me my money down,
He knocked me down with the end of a spar,
Pay me my money down.

The melody of this song had been co-opted for "Cindy, Oh
Cindy," but without its original feel. We put the song back into its
original groove, ignored the insipid lyric, and gave Vince a sound.

Cindy, oh Cindy,
Cindy, don't let me down.
Write me a letter soon,
And I'll be homeward bound.

We went into the studio with a bass player, a drummer, and Vince;
recorded two songs: "Cindy, Oh Cindy" for the A side of a single, and
"Only If You Praise the Lord" for the B side. Then we went in and
recorded an album of our own, which included "The Banana Boat
Song." I was living with Joan by now (Joni, to me), and she came to
our sessions. She sat unobtrusively in the back of the control booth at
the Columbia Recording studios, where we recorded, and kept track of
the snide things Phil Rose would say now and then. When I was feeling we needed a bit more space around our sound, and asked for it, for
instance, Rose remarked to his cohorts, "Erik's found a new word."

On October 13, 1956, "Cindy, Oh Cindy" with Vince Martin and
the Tarriers hit the top-100 Cash Box chart, peaked at No. 9, and was
on the charts for nineteen weeks. Eddie Fisher's cover of the record
came on the charts October 20 and got to No. 10.

One of the co-writers of "Cindy, Oh Cindy" was Art D'Lugoff's
brother, Bert, and they were all friends with Phil Rose. Did this have
anything to do with what followed? I don't know, but we were told
Glory would not release "The Banana Boat Song" until "Cindy, Oh
Cindy" was on the way down, and why didn't we go on the road with
Vince Martin?

8,000 reasons why not. If Carl Carlton wasn't on our wavelength,
Vince Martin wasn't on the same planet. We did not have to do this.
Nobody was holding a gun to our heads. But, we were all paying rent
on apartments and trying to keep mind and body together. I was en-
gaged to Joni, Bobby was about to get married, Alan and Jeremy's son,
Adam, had been born, and although we believed we were on the cusp

of success, we needed to bridge this gap. Nothing whatever in our contract said that the company had to release our record in our lifetime, even. Mistake number one.

When we signed the contract with Glory, we had also signed one with Art D'Lugoff for management. Mistake number two. He seemed to think teaming up with Vince Martin was a good idea, also. Everyone thought we could be a great act. We understood the impossibility of this, but we knew there was no way to explain why to a cadre of deaf people. At the same time, we wanted to be "good guys," fit in, not make too many waves, not look our gift horses in their mouths. It was a sellout on our part, for which we would not be forgiven; you make a pact with the devil, he always shows up with his lawyer and the contract you signed, with your blood. We chose to go on the road with Vince Martin.

When the earth was formed, God must have made sure that Buffalo, New York, would get plenty of cold, damp snow; and He wanted to be sure it stayed there all winter. The middle of winter in upstate New York is a hell of its own, but Buffalo really shows off. One of the first places Vince Martin and the Tarriers were booked was a huge supper club in the Italian section of Buffalo. The snow on the edge of the sidewalks was up to our hips, to our shoulders in some places.

These big supper clubs, all over the country, provided a circuit of venues for hit record acts as well as a mass of seasoned performers who filled out their shows. A comedian usually opened the show, followed by a belting jazz singer, and then the hit-record act. This place in Buffalo probably seated three hundred people at round dining tables with white tablecloths and cute little lamps, and the food was on the order of shrimp cocktails, oysters on the half shell, lobster, lasagna, chicken scallopini, steak, and eight kinds of pasta.

The act that we followed was one of the sexiest black female singers imaginable, accompanied by a sixteen-piece jazz band. We went out with our two acoustic guitars, a banjo, and Vince Martin, and did the first show. When we had finished, Bobby, Alan, and I were numb. The spotlight had been blinding, and we couldn't see or feel the huge, eating audience, although we could vaguely see the table lamps, dishes of food, water glasses, beer bottles, and dimly lit faces.

Vince had no understanding about what being on stage was about and no interest in learning. Getting him to understand timing, programming, introductions, and pacing had been like pulling the teeth out of a moose. Nonetheless, we got through the first show, and no-body had booed. It was now time to get out of our performance clothes, and hang out in the place until the next show. Someone knocked on the dressing room door. A voice said that the manager wanted to see us immediately. "It's okay, don't change your clothes," the voice said.

The manager's office was near the front of the club, on the left, as you walked down the side of the room. The walls of the club were black, as was the door to the office. The office was large with signed 8-by-10-inch photos of such people as Tony Bennett, Dean Martin, Nat "King" Cole. Sitting behind a huge, dark mahogany desk, the manager/owner of the place was right out of central casting for a 275-pound mobster wearing a rumpled black suit with white shirt and bow tie. This guy wasn't an actor with an accent, however; he had lit-tle accent at all, but he was the kind of guy you never talk back to. He gets to talk, you get to listen. When you meet someone like this, in the flesh, there is no question about it. I suppose it's like being one of those animals that knows instinctively who its natural predators are.

When we trooped into the room, there was no welcome, and the aura was thick, dull-witted, and quiet. We had to wait while he fin-ished doing some paperwork. This guy made Mr. Kohler, of Kohler & Kohler, seem like a guardian angel.

"You stink!" he said, when he finally looked up. "I ought to call your agent and send you the hell back to where you came from. You don't straighten that act out, that's exactly what I'm gonna do." He didn't sound dim-witted at all, and we had no room for any excuses whatever.

"Okay," Alan said, and we walked out without saying another word. Either we would manage to do it, or we'd be heading home in the middle of winter. We decided to open the show and do fifteen minutes, then introduce Vince. We picked which songs Vince would do, and the order, as well as how quickly we'd move from one to the other. Managing to stay the two weeks, we learned how to tighten a show so as not to lose an audience in the middle of their cracking the claws on their lobsters.

The Ohio, Allegheny, and Monongahela rivers converge at Pittsburgh, where at night we could see long barges moving out on the river and, if we found the right spot, the glow of a steel mill. Up the street from the club we were performing at was a pinball parlor with sixteen machines. I hope you don't ever get hooked on pinball, as we did. But it was better than twiddling our thumbs in a dressing room too small, even, for that. The club we were in was always jammed and had a long bar along the back wall, which meant we had to compete with the jangling of glasses, the cash register, and bar talk. But the sound system was great, so we could get people's attention. We were the only act on the bill, and it wasn't a big dinner place. After one of the shows, I was hoping to get out of the place and up to the pinball machines when a businessman stopped me, wanting to tell me how much he liked the performance. "You fellas are great," he said. "After the three of you finished that opening bit and that tall white guy came out and sang 'Casey Jones,' that was just great! Gonna stay for the second show. Bring the wife back tomorrow."

To this day, I wonder what shade of what color of what race he thought I was. Granted, Bobby was black, and Alan could have passed for a Greek, but I wasn't exotic-looking at all.

A big, powerful spotlight lit the nightclub in Boston we played, and the stage went out into the audience. Andy Williams had been the headliner the previous week. During our stint, we followed a male singer who closed his act with "Bye, Bye, Blackbird." You may not have heard that song, but it was part of the American soul at that point, and it's one of those songs that everyone sings on, and they usually cry. If they've had enough whiskey or beer, the entire audience will be weeping and hugging each other, swaying back and forth and crying over every pet that had ever died on them, or any time their hearts were broken in high school, or over any repressed disappointment until now. After something like that, when the audience is totally spent, you come out and do something like "The Rock Island Line," they're gonna think, "Where did these guys come from? Morocco?"

Added to that: this was good old Catholic Boston, and we were reviewed in one of the big papers. Vince's big song, "Casey Jones," got some reporter upset.

> Come all you rounders if you wanna hear,
> The story told of a brave engineer.
> Casey Jones was the rounder's name.
> On a big eight-wheeler, boys, he won his fame.

The song tells the story in eight or nine verses (I guess that's a ballad, all right), but it was the last verse that disturbed the reporter:

> Mrs. Casey Jones was a sittin' on the bed.
> Telegram came that Casey was dead.
> She said, "Children, go to bed and hush your cryin'.
> 'Cause you got another papa on the Salt Lake Line."

The reporter was irate that we were being disrespectful to Mrs. Jones's family, that Mrs. Jones never remarried and had been true to her husband. The article was endlessly long. What struck me was the trouble the reporter had gone through to research the Jones family history. I could not help but wonder, was this guy afraid we would lead Boston kids down to sin and destruction, because this folk tale had suggested adultery? (Only time would reveal the unforgivable sins that lay behind the stone walls of his own Boston churches, more heinous than anything that ever had been or would ever be sung by a folk singer.)

One place we were booked thought we were a dog act. We were billed: VINCE MARTIN & THE TERRIERS.

But we had to quit working with Vince. It was going against everything that had brought us to this music. We auditioned for Max Gordon, the owner of the Village Vanguard, and he booked us for three weeks. We played opposite the Clarence Williams jazz trio, the house band. They were easy to listen to and easy to follow on stage, everyone loved them. The Village Vanguard was twenty-five steps down from the street, with line drawings in white on its flat black walls. There were no dressing rooms; we got it together back near the kitchen. I'd seen the Weavers down there, Josh White, Ed McCurdy. Hallowed ground. The club served high-priced cocktails, sandwiches, and coffee. The *New Yorker* described it as "small and intimate." The audiences were close and compact, sitting at small, round, shiny black tables. In the back was a bar. As we waited for Glory Records to release "The Banana Boat Song," we were coming in out of the cold. In the *New Yorker* was just the one name: The Tarriers.

VINCE MARTIN and THE TARRIERS
Glory Recording Artists

Vince Martin and the Tarriers
(Photo: J. J. Kriegsmann)

THE TARRIERS   Glory Recording Artists

The Tarriers, sucked into showbiz. Alan, always in touch
with the joke of these moments.
(Photo: J. J. Kriegsmann)

21

"I sleep by sun and I work by moon,
Day de light, and I wanna go home . . ."

"The Banana Boat Song"

"The Banana Boat Song" came on the charts December 22, 1956, went to No. 4, and was on the charts for nineteen weeks. We had been right!

We had begun the calypso craze, however, and would be typecast as a calypso group, not as singers of folk songs. The T.V. show "Your Hit Parade" had production numbers of the song for eight weeks with dancers in costumes and sets suggesting bananas and Bahaman vacations. Except for the Ed Sullivan Show, every T.V. show we did had us sitting or standing in stage sets of dock pilings, barrels, netting, bananas, or palm trees. Steve Lawrence's cover of our record came on the charts January 12, got to 18, and was his first charted record.

Harry Belafonte was an emoter/dramatizer of folk songs and was, therefore, not of great interest to me. I'd never heard his version of "The Banana Boat Song," called "Day O," which had been released on an RCA Victor L.P. a year before ours but had not been discovered. RCA Victor covered our record with Belafonte's "Day O," which came on the charts January 12, went to No. 5, and stayed there for twenty weeks. With the power of RCA Victor, Belafonte's version became the better-known one and, for sure, sold many more records.

We were booked into the Apollo Theater in Harlem, with steel drum bands and the Duke of Iron, a calypsonian from Trinidad. This guy was for real, although a bit hard to understand because of his West Indies accent. In one five-minute song he sang (every night), all I ever got were the last five words: "Hitler sent back the codfish." But the man was a rhythmical genius, and this was authentic calypso. Calypsonian songs often wove stories around well-known historical people, such as King Edward, who gave up his throne for the love of a commoner.

> I know King Edward was noble and great.
> But his love would cause him to abdicate.
> It's love, love alone
> That caused King Edward to leave his throne.

"The Banana Boat Song," by the way, was not a calypso as much as a Jamaican folk song. Calypso came from the island of Trinidad and had a most unique and compelling sense of language, rhythm, and rhyme. The world of showbiz, by its nature, doesn't hear subtle distinctions like that.

The Macambo, Montreal, Canada—everyone speaking Canadian French. Ten acts were on the bill when we played this huge place. It had DayGlo tigers painted on its black walls. Workers would come in at 3 a.m. when they got off the night shift, put their lunch pails on tables, and drink out of quart bottles of beer. Being the headliners, we had to wait for those ten acts to finish each night, two shows a night, three on the weekends. They let us go on early for the last show on weekends.

Up in our beds—our rooms being not far from the stage—we'd hear the French Canadian singers doing their versions of such hits as "You Ain't Nossing but a Hound Dog." We went to sleep with those sounds. The bill also featured jugglers, clowns, and a guy who balanced on a billiard cue. He was a gambler who was always playing cards in the dressing room, taught us a great game of solitaire where you lay out all the cards face up, except for the kings, and he taught us a system for beating roulette. Joni and I would use this in Las Vegas. In short, we were becoming show folk.

Syracuse, New York, was in the midst of a bleak winter snowstorm, which lasted the two weeks we were there. We had been booked into the Three Rivers Inn, the biggest prom-night club in the area. The roofs of farmhouses, barns, fields, and sky were all the same shade of misty gray-white; if snow wasn't falling, it was blowing around, and only the walls of the houses and barns told you the shapes of their roofs.

Between shows, we sat at a huge, dimly lit, oval-shaped bar outside the main room. The opening act was a local group of female impersonators called "The Jewel Box Review." Seeing these guys in their sequins, dresses, and wigs across that bar for two weeks, in the middle of winter, was like being in a Fellini film. The reality of our dream, having a hit record and performing all over the country, was becoming quite clear. Yet, this film we were in did have its wonder in the flux of the human condition.

One of the things about being a performer is that you know, when you walk on that stage, it's a moment of truth. You've got the one chance to do what you do, and you can't do it over. This gives the event something you want to live up to. You can be nervous at first, until you find yourself mindful and carefree, giving it all that you've got. It's a place of elation and kindness, if you don't get thrown off.

When we did the Ed Sullivan Show, we had to perform "The Banana Boat Song" four or five times before we could do it for real: once for the cameras, once for the lights, full out for the sound, and full out for dress rehearsal. The nervous wreck of a director kept coming over and telling us to smile. He was a completely uptight and insufferable man who hadn't the slightest idea what we were about, what we were doing, or how we went about doing it. By the time it came to the final performance in front of the audience, with cameras between them and us, we had sung ourselves out. Our final performance was wooden, erroneous, flat.

Being on the Ed Sullivan Show, however, was something my mother and uncles in Baltimore, Maryland, could relate to, and they were impressed. The fact that Ed Sullivan seemed to shake my hand or touch it in some way as we left the stage was far more important than any music we might have done or not done, and how well or not well we might have done it.

From the producers of
"ROCK AROUND THE CLOCK!"
THE SCREEN'S FIRST GREAT CALYPSO MUSICAL!

"Calypso Heat Wave"

CO-STARRING: JOHNNY DESMOND, MERRY ANDERS,
MEG MYLES, THE TRENIERS, THE TARRIERS, THE HI-LO'S,
MAYA ANGELOU, PAUL LANGTON, JOEL GREY.

Hear THE TARRIERS sing their big
"Banana Boat" Hit!
Every cat is crazy about these
CALYP-STARS!

Screen Play by DAVID CHANDLER
Story by ORVILLE L. H. HAMPTON
PRODUCED BY sam katzman
Directed by FRED F. SEARS

Those were the blurbs on a theater poster advertising the film. Although the entire film was shot in ten days and was never worth seeing, it was a thrill to be on the back lot of a Hollywood studio. We watched Maya Angelou moving among barrels and dockworkers while she lip-synched one of her songs; huge speakers played her performance track music. It all came to a halt when the director would cut off the music, sending all the dockworkers, actors, dancers, and Maya back to their original places, ready to shoot the scene over for some little change. When it began once again, it was, once again, real. Maya was beautiful to watch, a wonderful singer, and she moved like a leopard. The Hi-Lo's were a jazz group, as their name suggests, and could probably have sung any intervals anyone ever imagined, completely in tune.

When we lip-synched "Chaucoun," a Haitian folk song, even though we were lip-synching the song, I got into it enough to be crying. No matter what context you're in, I discovered, the emotions that hide in a song can come forth.

Las Vegas, Nevada, the city of silver dollar pancakes, bright lights, gambling, and the country's top entertainers. We found that no motel would take Bobby. We hadn't come up against this. Not having grown up in the South, having been raised on a lake in upstate New York by a painter who had not a prejudiced bone in his body, this Las Vegas reality check was not in my frame of reference.

Although I had heard the "n" word (who hadn't?), it always came as an unpleasant shock, and lynching was, for me, only a horrid idea, not a reality. And I'd never been in the South, never seen signs that read "WHITE ONLY."Looking back, I'm sure there were many who wanted to lynch us for being a "mixed group." We never were booked into the South, come to think of it. We were just guys from New York creating this music and just hadn't thought about this as a thing that would get in our faces.

We found a motel in the black section of town that would take all of us, but the chlorine in the pool was so strong it permeated the rooms on the second floor. Next day, Joni got on a tear, calling every motel in the book. She found one, a short way out on the strip, that had no color code.

The room that we played was in the El Cortez casino, downtown, and was the smallest place we had played. I don't think it seated more than two hundred people. They had a small band that played in a cramped orchestra pit, stage left—bass, drums, piano, and saxophone. They accompanied the opening act and expected to accompany us. After the first rehearsal and sound check, we decided we did not need a band whose sense of time was based on the show-tune milieu. And we discovered that the stage was a 20-by-30-foot ice rink.

A mike stand had been set on the ice, downstage center. They could have lowered a mike from the ceiling, but we were used to gathering around a mike stand. Not only would we have to cross twenty or so feet of slippery ice to get there, but once we got there, we found that our natural movements had us losing our footing, and the bottoms of our feet were getting cold. They ended up putting a large rubber mat under the mike, and that meant that, once we got to that island of safety, we were home free. Except that, if a metal pick came off one my fingers and bounced onto the ice, and I had to move off that mat to bend down and retrieve it, I was in serious trouble.

The room being small and the sound system strong gave us a control of that place like no other. The opening act consisted of showgirls on skates and a singer of sorts, who sang into the mike that came down from the ceiling. It was a good act to follow for us; we were a perfect contrast to bass, drums, piano, and sax. The unique sound of the banjo and guitars took over that room, the waitresses gradually stopped serving during our songs, and the room became ours. When waitresses stop serving like that, except between songs, it is one of the best compliments you'll ever get. And that you take with you. But no matter what you take with you, it doesn't always apply to what's going on later; life can get denser, and the great value of *hanging in there* can always apply, as it sure in hell would in my case.

The Tarriers at RKO Palace
(Photo: Arsene Studio)

At the Apollo
(On the bill with the great Duke of Iron)

22

"I am a roving gambler. I've gambled all around.
Where'er I see a deck of cards, I lay my money down . . ."

Wee Kirk of the Vale

Joni and I had been waiting for this: the roulette table at the El Cortez was nearly deserted one night.

The system I had learned from the gambler at the Mocambo revolved around the three sets of twelve numbers on a roulette table you can bet on, as sets. If any one of those numbers comes up in your set, you double your money. The system was this: you wait until one set of twelve numbers has missed in twelve spins of the wheel; then you start betting on the thirteenth spin, on that set of twelve. If that set misses again (and you lose), you double your bet for the next spin, and you keep on doubling it until one of those twelve numbers hits. It computes to a quarter, then fifty cents, then a dollar, two dollars, four dollars, and so on. Once it hits and you win, you start over, waiting for another twelve misses on one of the sets. You won't win a lot in a hurry, the gambler had said, but you'll keep winning steadily, and you don't need a whole lot of money to start.

Joni

We didn't have the patience to wait for twelve misses again and again, and casinos don't like you sitting there taking up space and not betting, so we changed it to eight misses, then bet. We agreed to start with eight dollars, play until we were eight dollars ahead, put that money back in our pocket, so that we would only be playing with money we'd already won from the house. The gambler had told us you need at least eight dollars to start.

I'd always assumed that having a hit record would solve all of life's problems, at least the financial ones, anyway. Doesn't happen. You need at least three. With one record, you might end up with a new car, but not much more than that. The expenses of travel and lodging and food, putting money aside for living back home, for down times, for when you don't have a hit record, and paying your taxes— it all eats you alive, like it does anyone else.

We ran the house's eight dollars up to sixty-four dollars, and began thinking new clothes, a vacation, a new couch, easy strect. On the next go-round, we had to keep betting until we had the sixty-four dollars out there, twenty spins of the wheel had missed. And it missed once again.

It was over.

There was no way we could double the sixty-four dollars into a hundred and twenty-eight dollars. We had been playing for peanuts, of course, on our way to big bucks, but when we left the casino and walked down the street, it felt as though we had lost all of those dreams. Yet we had lost nothing. Dreams of something for nothing. Joni and I never had an interest in gambling again.

We had decided, however, that we would get married this trip. It was something we wanted to do on our own. My family had not been a family for as long as I knew; Joni hadn't felt overly loved by or validated by hers. She was an actress, I, a musician, we would do this together, by us and for us, and with our best friends. It was our way of standing alone in the world. Why in Las Vegas? I guess we'd seen those little wedding chapels in movies, and the place seemed more celebratory than New York, somehow. This made it easier for me to deal with my mother, as well. I didn't think she had understood my connection to Joni, in any event, just as she hadn't seemed to understand my connection to anything else. I did not want her at this event in my life. That was sad, I suppose, but it's just how it was. Out of town made everything easier, none of the relatives, nobody slighted, and, at the same time, Las Vegas, Nevada!

Alan and Bobby were best men. Jeremy and Bobby's wife, Harry, got a whole bunch of tacos and sparkling burgundy for our celebration back at the motel. It was a great day. Joni wore a special blue dress we had bought in New York, and a rabbi, at a little blue-and-white clapboard house called the Wee Kirk of the Vale Wedding Chapel, performed the ceremony. It was like in the movies.

Except that during the ceremony, I began laughing and had trouble saying my vows. I was frightfully embarrassed, guilt-ridden, and worried about what Joni would think. I carried that guilt until over forty years later, while writing this book, when I finally asked her how she had felt. "We both had trouble keeping from laughing," she said, "because the rabbi had a waxed handlebar mustache and wore a frock coat, a string tie, cowboy boots, and a cowboy-like hat. He had everything but a tin star and spurs. Your laughter seemed perfectly natural to me; that's why we should have been married. Think on the positive side."

There you have Joni.

It turned out, as well, that our cowboy rabbi was also the head of the local NAACP. It all fit together.

The big shocker came after the ceremony, when the fat lady in the cotton print dress, who ran the Wee Kirk of the Vale, asked if I wanted a recording of the ceremony, for an extra ten dollars. I could think of nothing to say except, "No!" She'd never asked if we wanted it recorded in the first place, so the invasion of privacy boggled my mind. (And my laughter, recorded?!) I was incredulous. To this day, I wonder if that recording isn't out there somewhere. It could be. It could turn up on eBay.

After our last show of the night, without changing into our street clothes or taking off makeup, we often rushed out to the Sands to feast on the buffet before it closed. Three dollars bought all you could eat: lobster, shrimp, ham, prime rib, small sweet pickled apples, and desserts of every description. On one of those evenings, Nat "King" Cole, who was playing the big room, came ambling through the lounge with some friends. A guy sitting in the lounge shouted, "Hey! Come on, you could do us a little favor. Sing us a couple a tunes." Cole ambled over to a mike while the bass player, drummer, and guitarist, on a break, got to their feet and filled in behind him.

Cole's music was of the kind that was part of the American experience, almost a backdrop. I took it for granted; I'd seen him on T.V. and in movies and wasn't particularly impressed. In person, however, the elegance of the man as he stood there and sang was a grace of the creative spirit that explained why he had been so successful. Success of that kind has its reasons for being. He exuded a grandeur of humanity, but so unadorned and fine-lined that his presence was mesmerizing. He put no spin on it, no extraneous emoting, no ego, no attitude; it wasn't an issue of showbiz. And the whole thing just happened: no curtain going up, no introduction, no hats, not dancing, no razzmatazz of one kind or other. Then it was over. He offered thanks and walked off.

We didn't learn until later that one of the reasons he probably stopped and sang a few songs was that blacks weren't allowed in the lounge. When I heard that, I wondered if they allowed him out of his hotel room during the day? Good thing they hadn't spotted us. And although Bobby seemed to take it in stride, our trouble when we first got to town, the fact that that stuff was alive, made me wonder how he felt. What that must be like. If there are things you can do to put that aside. Or if he even knew what it did. I never asked. I hadn't learned how to get real. But I knew it was something that protest, or law (by itself), couldn't change. Not the heart of the issue. And it was at the heart that change had to happen, at the heart of the brain, however and wherever that is.

At a urinal in the men's room of the Sands, a guy next to me said, "Where are you working?"

It had to have been the makeup I hadn't had time to take off, and maybe the shirt. It was just a striped shirt, but it didn't quite look like street clothes (Kameron had told us never to wear clothes from the street on the stage, it should be something that nobody in the audience has in their closet). It turned out that this guy was from one of the lounge acts. He asked what type of stuff we were doing. I said kind of like folk music. "Hey, that's a good thing," he said. "Yeah, get something new. Always good to get something new." There was no way I could have explained that it wasn't a choice of that kind, but it pointed up a difference between us and a lot of entertainers out there.

Then we found a piece of existence one night. And a moment I'd never forget. The room was nearly sold out, and it happened that there was a table reserved for fifteen people, Liberace and friends. He was so well known that I could not help but be somewhat impressed. And, of course, they all bustled in during the middle of the last song of a set. You couldn't miss Liberace with his rings, his huge face, head of hair, smile, and voice. Even though we were interrupted, there was a positive energy, as the group was respectful, and there to have fun. We looked forward to the second performance.

We knew the room at this point, knew where the walls met at the corners, so to speak, knew where the entrance door was. We were loose and at home and had begun playing around with the rhythms of songs, adding new musical lines here and there, beginning to grow. But on this particular night, as we began the last show, we found we were swinging our asses off. I don't know how else to put it strongly enough, or precisely how to explain what took place. It wasn't the kind of thing where one of us said, "Hey, let's really do it tonight." Yet, as the moment's awareness gathered us to it, each of us knew that any one of us could change what we were doing as a group, and that the other two would be there behind it. Yet, at the same time, each of us knew that the others would not change a thing. It was like knowing what somebody's thinking, but from inside his mind, and in this case, inside two other minds. We were floating and totally focused. It was nearly bizarre, in contrast to the rest of our lives, except that it felt so alive.

It was beyond the idea of performing on a stage to an audience, more like a moment of having walked into a room of pure consciousness, where no permissions or thank-yous had to be received or given. We were now free from having to explain or be liked, like innocent children who haven't been harmed.

I'm not sure what it means to be fully present, if that's what took place, but it was as if we had melded into an acute understanding of what we could become as a group, with each of our individual talents. And it was time to become that, without letting it blow us out of the water. We kept the thing going. It was the reason to be there and the ultimate reason for doing this work.

At the end of the show, we got an explosive standing ovation. This was with songs that most of the Las Vegas audience would never have heard of, such as "Drill, Ye Tarriers, Drill," "I Know Where I'm Going," "Shadrack," "Rock Island Line," "All My Trials,"—folk songs. We knew we had earned the ovation in the best of all possible ways. And it was as if we were able to say to the prejudice we had encountered, to the performing on ice, all the way back to that Buffalo gig, to all craziness, maybe: "We have our wings and we're flying away!"

It wasn't with a sense of pride that we left that performance behind. It was with a sense of amazement, and something you can't get a prize for, or even understand fully, because you can't find its edges. We had moved up a notch, as we headed for the next phase of our journey, as we headed for Europe; perhaps it would give us an edge where the cultures were different from ours,

And Joni and I were now husband and wife. On record, in fact.

23

"What was your name in the States?
Was it Thompson or Johnson or Bates? . . ."

America Visited

Alan, Jeremy, and Adam (the baby), Bobby and Harry, Joni and I, arrived at Le Havre, France, and boarded the boat train to Paris. The food from the vendors on the train was ham and cheese on fresh French bread, with small bottles of wine. The bread is always fresh in France, as we would learn well.

When the three weeks' engagement was over, Joni and I moved in with David and Gloria McAdams, friends from the States, who lived on the outskirts of Paris on a cobblestone street, where no one spoke English. We were there for a month.

We had come over to Europe by boat, on the *America,* and had managed to get bumped up to second class by agreeing to perform in the ballroom of the first-class lounge. We would get into our outfits, tune up in one of our staterooms, and wend our way up through a system of passageways. They put a mike on the dance floor in front of the bandstand, and while we were singing, people got up and danced. Meanwhile, the boat would slowly list over to one side, then way back to the other, and the dancing people all slid to the lower side of the dance floor. It was all we could do to keep from laughing long enough to sing songs. After our weeks on the ice and now this, it was getting to be a bit much.

When we slept, when we ate, when we played cards, when we walked on the deck, the boat listed. All of us were on the verge of seasickness. When the five days of crossing the Atlantic were over and the seven of us settled in on that boat train, with the wine and the simple French food, the click-clack of the wheels and the jerk-back-and-forth of the train were like heaven.

The owner of President Records and some of his cohorts met us when we got off the train at the Gare du Nord, in Paris. We split up among four small taxis and then were driven at high speed (I mean crazy) to our hotel, which was within walking distance of the Olympia Theater, where we were to play for three weeks. We had insisted on a hotel close to the theater so we wouldn't have to deal with subways and taxis, at first. The women and the baby remained at the hotel to get settled. Joni went out to a drugstore to pantomime for disposable diapers.

The owner of the record company whisked us to a press party—everything frenetic, happening at once. We were told President Records would be recording us live at the theater and then selling that record in the lobby. We weren't sure how happy we were at being recorded and having no control over what was released, but this was the way things were done.

The press party was held at a restaurant with *hors d'oeuvres* and wine. Three of the most beautiful women we'd ever seen were there, dressed in the most simple but elegant clothes. French clothes, at the time, were the finest in the world, down to the stitching on the inside of lapels and along inner seams. The clothes these women wore seemed to flow down their bodies like cream. It wasn't a matter of romance, or even sex, I suppose, because we didn't know who these women were, and we were, each of us, fully involved. But some women you can't take your eyes off. And then someone let us know they were brought there for us! This was their idea of "a welcome to Paris."

I don't know how to explain what that's like, either. Knowing so little, at that age, about human relationship or about French ways and means, it slips in on you at a 180-degree angle. We informed the promoters that we were married and had to get back to our wives. "Why on earth did they bring their wives?" exclaimed one of the press team, according to the guy from President Records who had become our translator.

At the theater, they wanted us to perform with bass and drums (and the musicians were good), but they wanted them to be hidden behind the thick curtain. We would perform on the apron, and somewhere back there would be our drummer and bassist. For the life of me, I could not understand why it was so important that the audience not see those musicians. Then there were issues about programming. To look in your little English-to-French book dealing with issues like this was impossible. Fortunately, someone spoke enough English to translate. But right when it came to a disagreement, they would not understand. Could they really not understand, or was this their game? It was driving us crazy.

Then there were the taxi drivers. Once they understood we were foreign, they'd take us the longest route possible, or they'd tell us they had passed into a district that imposed a surcharge. Such districts did exist, but we didn't know if they'd driven into one or not. Paris was made up of so many twisted, one-way little streets that sometimes the only way to get to wherever it was, was necessarily circuitous, seemingly crazy, as well. I wondered if the way the streets were laid out had an effect on their national psyche, or was it the other way around?

Since we had arrived, there hadn't been time to catch on to the fact that the only hotel that was as close to the theater (as we had requested) was a hooker hotel. People coming and going all night. Joni found a hotel on the Left Bank, on a quiet little one-block street, Rue de Montholon. With the price came breakfast (brought to your room), which consisted of eggs, croissants, butter, sharp marmalade, and hot chocolate or coffee. The windows were six feet tall, opened inward from the street, and had heavy, dark green velours curtains. The bedspreads were heavy red-silk-covered quilts. Made you wonder what *this* hotel was about.

The night concierge was an old guy who had been a professional soldier and had fought in the armies of the White Russians, the Italians, the Germans, and the French. He spoke enough English to entertain us with his views on the character of these different peoples, according to how they fought wars. Diagonally across from the hotel was a restaurant we ate in a lot. It served rabbit stew, much as my father had made it. *"Messieurs-dames,"* the woman sang every time we came in, throwing her arms up in a welcome. When we got to know her, we discovered that she thought we were English.

Next to the lobby, with a doorway connecting it to the hotel, was a small, dark-wooded café that served cognac, wine, and espresso. An ex-ballerina owned and ran it. A huge, passionate photograph of her hung on a wall. One night, Joni and I were having a couple of cognacs before heading to bed, when a Frenchman came in with a man from Oklahoma. The Oklahoman wore a brown suit, white shirt, string tie, beige cowboy hat, and brown boots. Neat and expensive, had already had too much to drink, but kept ordering more, and he got louder as the minutes wore on. "I bet you this . . . and I bet you that." My guess was that he felt it was all a big joke: the money didn't look real, the French couldn't understand what you said, and who are they anyway? Back in Oklahoma, the rules of the road had probably kept him congested since he was a child. He began spewing out sexual epithets and fantasies that I'd never heard anyone in my life express in public, or anywhere else. Any low dive in the States would have thrown him out.

He must have taken us for French, because he turned to us and he bellowed, "I bet when you go upstairs, you stick it in her ass. . . ." The Frenchman with him didn't seem happy, but he was taking his money, I figured. We paid our bill and left quietly, having seen through the keyhole of one of America's cowboys in Paris, and the underbelly of middle America.

The majority of French people seemed to have motorbikes, motor scooters, or those little gray *Deux Chevaux* cars that were called "sardine cans," the roofs consisting of a piece of stretched canvas. During rush hour, twenty-five to fifty of these putting vehicles would sit, axle to axle, fender to fender, scooter to scooter at a red light; when it changed, the sputter and crackle was something that can't be described, except to say, "Paris."

Many of the buildings were in shades of pastel and had been there forever, with baked-enamel house numbers. A woman could walk anywhere, safely, at night. I felt I could get to love Paris, once I learned enough French to handle the taxis.

Joni managed to find an English production of *A Streetcar Named Desire,* and got the part of Blanche. One evening, a couple from the theater group invited us over for coffee. Their apartment was literally eight by ten feet, with a narrow bed, a hot plate, a sink, and a closet, the door of which was covered by a thin bedspread. All the apartments on that floor used the one bathroom down at the end of the hall. They explained that most French apartments were small, like this, which was why people went to cafés to meet friends all the time.

Coming in contact with the French, as a people, in subways, cafés, and streets, it dawned on me that there was something French about everyone. Like a similar skin tone, a jaw set, a broad stylistic attitude with many gradations, inclusions, and nuances: how they pursed their lips with certain expressions; or two cab drivers refusing to back up if they happened to meet in the middle of a one-way alley. Bobby and Harry went to a basement night club where sex was performed on the stage. There were artists along the Seine. La Bonne Crêpe was a restaurant that made *crêpes* on little round stoves at gray-painted picnic tables, where students could eat inexpensively. La Pomme Frite served potatoes and little steaks cut across the grain, cooked three feet in front of you on a huge five-foot griddle. You couldn't get out of there without smelling of steak—another page out of my father's house. A subway line ran on rubber tires and the tires on wood, noiseless and smooth. It was so unlike a subway, yet that's what it was. At an immense flea market, I found a bunch of antique watch faces with tiny garnets and sapphires, for 25 to 50 cents apiece. Thought I would make a collage out of those when I got home. Paris was a city of watercress, snails, sauces and soups, and sounds that were foreign. Even French poetry had a romantic sound, so you didn't have to know what it actually said to think it meant something profound.

And then came Edith Piaf ("The Little Sparrow"). I think she had the heart of the French. She came into the Olympia Theater after we left, but we happened to see her backstage, before we had finished our gig. She was shockingly small—well under five feet. But, when we saw her on stage, it was an epiphany. Her presence and voice filled up the hall, and the world around it, beyond any restrictions. The size of her passion and soul was a thing that remains in your person forever, along with her attention to detail: timing, and movement on stage, no matter how small. Consummate. An order of human perfection. Like a great concert pianist. We saw every performance she did in that place, including all matinees. Since we had performed there, they let us in whenever we wanted.

She made us feel like all is not lost, even though she sang of much pain. She was a model for telling the truth and leaving no corners untouched. All by herself, as small as she was. The absolute height of performance on stage. The Little Sparrow.

Out of all that was French, I realized that I'd never had a conscious sense of being American. I had no sense of my own cultural identification, per se. In Paris, I felt like a camera, a neutral observer. I felt more or less blank about my own cultural psyche, unselfconscious about it at all, until one day, when strolling through a park, we noticed, at the far side of the square, people were gathered for some kind of procession. We ambled across and joined the onlookers just as a motorcade passed.

Standing in the back seat of a large American-made convertible, with fins, were Dwight D. Eisenhower and General Charles de Gaulle, side by side: de Gaulle in his olive-green hat and olive-green uniform, and then Ike in a blue suit and striped tie. I'd never seen either of these men in person. Ike's ruddy complexion, his blue eyes, which could have been seen from a mile, contrasted dramatically with the face of de Gaulle, which was somber and closed, his skin color a soft variation of the olive in his uniform. Ike's face was American, and de Gaulle's, French. I could see the G.I. in Ike's aura, the openhearted grin, as if America had never grown up in some way, or had cast off the rules of European decorum left over from divine rights of kings and their offspring. Yet, he wore the term "presidential" so well: no arrogance to him. It was the first time I understood that part of being an American had to do with an innocence, I think, and a lack of emotional secrecy. I felt a sense of my cultural heritage for the first time in life. Some part of me resonated with what Ike was about. Maybe it was about being nothing in particular or about being able to dislike many things in my country, yet feeling free to do that, yet not knowing quite where that came from. It just was, in some way.

We were booked into Stuttgart, Germany, for one concert. We left Paris by train and were awakened sometime in the night to show our passports. At breakfast, in the dining car, we were already in the middle of the German countryside. By contrast, Paris had felt soft, disorderly, creative, romantic, loose-footed, a mixture of order and chaos; some of the older buildings were supported by long wooden poles that angled into the ground. The German farmhouses were straight-walled, made of cut stone, orange-tiled roofs, sturdy, in order, secure. What a relief, so it seemed.

A man with a black diesel Mercedes met us at the train station. The car's engine sounded like a clock ticking. "Now that's the essence of engine," I thought. And the seats were tan leather, sweet-smelling in winter. He drove us right to the hall to check out the sound. The Neumann mike, which was already set up, was a cylinder the size of a flat-ended fountain pen. The damned thing picked up every sound that we made and delivered it to every corner of the hall, metallic and crisp. One mike. Germany seemed to know how to make automobiles, farm houses, and mikes, that was for sure. It didn't take more than one song to check out the sound and the lights. Our man with the four-wheeled clock then drove us right to our little hotel, two stories high. Everything neat and in order, and tomorrow we'd sing.

A party was in full swing at the hotel. This was the time of *Fasching,* a German holiday similar to our Halloween, where people dress up in costumes. After drinking for hours, the merrymakers were now caterpillaring around the hotel in a long line, each person holding the shoulders of the person in front, everyone singing, with side-to-side swaying. Just as we entered the hotel with our bags and our instruments, ready for sleep, the front end of the line came through the small lobby. Leading the line was a person dressed up as Hitler!

It didn't feel funny, or merry, somehow, being that we were two Jews and a black guy, and we had no idea what this was about, no idea about *Fasching* (and even if we had). I didn't sleep deeply that night, despite being under a six-inch down comforter, with the window wide open, and breathing cool air.

Early the next morning, women were out in the street on their hands and knees, scrubbing down white marble doorsteps of stores. I went to a drugstore for an aspirin. The man who waited on me was a tall, broad-shouldered, big boned, distinguished looking middle-aged man you might see in a film shot on-location for a 1942 World War II movie. A Kurt Jürgens type. Only he walked with a limp. I could not but wonder if he had been wounded in the war. A war we had won. I felt like an American, then, and it felt odd to be facing this formidable man, waiting on me, who would surely have been a commander. I was small-boned and just a musician, yet I was the victor.

Everything about Paris swirled around our involvement with the work. As large as it was, the Olympia Theater, with its huge balcony and wide stage, felt intimate and alive. The producers never gave in on the placement of the bass and drum player (behind the curtain). "To hell with it!," we said among ourselves. "We'll play it our way, and if they can't follow us, that will be their problem." Only they didn't have any problem.

We didn't give in on the programming. One thing about becoming an artist is that you learn how your work works, and you do not let people mess with it. The recording "Les Tarriers, à le Nouvel Olympia Panoramique . . . votre Music Hall" turned out to be the best stuff we ever recorded. The bass and the drummer stuck with us like glue, and the French loved us more than any other audiences anywhere, save for that one night in Las Vegas. Nobody came to the Olympia to drink or eat food, they came to hear music. That gave us an edge.

When we got back to New York and I took a subway the following day, I was struck dumb by the sight. Slowly taking in the entire population of the car, I saw that they weren't all French. No two people were the same color or complexion, or had the same cultural attitude. It was with a sense of peculiar amazement that I absorbed what this was. I had been gone long enough to have forgotten New York, and America. And I thought it so odd that I'd never seen this before.

When we came back from Europe, Phil Rose had the brilliant idea of releasing two singles at once. The A side of one was a mediocre calypso-type song from our album "Pretty Boy." The A side of the other single was a country waltz, "Those Brown Eyes." He let the D.J.s decide which was the hit. The D.J.s, of course, all jumped on "Pretty Boy," because it was a "calypso." Two D.J.s in Minneapolis/St Paul, however, jumped on "Those Brown Eyes," which became a No. 1 hit in those sister cities. "Pretty Boy" was an immediate bomb everywhere else in the country, as well it should have been. Had it only been "Those Brown Eyes," the course of our history would have been different.

We flew out to Minneapolis/St Paul to be in a Fourth of July parade. Like war heroes, we sat up on the back seat of a Cadillac convertible, while they played the song through loud speakers. When the parade stalled now and then, we sat in the hot, humid, midwestern sun with our sense of being heroes diminishing.

The feelings among us were strained. Before long, we knew Alan would be leaving the group. While we were in France, he had broken the news that he needed to follow his passion and go back to acting. Everything on the journey—from Art D'Lugoff to Phil Rose to Vince Martin to, most of all, our own ignorance—had taken its toll. As far as the group and my life were concerned, this was disaster. And I knew Alan was right. It was the main lesson to learn: that in the true bloodline of the creative soul, it is always "To thine own self be true."

Not long before Alan was leaving the group, the music business changed dramatically. This change was one that the Tarriers could have thrived in, had it all happened sooner, had we been the flower instead of the seed. Phil Rose had kept asking us to come up with another hit song, so it remains a complete mystery why he didn't release our version of "Tom Dooley" when it hit the charts in September 1958, as sung by the Kingston Trio. The song was on our L.P. from two years before.

While the Kingston Trio's form of folk music was climbing the charts and transforming the musical taste of the nation, we found Clarence Cooper, a wine salesman from Harlem, to replace Alan in the Tarriers. He brought a repertoire of extraordinary spirituals to the group. I thought the world would love them. We recorded an L.P. for United Artists and, although I was not wrong about those songs, I was wrong about the world loving them. To listen to stuff you've recorded, know it's magnificent, that it does all you need it to do, for itself and your own sense of musical purpose, and then to understand how it does not resonate with what's going on in the street, this is perplexing. And this is the game.

The Tarriers, with Clarence Cooper
Bobby, Clarence, and me
(Photo: Ray Sullivan)

Erik   Alan   Bob

LES TARRIERS

EXCLUSIVITÉ
DISQUES

PRESIDENT
Records
HIGH FIDELITY RECORDING

Les Tarriers
Paris

24

"If I had known my captain was blind, darlin'.
If I had known my captain was blind, darlin'.
If I had known my captain was blind,
Wouldn't gone to work 'till the clock struck nine, darlin'."

The Lesson from Clarence

Softspoken, clear-speaking, intelligent, Clarence seemed to be living his life with wisdom, even though he didn't say a whole lot. The sense of his wisdom came more from a smile or a look in his eyes when he recognized something as true, than through something he'd say. He always dressed well. Part of his being a salesman, I guessed. He was blacker than Bobby, and although he lived closer-in to the black culture than Bobby, his sensibilities seemed to be, as I heard them, less about being black versus white, than about what life was about beyond all of that. As if to say, "The crazies live everywhere, so let's get along where we can." He was easy to be with, and if one description fit him more than anything else, it was that he was a gentleman. He had a personal deference to getting along (without selling out) that you simply don't see very often.

Through my respect for his music and what he brought to the group, I felt a friendship existed between us, a bond that allowed a degree of intellectual freedom, a shared sense of humor, a willingness to play with what is. No racial tensions whatever arose between us. But there was this one time when I thought I'd be cute, yet serious, too, around the idea that I did understand, at some level at least, that the way of the white world was stacked against him, a world that, of course, I was a part of, but that I took nothing for granted. After rehearsing at his apartment in Harlem, as we were all leaving, about to walk out the door, I stepped to one side and said, as I beckoned with my hand, "You first . . . for once."

"Oh, that's okay, man," he said, not missing a beat, with a smile, no edge to his voice whatsoever, "I'm used to it." He had spoken with the same sense of good will and play as I had, and sort of like stating a fact. As if not a big deal. I was pretty much quiet for the rest of that day, as I pondered the echo. "No laws on this planet can change how it is" crossed my mind once again. It has to come from a shift in a pattern of soul and of heart among people. I felt then and feel now that this sort of sickness living in the sinews of our culture, hidden as it is, will fester and hurt for a very long time. It is a terrible sadness and one of the reasons we needn't be an arrogant people.

I asked my captain for the time of day, darlin'.
Asked my captain for the time of day, darlin'.
Asked my captain for the time of day,
He got so mad he throwed his watch away, darlin'.

Book III

The Weavers

25

"There once was a ship, sailed on the lowland sea . . ."

The Weavers

Pete Seeger had left the Weavers, and they were looking for a replacement. The number of people in the country who fit the requirements could have been counted on the fingers of one hand, and I may have been the only one in New York, at the time. It had to be someone who played the five-string banjo, knew their music, and had been on stage enough to know that you show up on time. Because of the place they held in my psyche, when I got the audition call from Fred Hellerman, I felt equal parts of excitement and trepidation. I could not help but wonder if I could live up to this call.

I did know that the Weavers had been brought down by the blacklist and labeled as "Reds," whatever that meant. It had little meaning to me, not being a political person at the time. In my father's house there was seldom a newspaper, to say nothing of political discussions. He'd always say, "Somebody got married, somebody died, there's a war going on, and I don't need a newspaper to tell me that stuff." And music, to me, was not about economic theories; it was about finding emotional reasons for living. Much more to the point was the fact that this group had inspired the very essence of me, created a space which I hadn't had. That inspiration had given me the Tarriers. I came to the decision that if somebody wanted to taint me as a Red, so be it.

We sat around and sang a few songs, that's how the audition was held. No pressure. Having sung a lot of their songs in Washington Square and having been through a world of harmonic ideas with the Tarriers, it wasn't hard to find where my voice needed to go. At first, they presented it as wanting to finish an L.P. they had started with Pete; after that, we would see.

For some time, I rehearsed with the Tarriers as well as with the Weavers, treading an awkward line between the two groups, until the Weavers asked me to rehearse for three weeks at Crystal Lake Lodge in the Catskills. The lodge had agreed to give them free room and board and a place to rehearse, in exchange for concerts on weekends. I accepted. Meanwhile, the Tarriers got booked into the Village Gate, and I couldn't make that because of the commitment I had made to the Weavers for the three weeks. Bobby didn't think I could work in both groups at once and felt they should go it alone. That ended my time with the Tarriers.

At times, I wondered how people would compare me to Seeger, as many of us had been drawn to the Weavers because he was with them. But, it was one thing to play Weavers songs at the Square, along with everyone else, and quite another to get the notes actually right, keep in mind the order of songs for a concert, remember where I had to retune the banjo for key changes, as well as blend in with the pattern their psyches created. I discovered that the group was a lot more than Seeger, and there just wasn't time in my head to worry about what people might think about anything.

Before I could feel I was holding my own, though, many concerts would pass. Our first Carnegie Hall concert was mostly unpleasant. I hadn't found a strong foothold, even though we had done many out-of-town concerts by then. On the intro to "Venga Jaleo," which Pete had invented, for example, I flubbed quite a few notes; I did a solo and left out some measures; and I had to keep looking (nearly compulsively) at the order of songs I'd Scotch-taped to the banjo. My island of safety was the song that had shifted my being when I'd first heard the group at Town Hall, and a song for which Seeger was particularly known: "Wimoweh." I felt more aligned with that song than anything else in the concert, and that was my goal. To hang in there until I got to that place.

As I got myself through one song, then another, it became a process of coping, being present for some songs and not there for others. When it was over, I remembered mostly the mistakes and my general discomfort. But Joni was there, and she remembered it this way:

> Pete was in a box, stage left, to my right, and everyone was watching to see what his reaction would be to you in the group. Me included. When you first sang, he sort of led the applause. Then, at

the end, when you sang "Wimoweh," he led a standing ovation for you. He passed the mantle to you in a most generous way, as I saw it.

I have no recollection of this, it amounts to hearsay for me, except that throughout the years, I've always known Joni to have the most annoying recall of events, such as who said what and to whom, and what actually happened. One thing stayed with me, however, as if it were yesterday:

> After that concert, you said that it didn't feel like you had dreamt it would feel. You had sat in the audience as a teenager and watched Seeger sing with the group, had even gone backstage and gotten your banjo autographed by him. But, now, here you were, being him, as it were, and the actual doing of it was not the magic and total cure-all for your life that you thought it would be. Both of us were beginning to find out, in those days, that nothing is that sort of thing.

Existing in a group is often like being in a dysfunctional family: one person comes ten minutes late, another doesn't like to rehearse, one is impatient, another is the salt of the earth; and issues of personal aesthetics are at stake, day in and day out. I was the tenor; Lee Hays, the bass; Ronnie, the alto; Freddie, the baritone; and no one was boss. It was for each person to work a way through, as best as he or she could.

There is a logic, of course, to the creation of music, the way melody and lyrics define what they need. But, within those parameters, every person is different, and you learn not to battle each tiny thing. Some you give in on, knowing you'll hate it forever. Others, the ones that you'd give your life for, you weigh in on as cleverly as you can. You stay out of the way, and you watch like a hawk for the moment to make a suggestion or voice an opinion on the side of another who hears it as you do. That's how I lived in the group. I was also quite good at bringing in Weavers-type songs.

Freddie, I thought, was impatient with me, even though I could see he was impatient with everyone else. And, as I imagined myself through his eyes, I saw me as lesser. He had a gift for arranging and a knowledge of music which I didn't have. I couldn't help but look up to the man. Yet, I never knew what to make of him or how I fit in. Joni's take:

> Freddie was who he was; he was shrewd, also smart. The meaning of the word *hyper* could have been coined around Freddie. I always

felt he respected you, but that his metabolism didn't allow him to take the time to tune his guitar, nor give you the time to tune yours. His whole energy ran so fast, I don't think he took the time to absorb the information he got.

I felt like Freddie was kind to me. Ronnie certainly was, but Freddie was, too. I can't put my finger on what it was, but it was like he was a good guy to me. Lee became our friend. We used to go to his house and hang out.

Dealing with three older and strong-willed people was far more complex than dealing with two guys my own age, as it had been with the Tarriers. Nevertheless, I was treated with the utmost respect, as an equal participant, not as the new kid on the block or someone that had to earn tenure; everything else was a head-trip of my own.

Out on the stage, it was as if a powerful gale came from back-stage and swept to the audience, and all I needed to do was to keep from being blown over onto my nose. Then, every once in a while, as I learned how to be there, as we learned how to be with each other, we sailed like no other group in the world. Our topgallants, royals, and skysails flying. It wasn't as it had been with the Tarriers, where it seemed like we swung from inside each other's brains, it was more side by side. When I was singing the lead on some song, I could feel each of them extending their power, timing, and eagerness to me, helping me live in that moment. They supported my artistic merit, whatever it was, every time. But, it was as though they had been given a gift of some sort, and I was given the privilege of visiting there, in the temple they sang from. They seemed to lift up their voices and sing to the entire world, whereas my tendency would normally have been to speak to the person out there who sat all alone, yearning to make a little more sense of it all, and hoping to find a resonant voice of authentic feeling, confirming that his or her life was as important as anyone else's. That the struggle is worth it. That the bell tolls for us all, each, for our own unique way. At the same time, many of the songs the Weavers performed reflected the sort of gritty, down-to-earth passion for the human condition which had drawn me to folk music in the first place. "Buttermilk Hill," for example, a solo of Ronnie's, spoke not only to the depth of love that a woman can have for a man, but to the depth of sorrow that goes with losing that man, along with the twist of fate that brings her to buy him a "sword of steel" in the hopes it would save him, while knowing it might get him killed. And then, later, that it did. This is Shakespearean. A deep, personal tragedy, that expresses the value of an intimate love.

> Here I sit on Buttermilk Hill,
> Who can blame me cry my fill.
> And every tear can turn a mill.
> Johnny is gone for a soldier.
>
> I sold my rack, I sold my reel,
> I even sold my spinning wheel,
> To buy my love a sword of steel.
> Johnny is gone for a soldier.
>
> Me, oh my, I loved him so.
> Broke my heart to see him go
> And only time can heal my woe.
> Johnny is gone for a soldier.
>
> Here I sit on Buttermilk Hill,
> Who can blame me cry my fill,
> And every tear can turn a mill.
> Johnny is gone for a soldier.

Or take "McPherson's Lament," which speaks to the sanctity of music, the right to one's soul, and all that that means in the end.

> Farewell, ye dungeons dark and strong,
> Farewell, farewell to thee.
> McPherson's song will not be long
> Upon the gallows tree.
>
> Say rontonly, say wantonly,
> Say dauntonly played he.
> He played a tune and he danced it aroon.
> Below the gallows tree.
>
> Oh, little did my mother know
> When first she cradled me,
> That I would become a roving boy
> And die on the gallows tree.
>
> Untie these bands from off my hands,
> And give to me my bow.

I've not to leave my brave Scotland
But a tune before I go.

There's some come here to see me hanged,
And some to steal my fiddle,
But before that I do part with her,
I'll break her through the middle.

He took the fiddle in both his hands,
He broke it o'er his knee
Sayin', "When I am gone, no other hands
Will ever play on thee."

Say rontonly, say wantonly,
Say dauntonly played he.
He played a tune and he danced it aroon.
Below the gallows tree.

I'm reminded of a story Lee told me of Seeger. Lee and I hung out
on occasion, drank beer (he more than I), and talked about life. We
both had grown up in the country, and that gave us a kinship, I think.
This had to do with some concert the original Weavers had given, and
they were at somebody's place after the show.

Seeger had taken his banjo and smashed it down through a glass
table. The neck broke, and Lee was elected to take it somewhere for
repair, while the other three Weavers fulfilled some obligation. Lee
said he would take care of the banjo, but only if Pete told him why
he had done that. Pete's reply, according to Lee was, "Sometimes I
feel like I've got to either kill someone or smash a banjo down
through a table."

I never understood why Lee told me that story until now, perhaps, after reading the lyrics of "McPherson's Lament." But, I've had
those sorts of feelings, as well, and I've broken my share of instruments out of one kind of frustration or another. I recently asked Pete
about that event, which he remembered. He wrote me this note:

"Tiny" Hill weighed three or four hundred pounds and led
a country band at a nightspot in Denver. It was 1952, perhaps,
1951. I smashed the banjo because "Tiny" and the Weavers
wanted me to drink with them, loosen me up. Since I don't drink,
except for an occasional beer or glass of wine, I got mad instead
of laughing at them. But I didn't feel like killing anyone, as best
I remember.

Darling Corey

Wake up, wake up, Darlin' Corey,
What makes you sleep so sound?
The revenue officers are comin',
Gonna tear your still house down.

Well the first time I seen Darlin' Corey,
She was standing by the sea.
Had a forty-five strapped to her shoulder,
And a banjo on her knee.

Go 'way, go 'way, Darling Corey,
Quit hangin' around my bed.
Bad liquor has ruined my body,
Pretty women gone to my head.

Oh yes, oh yes, my darlin',
I'll do the best I can,
But I'll never give my pleasure
To another gamblin' man.

That was an interesting woman, I thought. A singular lady. She had a forty-five strapped to her shoulder and a banjo on her knee, and she didn't want to make love to someone who gambled. Like so many folk songs, it reverberates in many directions at once, such as our war of independence being started over issues of revenue agents and unfair taxation. And in this case, love isn't something to bestow on a gambler.

Lee Hays was from Arkansas, and remained so, I believe, though I'm sure he would never have gone back. Had he drank less beer, been from somewhere else, and weighed less, he might have been delighted when we got the news that a promoter in Israel wanted to book us for a tour of that country. We would get to Great Britain, as well. Lee sat there and looked pale, with a typically inscrutable silence, maybe poking his glasses up on his nose (a habit he had).

I wasn't eager to schlep all the hell over there, either. I felt I'd been there and done that. Not wanting to make waves, I kept my mouth shut, hoping this would blow over. Lee's silence and passive-aggressive behavior had me believing he'd get the job done. I sat back and waited. Not a good choice.

One of the Weavers' themes was the idea of people all over the world getting along and living in peace. Intellectually, going abroad fit with that theme. Freddie and Ronnie were eager to go, but then Ronnie was eager for life as a whole, no matter what it contained. In fact, Ronnie was the center of gravity that allowed the rest of us to spin out of orbit at times. Whatever the case, my strategy lost.

Lee, Ronnie, me, and Fred
(Photo: Joe Alper)

Me, Ronnie, Fred, and Lee
(Photo: Joe Alper)

26

"I'm bound away, 'cross the wide Missoura . . ."

The Yarkon River

Here we were, booked to do forty-two concerts in five weeks, and just before we began our descent into Israeli airspace, I discovered I had a sore throat. Not only that, but the back of my throat showed white spots. Scared the hell out of me. Further, to get visas to work in Israel, we had to agree to perform a number of afternoon concerts for the army. I know of no sober performer who likes afternoon concerts.

When we stepped off the plane at the Tel Aviv airport, it was like stepping into a total inferno. The heat came from in front, from behind, from below, from both sides. I thought to myself, "See what you get when you keep your mouth shut?" Stepping into Dante's inferno, I was one unhappy camper.

An odd thing was that Pete Kameron, one of the Weavers' earlier managers and helper of the Tarriers, had somehow been put in charge of being the road manager for this tour. Joni, as well as I, had informed Kameron of my condition before the plane landed. He said he would take care of getting a doctor, first thing. Since the days of the Tarriers, however, I'd always had my suspicions about him. You couldn't tell who he was. You couldn't be sure, from his manner, that he'd ever do what he'd say. Although his midtown office had been spacious with dark carpets, tall windows, a big desk, and he managed the Modern Jazz Quartet, he dressed in a self-consciously hip way, affecting the use of a cigarette holder. His eyes always darted away, as if he wanted to keep track of who was listening: he reminded me of a Peter Lorre type, who had maybe smoked a pipe bowl of hashish. At the same time, Kameron knew a lot about stage presentation and programming. What he'd taught the Tarriers had saved us in Buffalo.

Our motel was not far from a waterway known as the Yarkon River. The only unpleasantness, at breakfast, was in those moments when the wind came in off the Yarkon River, which emptied into the Mediterranean and was simply raw sewage. At all other times, it was out of nose, out of mind.

All the rooms opened onto a swimming pool, and the inhouse restaurant tables spilled onto a shaded patio, always with fresh white tablecloths on them, and had heavy creamers like old railroad silver. These were surely nice things for a desert existence, but they meant nothing to me at that moment. I needed a doctor. Our take on Kameron's present demeanor was that he had brushed us off with empty assurances, and that he would end up doing nothing about getting a doctor right off. But, we didn't want to get a doctor on our own, in case our instincts were wrong, and have two doctors show up, as well as showing disrespect for Pete's word and the idea that he was the man.

"He was the slickest little cannonball showbiz weasel," Joni remembers. "And newly married to this tall, beautiful model. He was Mr. Commercial, compared to Harold Leventhal (who managed the Weavers then), who was Mr. Integrity. Pete Kameron was very busy honeymooning with his new wife."

The point is, a doctor never did show. I called Joan Greenbaum, who used to hang around Washington Square, then married and moved to Israel. She gave me the name of a doctor, who showed up within a half hour. Within a day, my infection was on its way out, and our updated understanding of Kameron was in. To be fair, if he was your manager and making a deal with some other weasel, he was what you would have wanted. Everyone fits, it would seem, at one level or other. You just have to keep track of where.

The tour people drove us from one place to another in old New York taxicabs with jump seats, so five of our troupe could fit into one cab. No air conditioning. They were DeSotos or something, not Checkers. How in hell they got over to Israel I never found out, but that's what they were, repainted a beige sandy-brown; a camouflage color, harder to see and shoot at.

The heat never ceased, even at night. Under the stage lights, it was next to unbearable. We wore light, cream-colored, tuxedo-like jackets, black pants, and bow ties, and Ronnie wore light, hot-weather dresses. None of that seemed to help a whole lot. We were so explosively received, however, that we accepted the heat. Looking out at the audiences, we knew why they were always a sea of white, short-sleeved shirts and no jackets or ties.

From one *kibbutz* to another, we drove, seldom stopping for breaks. There were no off-the-road diners and that sort of thing. The *kibbutzim* all seemed different: some run by people from Europe, others from Brooklyn, or Russia, that sort of thing. And they usually manufactured something—wheelbarrows, motorized farm equipment, glass—or grew vegetables. We ate lunch in the communal dining room of a *kibbutz* that seemed to have lots of people from Brooklyn. During the day, the children were educated away from their parents, but the families gathered for lunch, all in one huge dining room. The noise was so loud in that building that I couldn't think, to say nothing of talk. But, I never saw fresher, more beautiful vegetables, or happier children—or louder, at least.

Ein Gev, in the north, a *kibbutz* next to the Golan Heights, was known for its amphitheater and sculpture. We arrived in daylight and were shown around the *kibbutz,* which nestled next to the Sea of Galilee (wherein I took a swim). The bullet holes in the sides of school buildings and the trenches from one building to another dug for the children woke me up to the reality of where we were. At that time, the Golan Heights were in Arab hands, and the Arabs had to be notified if a concert was happening, as people would be traveling in trucks, at night, from other *kibbutzim.* If the Arabs were not notified, it could look like an invasion in progress, and that meant a counterattack.

The amphitheater stage faced the Heights, with the audience, then, facing away from the Heights. This meant that from onstage, we were seeing the Heights and the audience wasn't. In the middle of this concert, I saw a light coming slowly down the Heights above the heads of the audience. As is often the case, we couldn't see most of the audience because of the blinding stage lights, but I could still see that light, high in the blackness out there. "A sneak attack by the Arabs?" I wondered. "Are we about to be shot?" We were sitting ducks in those lights. I was seeing the headlines: "AMERICAN FOLK SINGERS SHOT IN ISRAEL: NEW WAR ERUPTS." Then, I figured it couldn't possibly be an invasion, these people would know, they'd have lookouts out there all the time. Yet, it was totally possible, and it could surely be that I was the only one who happened to notice this light; a lot stranger things have happened in life.

The big question was: "Should I stop the concert and tell them?" I'd save the day, be a hero, and we wouldn't be shot on the stage. On the other hand, if I were wrong, how utterly silly I'd look. I was literally sweating this out while trying not to keep staring at that light all the time, and, at the same time, sing the damned songs, none of which mattered. We could be history in minutes.

Finally, came intermission.

The stage lights went down and the theater lights up. Now I could take action. As I peered out from backstage, I could see that the amphitheater seating was far higher than I had remembered, and I could see that the light had been somebody's cigarette, somebody smoking. I came that close to making an international fool of myself.

We headed back to Tel Aviv that night in three cars. A long drive. Kameron and his elegant wife were along, one of the roadies and his wife, and Joni. Altogether, with the drivers and grips, we were probably eleven. It was late when we reached an older road that took off to the left from the main road we were on. Right there, sat a tank!

I had never seen a tank in real life, ready to blow something away. Its rounded turret looked efficient, and the entire tank was more modern than any I had seen in the movies or on display in front of an armory in the States. It had a chilling effect and made more of an impression than the bullet holes in the school buildings. It turned out that this older road was a shortcut that would save at least two hours, and only one percent of the people who traveled that road were killed, so our drivers deemed it pretty safe. ("One percent? *What the hell does that mean?!*"). According to the tank commander, things were quiet, and everyone wanted to get home as soon as we could, me included. You never figure something will happen to you. The shortcut was it.

About an hour into this road, one of the cars got a flat. As the tire was being changed, I took it upon myself to walk out into the darkness in back of the cars, keeping a lookout, as I saw it. It was pitch-black, no moon, and the darkness felt thick. It had crossed my mind that changing that tire in the middle of this blackness, with a necessary light shining on it, made us sitting ducks once again. Kameron's wife was terrified and was crying quietly inside one of the cars.

I could tell Lee wasn't happy by how resolutely quiet and pinched-mouthed he was. Joni was fine, probably thinking the whole thing was funny. She's one of those people who usually figures things will come out all right in the end. On the other hand, when she got angry, it was as if all hell had broken loose in her bones; something got triggered from childhood, and she would feel invincible. One of those women you don't want to argue with a whole lot. Let me tell you.

Far enough out into the dark and away from the light on the tire, I noticed a dimly lit window, like with a kerosene lamp, maybe one hundred yards down the road. I couldn't see the outline of the house, it was too dark, but I came back and informed the Israelis of what I had seen. They said Arabs lived in this section, and that they were peaceful Israelis. Nonetheless, I felt that if I went back out into the dark, I wouldn't get picked off right away, and that would give me a chance to take some sort of action, if trouble began. And do what? I couldn't have told you, but that's how my mind dealt with the event. I stayed out on that road until we were ready to leave.

Some newspaper, the next day, had an article about our incident. It said that the wife of Erik Darling had stood out on the road waving her American passport!

In the first place, how in bloody hell did the event get into the papers at all? And why? Who thought up that story about Joni? The two of us were incredulous. Was it someone's idea of how to get publicity? Help sell out concerts? There was no way to find out where the story had come from, and it really was not all that important, given all else, except for one's sense of the unfairness involved, and that we could do nothing about it. I've always thought it was that little weasel, Pete Kameron.

And that's showbiz.

Cold, fresh, deep-in-color orange juice, goat cheese, English muffins, fresh butter, tart marmalade, black coffee with pitchers of fresh cream, and the greatest-tasting melon in the world were served for breakfast at our home base motel. This was the best part of the entire trip. And it would only get weirder and harder as the heat would continue to tear at our edges.

27

A Campari on Ice

Lee was in pain. The Middle Eastern foods, or the water, or the heat, or his size, or a combination of all, made his body quite sick. At one point, he showed Joni and me these red welts which were the size of silver dollars, all over his body. We were far more shocked than we let on; you don't see those sorts of things except in medical books. He asked that we not tell the others. This group hadn't ever shared feelings or problems of a personal nature, and we felt we could not betray Lee's trust or the honor of his friendship.

"The State of Arkansas" was a solo of Lee's, with me on the banjo. It was a long, half-spoken, half-sung piece of Americana he had learned from a Mrs. Emma Dusenberry, a blind folk singer of the Ozarks, once his neighbor. He wanted to cut it out of the show because of his physical pain. Freddie and Ronnie wouldn't hear of it, not having the slightest idea of Lee's problem, and said we couldn't "short-change the audience," and we didn't have something to replace the song with.

State of Arkansas

My name is Charlie Brennan,
From Charleston I come.
I've traveled this wide world over,
Some ups and downs I've had.
I've traveled this wide world over,
Some ups and downs I've saw.
But I never knew what misery was,
'Till I hit old Arkansas.

I dodged behind the depot,
To dodge that blizzard wind.
I met a walking skeleton,
His name was Thomas Quinn.
His hair hung down like rat-tails
On his lean and lantern jaw.
He invited me to his hotel,
The best in Arkansas.

I followed my conductor,
To his respected place.
Where pity and starvation
Were seen on every face.
His bread it was corn dodger,
And his meat I could not chaw.
But he charged me a half a dollar,
In the State of Arkansas.

[Spoken:]
Then I went out and got me a job on a farm,
farmin'. But, I didn't care for the work,
nor the farmer, or his wife, nor none of his children. So, I went
up to him one day and I said, "Mister, I'm gonna quit this here
job, and you can just pay me off right now."

He says, "Okay, son. If that's the way you feel about it." Then
he took me out in the barn and he handed me a mink skin.

I said, "I don't want this thing, I want my money for the work
I've done."

He says, "Son, you may not know it, but mink skins is what
we're usin' for currency down here."

So, I took it, went into town, hunted up a place, put my mink
skin up on the counter, and darned if the bartender didn't toss
me a pint.
Then he picked up my mink skin, blowed the hair back on it,
put it under the counter and fetched me out fourteen rabbit
skins and three possum hides, for change.

[Sung]:
I'm goin' to the Indian Territory,
And live outside the law.

I'll bid farewell to the canebrakes,
In the State of Arkansas.
If you ever see me back again,
I'll extend to you my paw,
But it'll be through a telescope,
From hell to Arkansas.

Lee's strategies were usually passive-aggressive: if he had a problem, he would essentially pout, attempting to use people's caring for pouting against them. In this instance (perhaps getting back at Ronnie and Freddie who hadn't succumbed to his pouting), he performed the slow, ambling song at the speed of a hoedown, throwing his discomfort, pain, and frustration at the audience. "You won't let me cut it? I'll show you 'not cut it.'"

Freddie and Ronnie were furious. It was all I could do to keep from telling them what Lee asked us not to. I decided to let them stay as they always had been, long before my arrival. The misunderstanding and the distance was sad, yet a microcosm of the rest of the world.

Lee and Fred

A Tel Aviv couple, both actors in the Israeli theater, invited us over for dinner. They had heard Lee half-joking about wishing he had some good old Arkansas cooking, like bacon, grits, pork, or the like. In Israel—being a Jewish state, pork not being kosher, and the super-orthodox Jews having sway over much of society—pork was not easy to come by. This couple had graciously gone to the black market to purchased some bacon. It was a great deal of trouble, acquiring this unfamiliar and forbidden food. At least Lee would have this one hint of home.

When we walked into the apartment, we could see into the dining room, where a table was beautifully set: a white-on-white table-cloth, full sets of fine china, cloth napkins, candles, and beautiful silverware. And carefully placed in the center of each *hors d'oeuvre* plate, was a slice of *raw* bacon!

Nobody said a word.

After passing the dining room table, silently, we settled ourselves into the comfortable living room furniture. I wondered how I was going to get that raw strip of bacon into my mouth and down into my stomach, remembering it wasn't easy to cut, uncooked. Was I going to be able to swallow that stuff out of some misbegotten code of manners I held?

Ronnie understood the mistake, quietly took our hostess aside, and informed her that the bacon had to be cooked. As we sat in the living room talking, I noticed that the bacon was quietly transported to the kitchen by a dutiful (now knowledgeable) host. A few minutes later, Ronnie went into the kitchen to see if she could help further, and we heard her laugh. Nothing unusual, as she delighted in life, as a general principle. But, she beckoned to Joni, whom she could see from the kitchen. I followed. Eventually, everyone followed. Even Lee had to smile. The bacon was in a large frying pan, churning over and over in fast-boiling water.

The extra concerts for the army got to be more and more painful. There's nothing harder than having to get it up to perform in the middle of the afternoon somewhere in the middle of the desert. It was a deal that was made in Leventhal's office, back in Manhattan, where a few afternoon concerts were just afterthoughts, wisps of the mind.

In contrast to the grueling schedule, whenever we got back to the motel, next to the pool and the river Yarkon, Joni and I would be trying to discover the meaning of life, trying to become more-evolved human beings. Joni had been introduced to the writings of P. D. Ouspensky, a Russian philosopher/psychologist who wrote a book titled *The Psychology of Man's Possible Evolution*. Exercises in it had to do with getting rid of your ego and the erroneous things that would keep you from finding a true balance in life.

Early in the cool of the morning, I would sit out on one of the benches between our room and the pool with my eyes mostly closed, meditating, trying to let go of worldly concerns and the idea that the sun would be unbearably hot in an hour or so. I did this while keeping an eye out for those harmless little desert lizards, not wanting them to crawl on me by mistake. Joni, being more advanced than I was, I think, didn't care if they might crawl upon her. At moments, I actually felt like I was going to a place that was beyond all of this.

Near the end of the tour, we were driven south to Beersheba, past areas of desert where we could see the low, dark brown tents of the Bedouins, living as life had been lived long before plumbing. Farther south, we could see the remains of shot-up tanks rusting away. The farther south we headed, the hotter it got in the old New York cab. We could only sit there, knowing the trip would eventually end, and that the sun would go down. We would hang in there and get the job done. What I did not understand and what I was to learn, was that, for me, there could come a point where it was possible to lose it. It would take place during "Bye, Baby, Bye," a sweet Southern lullaby we did at the end of the concert.

Bye-o, baby, bye-o,
Bye-o, baby, bye-o,
Papa's gone to the mail boat,
Papa's gone to the mail boat, bye.

Close your sleepy eyes,
Close your sleepy eyes,
Papa's gone to the mail boat,
Papa's gone to the mail boat, bye.

Stars shining, number one, number two,
Number three, good Lord,
By 'n by 'n by 'n by, good Lord,
By 'n by . . . by 'n by.

It was a lovely song to be singing in the heat of the night. As well, it had become one of those moments when the four of us may have found a degree of relief from the unrelenting routine which was taking its toll. Ronnie would sing the first verse, with Freddie playing a few simple chords, and the rest of us would come in at various intervals, created an airy, delicate fugue.

In back of the group, as the delicacy of the song began, I waited with Lee, ready to come in on my part. But, somewhere within the vast tubular depths of Lee's body, gurgles began! I'm talking GURGLES. Surely they were picked up on the mike, I thought.

And then the big body burped, or whatever it was. It was like a quake; it seemed like I could feel it move into the wood of the stage. I wondered what would come next?

As I shot him an involuntary glance, which I immediately wished I had not, I could tell he didn't think this was funny. And that struck me as funny. In fact, I had never thought of anything funnier in my life, and I was not going to be able to avoid what was coming. The inevitable physiological rise of my laughter was like knowing an asteroid was heading for the town I was in and for the place where I stood, with nothing on earth I could do.

Then it was on top of me.

I didn't dare laugh right out loud, but I sure couldn't sing, though I desperately tried. You would not believe how I tried. How I wanted to. Nothing came out.

Ronnie carried the lead, and the others were doing their parts, so it may not have been obvious that one member of the group was no longer functioning. The big problem came with the next song, "Wimoweh," the number we closed with. "Bye, Baby, Bye," was the perfect setup for "Wimoweh."

For a moment, in back of the group, I got it together, as Freddie and Lee began:

"Hey up boy, Wimoweh . . . Wimoweh . . . Wimoweh . . ."

I started the rhythm part where the banjo came in (there was no banjo on "Bye Baby Bye") and then started the high, semi-falsetto wail. But that was as far as I got. The inner convulsion to laugh and the consequent panic brought the insides of me down as the asteroid landed. Singing was no longer possible. All I could do was keep strumming the banjo as loud as I possibly could, while making the movements of doing something important, hoping that facial gyrations might pass for some form of valid expression, regardless of what noise I might make. It was an African chant, after all. Unfortunately, we weren't a mime group, or African, either.

I don't remember how on earth we got off that stage, how we ended that concert. All I know is that in the dressing room, I couldn't look anyone in the eye. It remains in my mind as an utter and irretrievable disaster. I would lose that much control only one other time in my life. And in the not-too-distant future. The Weavers were definitely tweaking my psyche.

When we finally boarded the plane at the end of five weeks, Joni and I hadn't managed to find the nirvana or meaning of life we had hoped to through P. D. Ouspensky. At that point, I was trying to get through Ayn Rand's *Atlas Shrugged* and wasn't doing well with that, either. I had never been much of reader, whereas Joni read anything and everything she could get her hands on. Well, Rand asked that I think outside of my usual squares. After a half an inch of the book, I was ready to throw it away. Joni kept saying, "Finish it, you'll like it."

I kept thinking that I'd rather feel about things than think about them. Had I thought a lot about how good or how bad my voice was, for example, I would never have been in the business of singing. My singing came more from emotional needs and a sense about the importance of the essence of life than from thinking anything through. In a way, I hadn't the vaguest idea about who I was, where I was actually going, or even that I was a creative person, per se.

As the plane taxied for takeoff, I had a sense of having lived through a war; a war against heat, frazzled nerves, and more work than we could comfortably handle. And that, somehow, we won. Now, we were headed for a tour of Great Britain, and a three week hiatus before then. Kameron was allegedly looking into a concert in San Remo, on the Italian Riviera, and possibly one on the French.

We were in San Remo just a few days when we learned no additional concerts were coming. Lee, Joni, and I took the train west, to Nice, the center of the French Riviera. I don't remember where Ronnie and Freddie were headed. It could have been London or Paris.

The idea of our "Arkansas Traveler" in Nice, on the French Riviera, sipping a Campari on ice at a seaside café, struck me as a scene from a Fellini movie. I envisioned a close-up of Lee's petulant mouth, puffing a cigarette under a black fedora, absorbed with watching the sea birds as he peered through the lenses of tiny dark glasses.

Lee Hays in New York
(Photo: Joe Alper)

Lee explaining to Freddie the ways of the Arab street, as best he could. Not sure that Freddie was getting it.

28

"Bird in a cage, love,
Bird in a cage . . ."

Italy

Six-foot-three, weighing around three hundred pounds, a mystery-story writer, with a wry sense of humor, Lee was a character. He sparkled at anything to laugh at. My sense, though, was that, over here, he was deeply unstrung and wished he were home. Joni and I loved the mix of the man and smiled whenever we saw him, even though there was a hauntedness to him, a sadness over something we never learned much about. We were learning that people were far more complex than what we, at first hand, imagined. He was the son of an Arkansas preacher, had struggled through the Depression, and had found socialism as a salvation—but in some way that hadn't grown the man up, or balanced his sadness. I'm not sure that politics can. Up to then, I hadn't found a salvation of my own, and surely would have liked to. Joni and I had begun our search for some sort of answer through the writings of P. D. Ouspensky along with, of course, the stuff of our creative work. We hadn't landed on anything yet. Because I had found I could always draw a smile out of Lee, that made us close, and good traveling companions.

Joni and I visited Lee in his big white hotel, a block from the Mediterranean. We had become sort of a family, the three of us, having begun writing jingles together for Gold Medal Flour, which the Weavers would eventually record. It was odd, in a way, yet clearly a part of who he was, that wherever we went, he stayed in the biggest and fanciest hotel he could find, and resolutely refused to speak the language of whatever country we were in. And he'd always stay put in his room. For that reason, I was unable to buy him a Campari on ice at a seaside café, but I tried.

After what he'd been through in the Middle East, we suspected he needed to be hermetically sealed for a time, anyway. Still, we wondered how Lee afforded all this on the salary each Weaver got. Joni's and my expenses were more, being two, and putting money aside for the future, but Lee seemed to spend it like water. He ordered all food from room service, and if the food wasn't right, he sent it right back, in no uncertain English. This didn't fit with the Weavers' agenda of holding hands with all races and colors all over the world, but in no group do people believe the same thing and in the same exact way. Belief and behavior don't often mix well.

The French Riviera, along with the Mediterranean, lost any charm we might have imagined when Joni and I went for a swim, only to discover that raw sewage had blown in from offshore. Towns along the coast emptied their sewage through long pipes that went far out into the sea—just not far enough.

We got tired of Nice pretty quick, and the three of us left for Milan. Counting our pennies, Joni and I left Lee at another humongous hotel, across from the Duomo, a famous cathedral, and started walking with our bags and my banjo to a section where we were told we could find inexpensive hotels. The walk was humid and endless. We finally found a hotel with a room one flight up. It took us a bit to discover that the room had no toilet or shower. We found the communal toilet down the hall, but no shower. We were cranky and starved, and setting out for another hotel was out of the question. We found a delicatessen down the street, got a nice block of cheese, some salami, and some sort of uninteresting bread, and brought it all back to the room. There was no way this felt like a meal, however. I called Lee and asked if we could come down and borrow his bathtub in his big hotel. He wasn't eager to have us come down! But I didn't pull back on the quest; there are some favors in life you just bloody well need, and you do all you can to get them, even if they're not as forthcoming as you would have thought.

We were so tired by now that we splurged on a cab, and as soon as it pulled to a stop at Lee's place, two footmen opened the doors on each side of the cab. We found no way to enter the building unnoticed. Although the hotel didn't have a massive lobby, I never saw so much marble in all of my life. White marble on the floors and reddish-brown, white-veined marble on the walls, a white marble staircase, and marble floors in the hallways. The only wood anywhere was in the cubbyholes for the keys in back of the reception desk, and in the walls of the elevator. At least five bellhops in brown suits with brass buttons stood ready to serve us, and one in the elevator. The concierge used a house phone to announce us and told us that Lee was on the second floor, just at the top of the stairs.

Not wanting to deal with the elevator operator, who would probably be expecting a tip, we said nonchalantly, "Oh, we'll walk up the stairs." We figured we'd pass for some of those easygoing Americans. As we ascended the marble staircase, we felt the ten eyes of the bellhops on us; against all that marble, we looked like street urchins, and God only knows how we smelled at that point.

The white marble of the circular stairs, with no carpet, mind you, took us right to the top and went seamlessly under Lee's door. His room was surprisingly small, with two single beds, a white night table, white marble walls, white-and-gold lamps with white shades, a small white-and-gold desk with a mirror, and no windows. The bedspreads were white. The place felt like a modern sarcophagus of some kind. Lee was big in that room, and it felt rather small for the three of us. I could see why he'd hesitated having us over.

The bathtub was short but made up for its length by its depth. I had turned on the faucets, closed the bathroom door so the sound of the water against all that marble wouldn't make it impossible to talk, and came back into the bedroom to sit on the end of the bed next to the bathroom door parallel to Lee's bed a few feet away.

I was uncomfortable, at first, imposing on Lee as we were, but we needed this bath. Our life needed this bath. God wanted us to have this bath. After a bit, Lee seemed to relax, making the best of it. Joni and I had hoped he might think of ordering food, but that didn't happen at all. I sat on the bed, with nothing to lean on, and we chatted with Lee, who leaned back, much like a sultan, resting on pillows, his fingers entwined on his stomach, quite happy, it seemed. I would have loved one of the extra pillows that no one was using to lean on, but I didn't want to make any more fuss than we were already making.

It was going okay, everyone settling into this scene and making the best of it, until I noticed a nearly invisible puddle of water that had crept under the bathroom door and was heading toward the front of the room, straight for the hallway, with nothing to stop it. I jumped into the bathroom, turned off the faucets, and threw towels out to Joni to keep the water from slipping out of the room.

The only elegant thing about this place was the number of towels. While Joni dammed up the gap under the front door, I stood in the bathroom, now covered with a half inch of water, and looked in dismay at the completely full tub.

I was not unaware that marble and water make one of the slipperiest surfaces on the face of the earth. If I happened to fall, I could easily break a hip, or a wrist, or a hand, or even a finger, and that sort of thing doesn't work well with playing a banjo. Enough towels remained for Joni and me to begin toweling up water and wringing the towels into wastepaper baskets, of which there were two. She worked the bedroom, I worked the bathroom. My legs, my sides, and my arms began cramping from the strain of keeping my balance. To avoid slipping, I had to move in peculiar ways, hanging on to the towel racks, the side of the tub, and the toilet. It was the most dangerous and strenuous work I'd ever done. For one thing, a wet towel does not work like a mop. All it is, is better than nothing.

The rubber stopper was down at the bottom of the tub, where all stoppers are, but no chain was attached. When I reached down to pull out the plug, I attempted to angle my body and arm so my rolled-up sleeve wouldn't get wet, and my foot lost its grip. The top of me fell into the tub, causing more water to leap out and head toward the bedroom. I got myself up and stealthily went to the bathroom doorway to see how much damage I'd done, or if Lee and Joni had heard any part of the splash. The water was right at the towels along the bottom of the front door, but Joni was holding her own, not really aware that more water was heading her way. I noticed steam on the mirror above the small desk. I remained silent.

Lee hadn't moved. He was still leaning against the headboard of his bed, but his face had lost all of its blood, and there was never much there to begin with.

I had an idea of what scenario Lee's mind would have built: if the water could not be contained, it would creep all the way down the marble staircase to the lobby. The five bellhops would run up in search of the source. They would knock on the door and insist on coming into the room. And the unspoken question would be: what are these street urchins doing in this room with this man, running a bath? And all this, across from one of the biggest cathedrals on earth.

Once again, my soul crossed the line of what passes for sanity. I went back into the bathroom, closed the door to a crack, and then stood, half-bent, with my back against the sink. I started to shake. To the depth of my being, I believed that if I let it go, this time, if I started the laughter, it would be over for all of us, including poor Lee. We'd have to give up and let marble and water and Italian footmen take over. I was literally gripping my sides, hoping to God this would pass. I had to do better this time!

My convulsions subsided enough so that I could finally get the plug pulled out of the tub. Every time I saw Lee's face in my mind, however, it brought back convulsions, which (I knew well) could not be borne if the three of us were to survive. I saw it as all up to me. That made it worse.

Joni wanted to know if I was okay, as I had been totally silent. I made a sound of some kind, but it wasn't enough. She pushed the bathroom door open, I came out of the bathroom, but I couldn't speak. I lay on the bed, doubled over with biblical proportions of laughter—in silence. Maybe a squeak or a whine now and then.

She wasn't where I was at all; she simply thought it was mildly amusing, no more than that.

Lee remained ashen.

I couldn't help laughing when glancing at Lee, while at the same time feeling guilt. Guilt squandered in laughter.

Gradually, I gained a degree of control and went back to my job. The water was finally contained and toweled up. We never did get our baths. We made our way back to our hotel (on foot) and slept as if we had died. The next day, we found a hotel room with a shower, and within several days we came to.

We didn't see Lee again until London. That night was never, ever mentioned again, and I'm not sure he ever forgave us.

On the trek back to our hotel, in the small lighted window of a jewelry store, there was a gold ring with a ruby. I had always liked rings, since I was a kid. This ring had a sense of nobility to it, even a sense of salvation. The feeling I had was: *"If only I had that ring, all of my problems in life would be solved."* It would have been way too expensive, but I'll never forget it. The odd part of it was that if I could have afforded that ring, I would have been too embarrassed to wear it; I didn't recognize, at the time, that it was the same sort of thing as feeling that, if only I could learn one of those picking patterns, all of life's problems would vanish. And I couldn't see clearly that picking patterns were better than rings, but still not the answers to life. I hadn't found what I belonged to in life.

We rented a motor scooter and headed north to Lake Como. We got fouled up in the middle of traffic getting out of Milan, ending up in the middle of a four-lane street, next to a tall, black-haired traffic director who wore a white suit. He had signaled us to stop, right where he was, and had said something in Italian. The last thing I wanted was this, as I wasn't sure that the guy who rented us the scooter was completely candid about the validity of my license for driving in Europe. He had said this kind of vehicle we could drive, but it was a "Hey, don't worry. Everything gonna be okay, eh?" kind of thing.

I looked at the cop, said nothing, and shrugged in a way that I imagined an Italian would shrug; I mean, I had seen enough movies to know this. He smiled and motioned us forward.

The closer we got to Lake Como, the narrower the road became and the faster the cars—Ferraris, Lancias, Fiats—sounding like their tachometers were into the red as they passed. At one point, it seemed as if our scooter had slowed down enough to get off. Italy had no speed limits, apparently, or at least none that made any difference.

We found a small, three-story hotel built into a hill a few miles up the west side of the lake, across the road from the water. Our room didn't have a view of the lake, but it looked down through green leaves to the orange-tiled roofs of other lake houses. At dinner, the inexpensive white table wine that came with the meal was completely exquisite.

Overlooking the lake and stuck way up on a mountain not far from the hotel was a shrine. We made the one-or-two-mile trek up a footpath. One always hopes, I suppose, that some great shift in consciousness will happen in places like this, a personal proof that there is a God, something beyond the magic of everyday living. Bigger magic, at least. Other than a great view of the lake nothing was happening there.

The next day, we scootered the lake's circumference and then took a day to go into the mountains and paint. I'd packed a small watercolor set, some pencils, and a good pad of watercolor paper. I painted some church steeples and a dilapidated stone farmhouse with a red-tiled roof. It was a beautiful day with white, puffy clouds. The desire to paint that passed over to me from my father had never left me, and I'm not sure it could. When I walk into a place, the first thing I see are the paintings, or that there are none.

The one musical experience I had in this country was on this puffy white day, up in these mountains. I had to go to the bathroom, and it was going to be loose, and it had to be now! One of my least favorite things. I saw no reasonable place to pull off the road and get into some bushes or woods. Around a bend, we soon came to a small restaurant overlooking a valley with a creek running through it. As we pulled in and parked, I told Joni to follow me in and get us a table as I made a beeline for the bathrooms. Fortunately, they were in a small foyer just to the left as we entered the place. As quickly and carefully as I could, I walked to the door of the water closet, as they call them in Europe. It was a large, dark-wooded, elegant thing, with a brass handle and a large pane of striped, frosted glass. I opened the door into a four-by-four, blue-tiled room—with a hole in the center! Period. I'd heard of these things but never expected to use one, and certainly not in a situation like this. You had to squat there and aim at that hole.

I managed to take off my pants quickly, and while I held on to the grips on the walls, I finally had the courage to release. Courage? My time had run out. But in that very instant, the instant my stuff hit the floor, a loud jukebox came on in the restaurant. "It couldn't possibly be wired," I thought. "This has got to be a coincidence." But it happened that way, just as I've written. If this had been France, I could have believed it was wired, but not the Italians.

When I got myself put back together, I realized there was a flushing device that let water onto the floor of the room. When I turned the handle, it was all I could do to jump out of the way and open the door. I got to our table, overlooking the valley, and took a huge breath. The valley was beautiful. All sorts of coincidences happen in life, I figured. Get used to it. I had a Campari on ice, hoping its medicinal properties would help my insides.

By the time we got back to Milan, we had become brave enough to take a train across Italy to Florence. Someone back in the States had convinced us that we must see Michelangelo's *David,* which was in Florence. "Do not see the copy that stands in front of the Palazzo Vecchio," we were told. "You must see the one that's inside." This "must see" business had added a certain romance to this journey (right up our alley) and was one of the elements that compelled us to go.

Having not understood which coaches were which, however, we ended up sitting in a first-class one, which meant having to pay twice as much as we'd figured. The train car was crowded and hot, and the only thing first class was the price of the ticket. We decided to stop off in Venice, as that city came first and it wouldn't cost any more. Thomas Mann had written a book about somebody dying in Venice, and then there were the canals, the gondolas, and the Venetian glass. I kept grousing to myself that this trip had better live up to whose ever advice we had taken.

29

*"I sail the ocean blue,
I catch-a daplenty of feesh . . ."*

The David

To fall off a gondola, perchance, and have to swim to some steps to get out of the water struck me as a recipe for a hospital stay. No wonder Thomas Mann had one of his characters die in this place. Having grown up on a lake, I had always seen water as something you swam in as well as floated upon. Venice seemed like a dank, algae-infested theme park, kept alive only because of the thousands of bright-colored tourists who went there each year, taking home proof to south Texas that they were now cultured. I remember a kid, as he looked up at his big-Stetsoned father and shouted, "Daidy? Cain ah have fo' thousand leera?"

The city echoed a sense of the fundamentally despondent and depressed. Upstate New York, with its damp and gray winters, could be depressing, but nothing like this. The buildings looked like they were rotting away from within. The "romantic" canals were a pig-muddy green, and the infestation of tourists seemed to be doing nothing but supporting Kodak, whose home was in Rochester, New York, thirty minutes from Canandaigua Lake, from which we drank all of our water. The name I gave to the painting I did of Venice was "The City Morose."

"The City Morose" (E. Darling)
Venice, Italy
Watercolor, 15¼″ × 11½″

"North of Lake Como" (E. Darling)
Watercolor, 11" × 15"

Florence was beyond the antique. I had been raised by an artist and surreptitiously prepared for life by the man. It wasn't an issue of stealth, of course, but as I've suggested, something passed over to me from him about the appreciation of works that come from the creative process. His life was a reaching for more than the grease in yesterday's frying pan (even though he did that as well), and the life that we shared set me up, I suspect, for what was to happen in Florence.

Maybe art, at its best, always comes down to what life is about. Although life asks that question of each individual, and each person answers it differently, there are universals, I think. They go beyond politics and vomit and ego and misunderstanding and war.

Joni raised herself up within a family that had little or no understanding of where she was going. Her original father died of a brain tumor when she was six, and that didn't help. She fell in love with the works of Shakespeare and spent part of her life living out of a second-hand taxi, literally, so that she could afford to study under B. Iden Payne, a scholar of Shakespeare, at the University of Texas at Austin. The expression of the passions of life and of love as momentous was certainly the mark of Shakespeare, as well as of the Weavers, but neither Joni nor I could have foreseen the effect of the *David*.

I don't want to go berserk over this, but people have spent more than forty million dollars for an impressionist painting, and I don't think that's all based on some sort of acquisitiveness or hysteria. A great painting can move the soul again and again, and this movement is more life-affirming than knocking over a red-and-pink doll in a penny arcade with a baseball.

The *David* stands alone within its rotunda, with a slow, even light that encircles its form. You forget that it's light in the room; it's more like it comes from the stone, as if the stone has a life of its own.

On the way into that room, through a large foyer, was the Pietà, an expression of the essence of love a mother can have for the life of her child, and as he lies dying. But this can be felt only while standing next the work. You can never experience the essence of this in a photograph. Part of the magic takes place within the way the sculpture is finished, the surface of the marble: you want to reach out and touch it. Yet, in its presence, touching it would feel like an invasion of privacy. You don't feel the same way about life in its presence as you did in the street.

We couldn't stay with the Pietà, however; the room just beyond had a gravitational pull that drew us away like an outgoing tide, and we would be borne to its shore.

The *David* is Man.

Not *a* man. Not the warrior who fought Goliath with no more than a slingshot, nothing so simple as that. The work is a symbol of *Man,* of what man could be. Maybe the man in the statue is manly because he is completely at home in his body, with the only concern coming from the look in his eyes, the windows of thought. If a woman ever wanted a man to protect her while she was with child, I think she would want this sort of man, because he shows the warrior spirit as a thing without anger, vindictiveness, hatred, or fear. A reluctant warrior, perhaps, more watchful than anything else, a gathered protector of boundaries.

The *David* is not animal-man; he is man-man, for whatever that's worth.

It was like a salvation for us, another epiphany. It gave us a feeling of why it's worth being alive, why it's worth acting or singing or painting or reading or writing; why it's worth being considerate, honest, kind, strong. The experience was outside any kind of euphoria I could have imagined; and it held, within its expanse, the idea of all I was striving for, even though I couldn't have named what that was. And for the time I was there, I knew I belonged in that room. The words I found later, the words I use now, are only the map, of course, and the map is never the territory. It's what my father had been about, without words to explain it. But without some of the words, you can't hold it in mind; and if you can't hold it in mind, so that you can remember to nurture the thing, you can lose it. As I would find out.

Joni and I had no way to explain fully to each other what we had gone through, even though we couldn't stop talking about it. We both understood we were no longer the same, and this made us good friends.

Experiencing the *David* was when I knew that I had to affirm who I was, apart from all other things and events, including the *David*. I had to find what it was about me that I wanted to express about being a person, an artist, a person who sings about matters of life. And this meant, apart from the Weavers. When I joined the group, I did so because they had inspired my life, yet I knew they were musically different than I. I didn't think a lot about that at the time; I entered their realm of expression with total commitment. Now, I felt the need to move on, to follow my conscience, my own way of thinking and feeling. To thine own self be true, and all that. In more ways than I could have imagined, this was not going to be easy, but the die was now cast. At least, we had our tour of Great Britain before I'd have to face all of this. Great Britain was in all the old ballads we had sung at the Square, and I was intrigued about Britain.

30

*"I've just come from the salt, salt sea,
And 'twas all on account of thee . . ."*

The Kingston Trio

"Someday, I'd like to play the guitar," thought Allan Shaw. "I never did anything about it," he said. "In high school I began liking folk groups. Then came the Kingston Trio. With the earlier groups—like the Weavers, the Tarriers, and the Easy Riders—there wasn't the feeling that I could duplicate their sound. I first heard the Kingston Trio on the radio in May 1958, and then started college that fall. When 'Tom Dooley' became a huge hit, I went out and bought their first album, even though I didn't have a record player. I'd play it when I went home for Christmas. What excited me was that, with only three chords on the guitar, I could play most of the songs the Kingstons did. Once I learned to play the guitar, I took up the banjo and formed my own group; and for the next three years of college, I had that."

The explosion of "folk" as a pop-music category on the American scene began with thousands of similar thoughts in colleges all over the country. That explosion made it possible for the Weavers to work as steadily as they did when I was with them. Allan Shaw not only ended up playing this music, like thousands of others, but he gave up being a lawyer to devote his life to it, when he created Folk Era Records.

Before the Kingstons explosion, however, there were no folk groups in colleges, no large college concerts for singers of folk songs, no coffeehouse circuit. Folk music, per se, wasn't "in." The Kingstons' music may have been frat-party–like, but if not for their humongous success, there might never have been such performers as Bob Dylan, Don McLean, Peter, Paul, and Mary, Judy Collins, Simon and Garfunkel, Joan Baez, the Limelighters, the Rooftop Singers, the Seekers, the Journeymen, or the New Lost City Ramblers. Hundreds of thousands of people started with the Kingstons and found their way back to the Weavers, then all the way back to the original sources of the music, even to old English balladry, and to the people of an agricultural southland: the Carter Family, Flatt and Scruggs, and the old masters of the blues and the banjo.

When I spoke to Nick Reynolds of the Kingston Trio, and told him the importance I felt the group had, he said:

> You know as well as I do, a lot of people wouldn't agree with you on that. Three college boys from California coming into the folk scene and making a tremendous success of it? Bastardizing a lot of the music and kind of intruding on them? There was a "How dare you infringe on what I hold sacred and change it" sort of thing. But when we started, we never thought we'd make a penny. It was right after the Beatnik days and before the Hippie days, and there were these small coffeehouse clubs in San Francisco.

> The hungry i was started by Enrico Banducci [in San Francisco]. He booked people like Josh White and the Gateway Singers. There was a lot of interest in jazz and poetry—Ferlinghetti, Kerouac—and we were right at the end of all that. The Purple Onion seated about forty people, and we were packing the place, making forty dollars a week per person. We thought that was as high as it would ever get.

> Someone from Capitol Records showed up and decided to make a one-record deal with us. We recorded it in two days—you know, songs we were doing at the club, "Tom Dooley" being one of 'em. Then we flew over to Hawaii and were playing a little club at the Royal Hawaiian Hotel.

> Meanwhile, in Salt Lake City, a couple of D.J.s had been playing "Tom Dooley" and getting requests. Capitol put it out as a single, and all of sudden we had five songs in the top ten, all at one time in Salt Lake. Then people started playing the stuff all over the country. We got a telegram saying "Tom Dooley" has passed the half-million mark; get your butts back here and promote it.

> Irving Grant, from Jazz at the Philharmonic, arranged our first tour. It was ingenious what they did. In the old days, a college would have to take out of a student fund, like, five or ten thousand dollars to have entertainment for a big prom or a dance. They'd get people like Les Brown or Harry James, and they'd have to pay that money up front. What we did was say, "Pay our airfare and motel rooms and that's all—we just want 75 percent of the door."

> The college couldn't lose; they would have the top recording artist in the country and make 25 percent of it. It was an innovative way of getting to all the colleges, including those who couldn't afford even two thousand dollars. We traveled with people like Stan Getz or

Dave Brubeck; we'd have packages. I think one year we did 328 concerts; Capitol couldn't put out enough records. They made us record three albums a year, at least. We had a run of about twelve or fifteen gold albums. Guitar sales skyrocketed; Martin Guitars built two more factories and they were two years behind in production.

In and about college campuses and in the big cities, hundreds of coffeehouses sprang into existence: the Gate of Horn in Chicago; the Buddhi in Oklahoma City; the Exodus in Denver; the Ash Grove and the Troubadour, in L.A.; and the Bitter End and Gerde's Folk City (where Dylan got started) in New York, to name but a few. This meant, as well, that hit singles were no longer required for someone like Joan Baez or Judy Collins or Dylan to make it, and the audience for folk was in place.

Although folk soon became a household word, the actual process that created the original music—one person hearing a song directly from another and passing it on by word of mouth, like a story whispered around a table—the oral process, it was called—this process was now dead. This was the end of folk music. This modern folk era meant that everyone all over the country heard the same version of a song, pretty much all at the same time. Starting with Dylan, it eventually became an era of the singer/songwriter creating folk-like material. The folk process, as it were, would be strangled by the algae of mass popularity. It gave way to a new creative loam and a new way for acoustic guitar music to deal with life. Not necessarily lesser, but different.

For a while, all anyone needed was three chords, a guitar, and the gumption to get on a stage and sing anything in any haphazard manner whatever. Needless to say, this sort of thing couldn't sustain a large audience over great lengths of time, but it held for a while, and many who got with the music remained ever loyal.

Having seen what the Weavers had gone through with the blacklist, the Kingston Trio made a conscious decision to leave politics out of it, said Reynolds:

> We were not going to get entrapped by the McCarthy mentality of the time. We've been criticized for this, and rightfully so, because there were political things we could have supported, and our convictions were there. When we were at the height of our career, however, Judy Collins came to our hotel in New York and said they were

having this meeting at the Bitter End, because the Hootenanny show had blacklisted Pete Seeger. There must have been 300 people at this meeting. We decided to boycott the show along with everyone else. Hootenanny wanted us, of course, but we told them we wouldn't do it unless Pete did. We were then blacklisted for five or six years from doing any television ourselves. Then I'd turn on the Hootenanny show and see a lot of the people from that meeting who had said they weren't going to do the show. I thought this was curious.

From where I stood at the time, the Kingstons' music seemed rather Wheatena to me. But, I understood that they had made it possible for me to make my own way after the Weavers. A huge audience was there for anything folk. "Folk" had arrived.

31

*"There were three brothers in merry Scotland.
In merry Scotland, there were three . . ."*

Kings and Heroes

Hamlet, King Lear, Macbeth, Robin Hood, and the old English ballads "Lord Randal," "Henry Martin," "Barbra Allen," "The Golden Vanity"—they all had a meaning they hadn't before as I stood next to the huge stone caskets in St. Paul's Cathedral, in London. Beneath those ornate stone lids were the bodies of monarchs that all of that art was about. The doctrine of the divine right of kings came to mind (one of the few political things I remember from high school), and the struggle against all of that. Our Revolution. It all became real. Here were the monarchs, inches away from my eyes, alive in their deadness inside their stone walls.

And the Britons have a way with the language. No matter what sort of accent, or the odd words for things—such as daft, ring me up, fook it, straightaway, might have done—it never ceased to enchant me. I'd ask cabdrivers questions just so I could hear the music that came with their speech.

The Weavers toured much of Great Britain with Brownie McGhee and Sonny Terry, who opened the show for us. It was interesting that the English kids interested in blues were far more knowledgeable about blues and blues men than anyone I'd ever met in the States. Paul Robeson came backstage after one of the concerts. His hands were immense, and his voice you could feel in the bones of your chest.

Only one of our concerts sticks in my mind. It took place in a large, elegant hall in the middle of Glasgow, packed to the rafters. We were the only ones on the bill at this point. During the first half of the concert, in a silence between two of the songs, the voice of a Scotsman spoke clearly and loudly: "Sing 'Doon in the Mines'!"

We ignored it and sang the next song.

"Sing 'Doon in the Mines'!" the voice came again when the next applause had died down. He was louder this time; and you could tell he'd had a pint, maybe two.

Intermission came and went, and we hoped he had gotten "Doon in the Mines" out of his system, or left.

He hadn't.

"Sing 'Doon in the Mines'!" continued in between songs. He wasn't going away, to be sure. In fact, his ardor was growing. Seemed like he'd added a pint at the break. Ronnie stepped up to the mike and explained that we had worked up only so many songs, and that one we hadn't worked on as yet. And that we were sorry. She stepped back from the mike with a smile.

Came the voice once again: "Pate Sayger wudda soong it!"

It was the only time anyone ever alluded to Seeger's not being in the group, but nobody else seemed to mind that we didn't sing "Doon in the Mines," and it was one of our better performances.

Back in New York when my final meeting took place, when I officially tendered my resignation, we were all gathered in Harold Leventhal's office. We had been through so much together that I felt like I was disowning my family. A terrible feeling. Freddie and Ronnie were gracious. Lee looked away, let out a huge breath, and petulantly said, "Another career shot out from under me."

I left the office feeling like I had a hole in my back. I had trouble feeling I'd made the right choice. The Weavers were still bigger than life and had treated me with total respect, as an equal, while at the same time gently and quietly pushing me forward, beyond comfort zones, into playing more than I'd thought I could play: into singing better than I thought I could sing.

32

"Shoulda been on the river in 1910,
Oh oh oh, oh oh oh.
They was treatin' the women like they was the men,
Oh oh oh, oh oh oh . . ."

Leadbelly

On the lower east side of New York, in a five-story walkup, there was a small party. Leadbelly was there, along with my friend Tommy Geraci, who told me this story. A man showed up at this party who had loaned Leadbelly fifty dollars, and he wanted it back, right then and there. Leadbelly said he didn't have it. The guy grabbed the neck of Leadbelly's guitar and said, "Maybe I'll take this." Leadbelly had a stick he would carry, with a heavily weighted end, and he grabbed the guy's arm, threw him down, as if he were a rag doll, picked up the stick, and began beating the man. It was all the others could do to stop him, and the guy fled the apartment. Leadbelly was furious. He said, "Don't you ever do that again! He mighta been a pistol man."

Leadbelly had lived at a level of existence where he had commonly experienced that his life was in danger. A person like that brings a different perspective to his art than most of us bring. One of the great blues pianists once said, "They singin' about what they heard about. I'm singin' about what I live."

Because of the effect Leadbelly had on folk music and on my personal life, I felt the need to say a bit more of the man in these pages.

"Goodnight, Irene," the song that catapulted the Weavers into orbit, was a Leadbelly song, and the song remains part of the American psyche, while their other hits—"On Top of Old Smoky," "Tzena, Tzena," "So Long, It's Been Good To Know You" —have sunk into relative obscurity.

"The Midnight Special," a song that is said to have got Leadbelly (Huddie Ledbetter) out of the Louisiana State Penitentiary, was nearly the theme song for Washington Square. In all my years in New York, there was hardly a gathering at which the song wasn't sung. "The Rock Island Line," another of Leadbelly's anthems, was one of the Tarriers' pillars and remained one of the Weavers' most reliable songs throughout their career. In 1956, Lonnie Donegan began the skiffle-music era of Great Britain with his version of "The Rock Island Line," which reached No. 8 on the charts in the U.K., as well as in the U.S.

I spoke to Bess Lomax Hawes about Leadbelly. Her father was John Lomax, and Leadbelly had lived in their home. Bess's words speak volumes about who the man was:

> Being a black gentleman around a white woman teenager, Leadbelly was formal and polite. He was always reserved. Chances of us getting to be friends were small, even though he stayed at our house, ate at our table, and drove with Father. And I think he was what you could call institutionalized, had profound personality changes as a result of being incarcerated most of his life, and under extremely tough conditions. I think he had walled off most of his insides. I don't think people understand that about him. I think he was like a guy who had been flash-frozen and woke up two centuries down the pike.
>
> He was, physically, a very strong man. One of my most vivid memories was going in a car with him. There was [my brother] Alan, and Father, I don't remember who else, about six of us in a Ford. We were driving up to Connecticut in the middle of winter, roads covered in snow, and we got stuck in a snowdrift. We tried to drive out of it, back and forth, but we couldn't. We all piled out. Leadbelly walked to the front of the car, picked it up, and moved it over, then walked to the back of the car, picked it up, moved it over. Everybody got back in the car and we were off.
>
> He didn't even strain. He was just an enormously powerful man, and very fast. If you look at his pictures in his suits, he sort of bulged in them. That was all hard muscle. That's one of the reasons he was able to stay alive in the pen, I suspect. And, as a singer, of course, he flattened you.
>
> Because his music was rural, however, he couldn't play in the uptown places. He had to perform in low-class, dangerous ones. He was attractive to women, and a lady would start to make up to him, and some guy would come over and pull a knife on him. He would swat the guy across the room and the guy would be dead. And then, being a black man in the South, he would be charged with first-degree murder. But it was always a hot-blooded fight. Nobody ever said he

got up in the morning with the intention of going out to kill so-and-so. But there's no question he killed three people. It was kind of scary. But there you are. I don't know many people who have killed three people, do you?

I'd never known anyone who had killed anybody. Leadbelly, however, was a man who found himself in a context of life that called for certain behavior if he were to survive, and he rose to the occasion. There's a law of nature, I think, that says, "Okay, muck around on your wife, or your kids, or your dog, but you try that on a grizzly bear and you'll lose your life or a limb." And there's nothing unfair or tragic in that. It's the nature of things. Leadbelly was one part of nature that said: "You don't play games here."

When I first heard his recordings, I knew nothing about him, no back story at all, but I think that I heard who he was in his music. And it gave me a certain resilience, a thing to hang on to, something I wanted a part of.

As for the art of the man, there was a simplicity to his intention. It was not uncomplex, but there were no extraneous notes, no mugging, no posturing, no being somebody else. The great principle of art that says "less is more" was the essence of Leadbelly's playing: don't make it fancy, make it just what it is, let the listener fill in the blanks. Only Leadbelly didn't need all those words. I never came close to sounding like him, nor has anyone else, but there was something he did that I knew I belonged to, and, on the next leg of my journey, I was to reach for whatever I'd gotten from the him and put it out there.

33

*"Weep all ye little rains,
Wail, winds, wail . . ."*

Old Gold Cigarettes

As my father sat on the side of his bed every morning, having turned his legs out from under the covers and put on his glasses, he would take an Old Gold cigarette butt from an Art Deco ashtray and light it. He would inhale deeply, smoke there a bit, as he gathered himself, then put on his pants and go make his Medaglia d'Oro coffee. I don't ever remember my father without a cigarette, whether in the canoe, in the woods, or sitting on the porch at sunset. In October 1958, he died of lung cancer. I was twenty-five at the time.

When Dr. Mac Merrill, a close friend of ours, diagnosed that Dave was to die, and that it could be a matter of weeks, he called me in New York. "Should I tell Dave he is dying?" he asked.

How in hell should I have the answer to that? I'd never been here before. At that age, I didn't know what was involved any more than I knew what was involved in a marriage or much of anything else. I had never thought of his dying. I called my mother and asked what she thought. "Oh, don't tell him," she said. For damn sure, she wasn't the right one to ask, but I listened, and went with the game. And in all of the time I spent in upstate New York at the hospital, right to the end, we played it that way: we pretended, avoided the truth that lay there between us, avoiding our past, avoiding our love. Worst of all, we avoided our love, and what it would mean to be gone from each other.

I had wanted him brought to New York, to die with Joni and me in our apartment. Joni didn't think the idea would work well. The issue was confused and unpleasant between us, but part of me knew she was right. I didn't know what I was doing, and I desperately wanted to know.

I commuted to upstate New York from the city, 700 miles round-trip, and endlessly thinking about what not to say by mistake, how to hold feelings inside, how to deny and repress. I was already good at these games. We once had a dog—Blacky, we called her—a fine-haired, black-and-white English setter. We'd had other dogs—a beagle, a foxhound—but something about this little dog I felt close to. She was like me in some way.

Just north of the city, near Croton, New York, Dave taught art and shop at one of the boarding schools I had attended after my parents divorced. He'd left Blacky there for a couple of weeks, having made an arrangement with the school's caretaker, while we went to the city to pack up my summer clothes and some of his stuff from my mother's apartment. Then we headed back to the school, and from there we'd be heading to Canandaigua Lake for the summer.

When we got back to the school, I sat in the car while he went to the caretaker's quarters to pick up the dog. He was a while. When he finally got back to the car, he said, "Sonofabitch!" as he started the car and took off. Then he told me that Blacky was dead.

The story they told him was that she'd pushed her way through a screen door when they were fumigating one of the dorms and they didn't know she was in there. Dave didn't bother to tell them that it was all you could do to get her to go through a door when it was wide open.

I sat in that car and held back the tears. It was all I could do to hold back the tears. For miles, I learned how to hold back the tears.

Blacky and me

One afternoon, Dave wasn't looking at me as he shifted himself in the hospital bed, looking at his knees, which were upright. He suddenly said, "I'm a-goin', boy." I tried to ignore it. I held my breath and said nothing. How could he know? Where the hell had that come from? Or do they always know?

I got the call that my father had died at 2 a.m., October 28, 1958. I was awake, gathering things to take back to New York: penknives he'd whittled with, his favorite watercolor brush, a big box of oils, odd-looking rulers, French curves, old 6-B pencils—the stuff that was life between us. The call was a shock, even though I had known it was soon to be coming.

When I got home, the landlord had just refinished the floors in our apartment at 698 West End Avenue, and the living room was empty except for a very old sunburst Gibson J-45 guitar, which was leaning in a corner. I wasn't sure what forces were pushing me, other than anguish, what sort of crescendo I had climbed to its flashpoint, but I picked up and threw that guitar against every wall in that room. In the end, nothing was left except splinters of wood that couldn't be thrown and a set of orange-knobbed tuning machines, which had worked better than any I'd ever known. The strings were still attached to the broken off bridge and the tuning-machine head, no longer attached to the neck.

Years later, I realized how much had been stolen from my father and me by the game of denial. I never got to say how much I loved him, or even goodbye. We never got to experience our tears, and there would have been many, in making a closure, a bond, a last covenant with the love we had had for each other. It hurts to this day. How I hate all the games. And I wondered how one could ever find trust in doctors if they don't follow a code of telling their patients the truth.

A year later, my mother passed on from cancer of the liver. She didn't survive surgery, but I wouldn't have known what to say if there had been a goodbye. Tragically, closeness and love weren't there (or sadly, at least).

Every relationship seems to acquire its own set of insides over time. My marriage with Joni wasn't doing particularly well, on top of all this.

In the meanwhile, through the next eighteen to twenty-five years, I would look at the neat cardboard box up on its shelf that held the strange can with a pry-open lid that contained Dave's ashes, and feel that I ought to do something about them. I'd never wanted to open the can and look in. And it took me that long to finally let go, and decide what to do. I don't remember the exact date when the funeral was held. But, on a cool summer morning in the middle of a July, long before sunrise, I paddled our canoe and the ashes several miles to the deep cove on the north side of Black Point. This was his favorite spot on the lake. He always talked about how you could dive off the shore and not hit the bottom. It was shallow as hell on the south side of that point.

I had Gordon's London Dry Gin, dry vermouth, olives, and a martini glass. Above all, he had been a martini man. With a sense of foreboding, I finally opened the container of ashes and looked with surprise at how pretty they turned out to be—light shades of pink, gray, and brown, like tiny pieces of wood. I carefully sprinkled them just off the shore and watched as they sank to the bottom and settled in a long, white looking swath.

I got out onto the shore, pulled up the canoe, and sat on the shale. I made the martini, then let the green olives soak in the gin. When the sun edged its way over Bare Hill, on the other side of the lake, I breathed in the vapors and drank. I left the olives to the end, of course. I paddled back home with a brisk morning wind at my back, to a place that was mine, and no longer ours. A place that felt empty and no longer home.

34

"As I was a ridin' one morning for pleasure,
I spied a cow puncher a ridin' along."

Broken Bow, Oklahoma

My eyes on the road, hands on the wheel, foot on the gas, out on the road on my own, headed out West, and middle America. After leaving the Weavers, my first set of bookings: the Buddhi, Oklahoma City; the Exodus, Denver; the Inquisition, Vancouver, British Columbia. The coffeehouse circuit—and a concert in Victoria, B.C.

The farmlands and highways were drawing me forward and then disappearing behind. Maybe I'd never get back to where I once was. This didn't seem bad, just unfamiliar. I had always liked driving because of how thoughts drifted into my mind as the country went by. While I drove, I didn't feel like a solo performer, however. At the same time, another old song preyed on my brain, along with the idea of yet another folk group.

Okla means "red," *homa* means "people." Indian Territory. Not far from the Buddhi, in Oklahoma City, was a statue of a cowboy on a horse. This was the West. The Lone Ranger, Roy Rogers, Gabby Hayes, Red River, John Wayne, the Sons of the Pioneers, all of that stuff I'd grown up with reverberated here. True cowboys and Indians. The Buddhi was small; it felt good. The opening act was Hoyt Axton, a robust, good-natured fellow from Broken Bow, Oklahoma. I liked him right off. Definitely not from New York. He was simple, for real, straightforward.

By show time, the place was about three-quarters filled. I sat in the audience waiting my turn as Hoyt started his set, this first night, the first night of my new life on the road, on my own. Two college kids started heckling Hoyt. It was clear they'd had something other than coffee to drink before they got there. My first thought was, "Is this what I'm in for out West, in middle America?" I had figured the West had been tamed. They pushed Hoyt to a point where he put down his guitar, walked off the stage, knocked one of them out, and chased the other one into the street. Then he got back on the stage, picked up his guitar, if a bit out of breath, and finished his set, short a couple of songs.

When I got on the stage, I just stood there a while, shaking my head as I tuned my guitar, and then said, "How in hell can I follow that?" The audience roared, and from then on, the gig was clear sailing. Hoyt told me at dinner that night, over navy-bean soup and restaurant salad, that getting drunk on a weekend and looking for fights was what growing up in Broken Bow was about. Life gets arranged with different mindsets, I guessed, depending on where you grow up and what you get used to.

The Exodus, in Denver, was more of a citified, showbiz-type place, and the sound system, terrible. It wasn't a place that was worth doing. At the Inquisition, in Vancouver, "Bud & Travis" headlined the show, somebody opened, and I came on second. This place was hot. Bud and Travis were highly skilled artists and they bloody well knew how to put on a show, while paying the deepest respect to the Mexican folk songs they sang. They booked out of L.A. and were known in the West.

My concert in Victoria was as it had been with the Tarriers in Paris: people hadn't come to drink coffee or *frappes,* impress dates, or have frat-party fun; they came for the music. It was the only solo concert I did, as a whole other story was about to unfold when I got back to New York, because of that song in the back of my mind:

> Everybody's talkin' 'bout a two-way woman,
> Do you wanna lose your mind?

Not exactly the sort of hook that was going to sell on America's airwaves, that lyric from a 1920s recording collected by Samuel B. Charters, a jazzman. His book, *The Country Blues,* states that Gus Cannon and Hosie Woods, who recorded the song, had sung it so long in medicine shows, they had forgotten what it meant. I would end up rewriting "talkin' 'bout a two-way woman," but the concepts that would stick to the back of my mind were:

Walk right in, set right down, Daddy, let your mind roll on.
Everybody's talkin' 'bout a new way of walkin'.
Do you wanna lose your mind?

The idea of getting off your high horse, being more natural, less wired, letting more out, finding a new, more open way of handling life, was surely an idea whose time had come. I knew of few people, if any, who weren't uptight or confused in one way or other. I felt the song was a hit, but not if I did it alone; it needed a group and the sound of a twelve-string guitar, done as Leadbelly would have. What I wasn't aware of was how much the need for a new way of walkin' would apply to my life more than anyone else's I knew.

Book IV

The Rooftop Singers

35

"If I was a little sparrow,
And I had wings, and I could fly . . ."

Threads of Connection

With a silly little grin (which, later, would turn out to be typical), Lynne Taylor said she had something she wanted me to hear, this was right before I took off for the West and the Buddhi. I had gone over to visit her husband, Skip Weshner, a folk D.J. who had just moved his radio show from L.A. to New York. Lynne, Heidi (their infant daughter), and Skip were living in a cramped, two-bedroom apartment somewhere on the upper west side of town. I didn't know Lynne well, didn't know that she even sang, though I'd met her in L.A. She had made a tape of the second solo album I'd made, *True Religion* (recorded for Vanguard), and had overdubbed every song on the album with harmony! She had caught every nuance and phrase, and never got in the way. I was speechless. Had that been released with her voice doing that, it would have sold hundreds of thousands, I thought. On the road headed west, as the idea of this new group preyed on my mind, Lynne was the first person I thought of. It got so I couldn't hear the idea without her.

Although the *True Religion* LP, as originally recorded, did not make me famous, it had brought me Lynne Taylor, and later on, evidence that what I had set out to do with my life mattered—to somebody, somewhere. You take chances in art, you try things that don't work and go back to the drawing board, over and over. You can record things you love, and among everyone else, even your friends, nobody may particularly like what you've done, or not in the ways that you do. The payment comes more in getting something right, because when you hear it yourself, you know it, again and again.

In the case of this album, I learned that it mattered to at least one fellow artist, Tony Price. He wanted to meet me because of this story:

> It was in Victor Biondo's apartment on the lower east side of Manhattan. At the time, he was managing Ornette Coleman. Nobody would give Ornette a job, he was a little far out, a little too spaced. We were listening to all kinds of music back then. From about 1959 to about 1962, the jazz scene in New York was extraordinary. Folk was starting to come through the coffeehouse scene, and most of the music we heard was jazz or folk.
>
> Victor could spend half a day sitting there, listening. One day he brought in this *True Religion* L.P., said it was kind of a folk thing someone had given him. After hearing it once, I was dumbfounded that this might be the world's most perfectly balanced sound. Victor would play it ten, fifteen, twenty times a day, and it always fit in with whatever was going on. The way I heard this record, it just carried you out into a right place; it drummed in a kind of audio objectivity, gave you a feeling of distance, a lone soul standing there, screaming into eternity.
>
> I pictured you as having a long beard, living in a cave in Tibet, and you sprang out, somehow, to put out this record for this time. I kept saying, "Who is this guy? What else has he done?" Victor would shake his head, he didn't know. Then I must have lost the record while out in New Mexico on some mad adventure, leaving everything behind, and was never able to find another copy. But hell, what do I know about music? Just what I like, I guess. But that record spellbound me for a good year. And I wanna thank you.

Tony was a Santa Fe sculptor who made his works out of stainless scrap metals from the weapons industry, stuff he had purchased at the Los Alamos labs: atomic bomb parts, igniters, half spheres to hydrogen bombs, failed-experiment parts, every kind of odd-shaped form, from whatever constructions imaginable. The labs sold off this stuff from a scrap yard, once a month, for pennies a pound. Tony's intention was to plug nonviolent energy into the weapons industry system. "Pontius Pilate Fed Up with Nuclear Situation" was one of his pieces. "The Nuclear Last Supper" was another. His "Atomic Pig Bird Feeder" was a large pig-like thing, five or six feet long, with places for water and seeds, which jangled in the wind when it blew. The glistening metals, along with the compelling odd forms that looked like their titles, were insidiously subtle and made a powerfully visceral statement that nuclear fission is no way to go.

Bill Svanøe was the next person I thought of for the group, because I knew he could play anything I could, faster than I could, with a similar attention to timing, and his music had urgency; he didn't just do the math and go home.

And the key to it all, as I saw it, was the sound of the twelve-string guitar, which had never been heard on a popular record. I figured that if *two* twelve-string guitars were playing the same exact notes, then that Leadbelly sound could not be held back by some engineer who didn't quite get it. Bill was the man. In fact, he seemed to play music as Leadbelly had, every note being part of his life.

The fourth person I thought of was Tommy Geraci, whom I'd sung with at Bard, along with Nick Thatcher. Tommy knew Leadbelly stuff, so I thought he'd be perfect.

Lynne was a mystery. It was from Heidi, her daughter, that I found out who she had been, and I sure wished I had known. I could have been more of a friend.

> Mom was Miss Pennsylvania. She was two weeks into the Miss America Pageant when they found out she had forged the documents so they'd think she was older. She was kicked off the pageant, as well as dethroned as Miss Pennsylvania. The one thing that had hurt her forever, however, and that seemed to play havoc with the rest of her life, was once, when in a bathtub. She had just won a tennis match or some water skiing event. She was sitting in the tub, the door was ajar, and her father walked by and looked in. Not having the wherewithal to know that he'd be overheard, he turned to her mother and said, "My God, what are we gonna do about that child's breasts?"
>
> After that, she was gone. Her wings had been broken, and she carried those broken wings for the rest of her life. Till the day she died, I would never see her naked when she wouldn't cover her breasts from her daughter. Her saving grace was that she had known that her father was backward, that her mother was insane, and that she had to leave.
>
> She married a drummer when she was fourteen. It lasted three months. She had a girlfriend, a bit older, who had been on the streets a bit longer, who took a good look at what the marriage was about, grabbed her the hell out of there, and she got the marriage annulled. The drummer, however, had discovered she had a natural talent for singing. That same year, fourteen years old (she looked a lot older and used that), she auditioned at the Village Vanguard and got in for one

show. She stayed on for twenty-eight weeks; broke all their records. She had to leave only because they found out her age.

She then went with Benny Goodman and then Buddy Rich, where it didn't matter how old she was. She went on the road with Dean Martin and Jerry Lewis, [as] the "beautiful-chick-singer" they played comedy off of.

Lynne had no pretensions, no arrogance, no prima-donna thing going, and she wasn't trying to sell you on hipness or anything else, even though she was hipper than just about anyone I ever met. It was not about ego, persona, or intellectual postures, it was about sharing a moment of truth, a way that she actually was. When she smiled at you or the audience in the midst of a song, it was never a put-on. When she sang, it wasn't self-conscious, she held nothing back, and that gave her a sense of herself that nothing else did. Nothing else, anywhere. Every cell of her body and soul came through her pores around music. The stage was where she found her freedom.

Lynne, as we knew her
(Photo: Norman Vershay)

"The girl with the band"
(Lynne at 14)

36

"Oh, such a bunch of devils no one ever saw,
Robbers, thieves, and highwaymen, breakers of the law . . ."

Parchman Farm

Bill Svanøe was just out of Oberlin College when we first started putting this music together, and I'd known him from Canandaigua Lake, where his mother had lived, just up the lake from my father. I'd need to find out if he could hang in there and go for this music, even if the going got tough, which it seemed like it usually did. Lots of folks start out with the best of intentions but change when they see what the price is.

We became buddies, spent endless hours and days hanging out: playing tennis, skiing, and talking about painting, economics, and movies. Not much went on in our lives that we didn't share, except this one fact: that he'd been in prison just months before we had started this work. I don't remember how or why it finally came out, so many years after the fact, except that he wasn't a guy to brag about things, "Look what I've done," or wear stuff on his sleeve. But, the details of the story he finally told, had I known them, I would have known he could put up with the crap that was about to befall us.

He had left graduate school in May 1961, when a college friend mentioned the Freedom Rides to him. The two had heard Martin Luther King, and he had gotten their attention. They went down to Nashville in July of '61 to get nonviolence training, then to get arrested for sitting in the black section of a bus, and then to serve time in a Southern penitentiary:

> They put us in a county jail for one night, then into prison vans and drove us to Parchman Farm, Mississippi State Penitentiary.
> When we were first getting fingerprinted, they'd say to the white women, stuff like, "You free them niggers and they're gonna fuck you

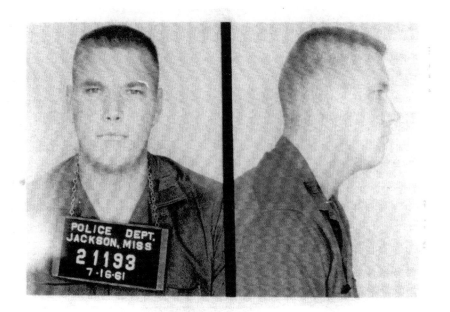

Bill Svanøe
Mississippi State Penitentiary

and rape all you women and screw everything up" or, "They multiply like rabbits if you let them screw. You should castrate every nigger there is."

You could tell they believed all this shit: "I was raised by a black nanny, niggers are our friends," they would say. "Rats got no feelings, just like niggers."

I was stunned. I knew there was prejudice, I'd seen it in New York, but this was a whole different thing. I realized, firsthand, what the blacks had been putting up with for so long. At that point, a lot of the songs began making sense, like, "Strange Fruit."

They put a bunch of us on death row, me and another white guy in one cell, black guys in other cells. There was a bank of eighteen cells with tiny windows up high, two men to a cell. My cellmate was a jerk, a radical Communist, always rabble-rousing, making trouble, trying to get himself thrown into solitary so he could say he had suffered. His and my politics were totally different. A lot of people went on this ride for different reasons: to further their politics, prove themselves as a person, rebel against their parents. But, a lot of them, to make the statement that this is a country founded on people being free, and that if they're not free, then we don't have the country we thought we had.

There was a shower at the end of a narrow corridor. Once a week, you walked down, took your shower, shaved, and went back. The cells had openings just big enough for a tray to fit through. I didn't eat for the first eighteen days. They would serve pork that had hair on it. It got so that when I'd stand up, I'd almost pass out.

The beds were bunk beds with a sharp metal lip that came up on all sides. The bed part was a metal sheet with quarter-sized holes, spaced two inches apart. You could only sleep in one position for about twenty minutes because your skin would sink through those holes, and if an arm or a leg would hang over and hit on that lip, that would wake you up instantly. I learned to turn, carefully, every twenty minutes.

There was a sink, a john, and no toilet paper, no toothbrush, and all we were wearing was a pair of prison-issue shorts. No shoes. This was Mississippi in the summer, hot and humid. There were bugs crawling everywhere: on the walls, on the floors, on the ceiling. I'd look up and watch. Every once in a while, one would drop down, and I'd brush it away. The worst thing was the bugs. Especially at night.

After three weeks, we were moved into a large room where all the other whites were. There were about forty of us. We had spring beds with thin mattresses, an incredible luxury. The beds were toward the center of the room, with windows all around three sides. The fourth wall was bars. That's where the guards were. They would sit there and watch us.

There was this whole little world, like Stalag 17. Two, four, five of us would get to know each other, and we'd form little cliques, and we'd go for walks around the perimeter of the beds, maybe a hundred times, take us an hour or so. There was a group that had saved their bread and had made a Monopoly set. They made dice out of the bread after it got hard, hotels, and the pieces to move. Someone tore off a section of sheet and made the board with grease markings from the food. Somebody had remembered the Chance cards, and the Community Chest. They had the whole thing. Somebody else, in another group, had made a deck of playing cards.

This was the summer the Berlin wall went up, and the summer that Roger Maris and Mickey Mantle were trying to break Babe Ruth's record. When anyone new came in, the first question was, "What's happening with the teams?" One guy smuggled in the components of a crystal radio set behind his balls. He either had a very small radio or very large balls. I never saw either. He would huddle in a corner farthest away from the guards and listen to the news. Then, discreetly, the news would get disseminated.

I was two days overdue for my day to be released, and if you didn't get released on time, it meant six months more of this stuff.

They were going down a list, calling out names: Harkness, Jones, Smith, whomever. Then he stopped. I knew he had come to my name and couldn't pronounce it. I called out, "Svanøe."

"Yeah, that's it," he said. They issued us out as quickly as they could, and a whole bunch of blacks met us and took us to the local Baptist church, where they threw a big party for us.

Lynne Taylor, Bill Svanøe, Tommy Geraci, and I were the players. Rehearsals were held at Skip and Lynne's place, as Lynne had to look after Heidi. This was on Jones Street in the west Village, one block over from Cornelia, where I had lived in the back of a store for a while. It was not to go easy.

37

"We've reached the land of hills and stones,
Where all is strewn with buffalo bones . . ."

The Devil and
the Details

Skip Weshner had an ego the size of a battleship and would order Lynne around their apartment as if she were a dog. Bill and I were appalled. Lynne's smile would suddenly fade, she would do what he bid, and then she'd come back with her usual good-natured face for the group. "Never interfere with man and wife, never understand. No matter who is wrong or who is right, oh, just show your sympathy," goes the old calypso.

After eight or ten weeks of rehearsal, I felt we were nearing the time to audition for Vanguard. The recordings I'd done with the Weavers had been for Vanguard; *True Religion,* as well. I knew who they were, I liked them, and we'd have control.

Out of the blue, Skip started talking about taking the group to Columbia Records, and the force with which he argued his proprietary idea was daunting. He had never been in the picture before, as a factor, so this didn't make sense. I didn't know if he'd already spoken to someone up there without asking us, whether he saw his wife's group as a meal ticket, or what. I'd gathered he didn't handle money well, and they were in debt; but he was a bully, and bullies don't listen. When he got on a tear, it was as if there was no space for anyone else in the room. And, for me, in terms of putting forth my point of view, not only did I think he was crazy, along with his being a bully, but I couldn't be absolutely sure that Vanguard was the best choice! You can't *know* those sorts of things. You use your gut judgment, but you never can know.

I trusted Maynard Solomon, the half-owner of Vanguard. You could talk to the man; he was a cellist and a pianist; he knew what music did. I had met Decca executives with as much sensitivity as a jar full of nails. The fact that Vanguard had never had a hit record meant nothing to me, for example, but that could be seen as an issue. But if "Walk Right In" were done right—meaning, as we heard the song—I believed it would go. I was also quite sure that if Skip got involved, he would wheedle his way into producing the group, and there would go our vision. He thought he knew all there was to know about music, as well as everything else in the world.

I lay quiet and placated Skip. Then, out of the blue, I said, "Maynard just wants to hear us, it's not about making a deal. We might as well audition for both companies, anyway," throwing a bone at Skip's cage. I felt Skip's resentment as it came out of the pores of his face and the sweat of his fatness, but this was a battle I was not going to lose.

We went in and recorded six songs, "Walk Right In" being one. It was a quick session with Jeff Zaraya, Vanguard's best engineer. The only sense I came away with, however, was that we had a big sound, and the twelve-strings were blazing away, as expected. I wasn't sure about anything else. The following week would be the moment of truth when we'd listen to what we'd recorded, with Maynard, and he would say yes or no.

It's one thing when you've got something you believe in and feel is compelling, something unique, but the people who could make the thing happen don't hear it. You keep moving on. That's simply the heat of the kitchen. It's when you hear it played back and you know it's so bad that you can't even say it, that's when it's tough. And that's how it was. It wasn't that the sound was big, as I'd thought, it was that it was heavy, thick, unattractive, un-swinging, impossible.

I began sinking before the first tune had ended. Music is life on a bed of sand, anyway. And if it is yours and you don't happen to like it, one thing's for sure: you can't expect anyone else to. I crawled up inside and I sat there, waiting for somebody else in the room to hear what I heard.

Maynard didn't say yes, he didn't say no, he thought it needed more work. He suggested we put in a couple more months. We'd already done that, however. I hated every word he said. It was all so irrelevant, I wanted to scream. He was even willing to pay Tommy's salary, as Tommy would have needed to quit his job for a time. I'd heard what was on the tape, and I knew that if we rehearsed for the next twenty-five years, it wouldn't get better.

It was Tommy.

Having him in this group, for me, was about giving him a gift for the years we had sung in the streets. And I thought I was making a family, and we'd all have a great time.

Tommy had all the love in the world for this music but, like Leadbelly, he was not a group singer. Lynne was like a fine willow that bent with the wind; Tommy was like an oak tree, strong but unyielding. During all that rehearsal, we'd simply gotten used to allowing for his way of singing.

I had been here before. When musicians don't swing, they don't feel that they don't, and they cannot understand what you're talking about. Tommy wasn't always easy to talk to, as well, but he was my buddy, my choice, and it was my job to tell him that he had to go. It would be thirty-two years before we'd get back together and become the friends we once were. When finally we did, a few years before he died of heart failure in May 1994, I asked how he had felt, and he told me:

> I felt that I had lost my best friend. Because that's what I felt towards you. It had all gone to pieces, and from then on we were no longer as close as we had been. It stayed with me for years. Maynard was even willing to pay my salary for a couple of months, because that was a big thing; I was married, we had Junie, Maynard was willing to carry me so that we could get it together. But you and Bill and Lynne didn't want to wait. It stuck in my craw, because I never got the opportunity to see if it could have worked out. I was left out in the cold. I remember Lynne's husband, Skip, saying, "Tom, just get yourself an accompanist, you could do it on your own." But I couldn't do it. I was shattered after that, for a while. But you get over things.

To attempt to explain to one of your best friends why he can't be in the group you eagerly asked him to be in—and at the same time, know he won't understand, because he just can't—is a terrible, terrible thing.

The rest of us went back to work. I didn't speak to Tommy again, as I said, because I didn't know what to say that would make the wound heal, and because of my own tunnel of darkness that soon clouded over my own sense of life, it all slipped away.

38

"Won't you think of the valley you're leaving? . . ."

The End of the Line

There are truths that can decompose any soul, if a person doesn't happen to know what they are. To escape this, a person can callous his or her soul with strategies that hide their existence, their patterns of being, and these can be soft or hard calluses.

What I mean to say is that a life can be lived for a while with familiar patterns of thinking, but patterns that don't sustain life over time. When people play games with self-perception, somewhere inside, they will *know* it. And then—depending on who they are—rehearsing music too long could lead to their death.

Two and a half hours of rehearsal, we found, was the limit. Nothing improved after that, our voices got tired, hands could cramp up, and we could begin learning mistakes. Day after day, we started at 2 p.m. and went until 6, with a big break in the middle. Lynne would make coffee or open some sodas.

Skip and Lynne's place, a third-floor walkup, was a loft with two windows in front, two in back. The refrigerator, stove, and sink were in a back corner, not easily seen from sitting in the living room, which was defined by two couches and an olive-green carpet. A steep flight of stairs went down to a first floor, where communications between Skip and Lynne were usually shouted. The stairs were so narrow that I never thought of the place as a duplex, though it was rented as one.

The air conditioner was broken on this particular day. It was sweaty and hot, and although the front and back windows were open, there was no movement of air. The whole city had been muggy for a week. Even the threadbare carpet was further remorseful. The failed audition with Tommy had left me more than discouraged; I was questioning, once again, if my life made any sense.

Bill and I had tuned up, we were ready, but lying around talking about letting it go for the day. Lynne brought some sodas from back in the kitchen.

After drinking a huge glass of Tab over ice, I got it into my head to find a chord for some railroad song. I wanted a sound, a feel, resonant with the weight of a railroad engine. I began pacing around, putting my fingers in various convoluted positions, a process of trial and error. My sense of discouragement vanished. Nothing like creative work to banish the devil. The chord became clear in a while and I drew a diagram of the finger positions on a napkin.

The chord had nothing to do with the song we going to rehearse, but that didn't matter. What mattered was that it had been three hours straight since I had started the search. It was nearly 5:30. What's more, I had completely ignored Lynne and Bill in all of that time. This was bizarre. Yet, Bill and Lynne had just sat there, drinking Tab, talking away, as if nothing was strange.

Then we began working on an old country song from my days at the Square: "I'm Just Here to Get My Baby Out of Jail," written by Karl Davis and Harty Taylor in the 1930s.

> "I'm not in your town to stay,"
> Said a lady old and gray,
> To the warden of the penitentiary.
> "I'm not in your town to stay,
> And I'll soon be on my way.
> I'm just here to get my baby out of jail.
> Yes, warden,
> I'm here to get my baby out of jail."

That gives you an idea of the story line. After six or seven verses, it ended like this:

> Then I heard the warden say
> To the lady old and gray,
> I'll bring your baby boy down to your side.
> Two iron gates swung wide apart.
> She held her darlin' to her heart.

She kissed her baby boy and then she died.
But smiling,
In the arms of her dear boy, there she died.

We were totally euphoric rehearsing this song, even though we had doubts we could carry it off or even use it with anything else we were doing. It wasn't our kind of thing. But by then, it was two hours later—7:30 p.m.— just like that!

After a break, we got drawn into its musical web once again, and we went on and on. Lynne flitted around, giggling, as Bill and I worked on the banjo and guitar parts for this thing, with Bill playing the banjo—something he had never done up to then. Then it was 2 a.m., twelve hours since we had gotten there. We finally let the song go and went home.

On the Seventh Avenue subway, jabbering our heads off the entire time, Bill and I kept saying how odd that we never got tired. We accepted it as some sort of zone we could slip into as a result of caring that much and working as hard as we had been to get this group right. You try to explain away things that have no explanation.

Then, in sharp contrast to all that euphoria, I found, the next morning, that I'd lost my voice, and had damaged a nerve in my hand, which made it impossible to play.

My marriage to Joni was over. She was in her own place. When we first split, I was convinced that our problems were hers, not mine. Nothing wrong with me, are you kidding? I was glad that she left. But, even if you don't get along with a partner, for whatever reasons, not getting along fills up a whole lot of space. And that space was now empty. The apartment felt empty.

Bill lived on 67th Street, right around the corner, between Columbus and Central Park West. I hadn't sounded too good on the phone, so he came over. There was nothing he could do, and I barely could talk. I said I was okay, and he went on his way. This left me alone once again.

Alone can be good. This wasn't good.

One of the great things I'd always loved about New York was the sense of life there, the feeling that you were never completely alone, even at night. The city simmers with all kinds of energy: you hear the car horns, the buses, the now-and-then siren, and out in the streets, you know there are people, a late-night bar, somebody walking a dog, a bunch of people on their way home from a party. The city lives in its streets. Then there was Chinatown, Little Italy, and Canal Street, where you could find any tool imaginable in the lofts or hardware stores there. All signs of life, and of hope, if you will. There was a midtown thirty-story building that had been torn down completely except for a tiny hat store on the ground floor. A meadow of bricks, twisted girders, wires, and broken-off piping completely surrounded this store with its glass and brass doorway, its clean little window filled up with its hats. Guess the developers couldn't buy them out of their lease. But that was New York, there were always those people who wouldn't sell out.

At this moment, however, in the middle of all of all this, in the bright light of day when the city is teeming, I found no signs of hope. The din of the city, if anything, seemed a reproach, a reminder of how separate I was from all human beings, and how fragile the threads of existence actually were. The material tools of this life are hard-wired, like a steel girder, a hammer, or the strings on a guitar, but how to use them is not.

In this state of mind, my perceived failures loomed as matters more relevant than anything else. I'd never learned to read music, for one thing. I couldn't go off and write music on paper, be an arranger, or be a composer of classical music—my first love as a child. Not reading music and living in New York, where some of the greatest musicians in the world read music better than literature, had me feeling uneasy about even saying I was a musician.

This folk music stuff was charming, ballsy, tender, sad, human, heroic, some of it funny, and it did have its artistic value, which couldn't even be learned by the reading of music, but I couldn't see that. I couldn't see that neither Leadbelly nor Ray Charles had ever read music. I wondered if maybe I had permanently damaged my voice or the nerve in my hand, that was my focus.

Both my parents had died within the last several years, so I was no longer somebody's son.

I was no longer a Weaver. My definitions were gone.

It was not a dark moment. I would have welcomed the dark; dark is a thing you can wallow in. This wasn't like that. I had no boundaries, no friend in the room. A numbing of the cells in my feet and at the edges of my ears had me knowing that something was dreadfully wrong.

Joni and I had lived here, at 60 West 68th Street, Apt. 2-D, my mother's old place. I walked through the rooms, and they didn't look real or feel right, although I had changed nothing since Joni had left. A full-length mirror hung on the closet door of the room I used as a studio, and I looked at myself. When I stood back from the mirror, I didn't look seeable, sort of. Everything had a sense of the "sort of" about it. I thought I should do something about whatever this was, but I couldn't call up my doctor and say, "I don't feel right."

He'd say, "What are your symptoms?"

"I'm terrified," I would reply

"Of what?," he would say.

"I don't know," I would say.

If you're running from some horrid thing in a dream, at least you've got something to run from and the idea of a place you run to, a sense of escape. There was no escape, here. The terror was in the sinews and cells of my body, like a nerve gas that goes into your pores, but from the inside. And it seemed to feed on itself, fueling its own degradation. That is, my fear of the fear seemed to engulf more of my being with each passing moment. I saw no way whatever of getting away from the vortex of this, and some reasoning part of me understood that I had to end this. You don't stay with a pain that's like this.

I took the elevator ten flights up to the top floor and got out. The door to the roof was at the top of the stairs in the building's stairwell. I'd been on the roof. It was covered with a thick, black roofing material that was acrid and unpleasant to smell. There was one of those water towers up there. I had calculated that if I jumped off the roof, the pain would end. I'd always been a practical person, good in emergencies.

Standing in the acrid smell of the roof, I thought about what the fall would be like, dropping past all those reddish-brown bricks of the building, and past all those windows. The idea that I would be dead wasn't as big an issue as ending the pain. I did not like the visual sense of the fall, however, or where I would land. Down, down, down the back of the building, ending up in a desolate place which was a dirty and smelly and plantless, an alley-cat place.

My sense of aesthetics held sway. I went back to the elevator, figuring I could jump later. I had the freedom and power to do what I needed.

Back in the apartment, I dealt with another possible option. (Creative work is always about looking at options, the gift from my father.) I got the idea that this pain had to do with my head, and perhaps I should call someone who knew about heads. I felt a tinge of losing face, calling Joni, because I was the one in trouble, not her. But I couldn't argue with myself about that, at this point. When I reached her, she gave me the name of the woman psychologist she had been seeing. I called right away, but she couldn't see me until later that evening. Hours to kill. I went out and managed to buy a pint of whisky, brought it back to the apartment and drank it, remembering that people drank when in trouble; that movie, *Lost Weekend,* with Ray Milland, came to mind. The liquor was awful, and it had no effect whatsoever.

Thirty-three blocks north and three blocks west, 101st Street and Riverside Drive, was my destination. It was still light when I began walking uptown. As people came toward me, they all looked like mannequins. I tried to walk as if I were normal. Joni's psychologist looked rather odd when she ushered me into apartment 10A. As the session wore on, the less odd she looked.

I wasn't going insane, I found out, and I wasn't the only one on the planet like this. All of the things I had used to define my existence—my parents, a wife, being in a well-known group, my ability to play music— were no longer there, all at once, and I'd had an anxiety attack. So this had a name. Panic. That helped me distance myself from the fact of this thing.

When I walked out of her building, the city was lit; darkness had come. As I turned south on West End Avenue, I began crying, because I could feel the tiny pebbles in the sidewalk through the worn soles of my sneakers. I realized that when I had made the trip up, I could feel nothing. I was now back in my body, at least. Joni came over and stayed with me that night, and that kindness may have saved me, because the panic came back, and when it showed up, it took over again, although I didn't tell her. But her being there made all difference. It only takes one really good friend.

But my structure had crumbled, and I knew I was no longer safe. And I had this question: would I forever be living this way, and one day would it win?

It was several weeks later, when talking with mutual friends who had also visited Lynne and had left with a similar kind of euphoria, that I knew she had spiked our sodas with something. The immorality of this, the invasion of ultimate privacy, was nearly impossible for me to grab hold of. She never denied it, when asked, nor did she admit it. She just gave us an "Oh, but wasn't it fun?" kind of look, childlike, innocent of evil intent. From where she had been living her life, she didn't know any better, I guessed.

There was no percentage in being angry at her, lecturing her on the sanctity of each human being. Further, I knew that it wasn't the drug and its morning after that took me to the edge of that roof, it was how I had lived in my head. I kept having once-a-week sessions with Joni's psychologist, but the panic still lurked.

39

"I have been a good boy, wed to peace and study,
I shall have an old age, ribald, coarse and bloody . . ."

Vindication

Vanguard released "Walk Right In" on November 21, 1962. One D.J. in Buffalo played nothing but that record for twenty-four hours, and that got it national attention. It began climbing the charts by the end of November, was edged out in December by the Christmas music, and then came back on the Billboard Hot 100 chart by January 5, 1963. By January 29, it had reached No. 1.

"Forty thousand." "Sixty thousand," Herb Corsack would say when Bill asked how many singles were ordered that day. Herb was in charge of Vanguard's promotion and was making this record's success single-handedly. Although I had developed an inner hesitation about Lynne, we had hung in there and done this together, no matter what other problems with life. In the struggle for this, we were allies. We looked at each other when we were alone in a hallway at Vanguard, shook our fists, and did one of those ear-to-ear grins. At one level or another, we were small kids and couldn't help giving each other permission to show the gratification and excitement we felt. That kidlike connection was always there when we sang, it was what we swung with.

The record took on an odd life of its own in relation to what I was feeling. Even though I had spent all that time hoping for this, the creative effort was over, part of the past. Now, the results came in at us, seemingly out of nowhere. In a performance, you work all the details of some song, the intro, the feelings, the instrumental break, and the ending, and the audience responds right away. Cause and effect. This had a delay which made it unreal.

Nonetheless, it was a vindication for Bill and me, because we'd come up with the peculiar arrangement of the song. Most songs had a ten-second hook, give or take, (the intro), to get you into the song. But, as we heard it, this song needed an entire verse-instrumental, and being that no D.J. had probably ever heard of a twelve-string, we felt this would work.

Maynard had thought "Tom Cat" was the hit, and we had said no. Fortunately, Herb Corsack was with us on this. It was a personal vindication for Lynne, as it was her style and voice that set off the record. For me, it was that I was right about Leadbelly and the twelve-string guitar; I could not help but remember the trouble my mother gave me for buying his record.

During one week, we could flip the radio dial and catch the song on several stations at once, and I could not help getting hung up on other hits while waiting for the song to come on. "Up on the Roof" by the Drifters was one, "Loop De Loop" by Johnny Thunder was another.

Vanguard started getting calls from venues wanting to book us, and we didn't have an act, had never set foot on a stage as a group. We got our feet wet with some performances at The Bitter End, Gerde's Folk City, and then into the Village Gate for a month. While we were learning to perform as a group, bookings started coming in for the summer. All of a sudden, we were into the business of getting on stage, working up concert material, finding out what worked and what didn't. In late February, we did *The Tonight Show* with Carson.

"Walk Right In" was thirteen weeks on the charts. "Tom Cat" was released and came on the charts the week ending March 23, got to as high as 20, and was on for ten weeks, but it got banned in Boston and some places in the South. And Boston was an important market for the rest of the country. Seemed like Boston was uptight about sex, even between cats.

Tom Cat

I got an old tom cat,
And when he steps out,
All the other cats
In the neighborhood,
They begin to shout.

"There goes a ring-tailed tom,
Struttin' 'round the town.
And if you've got
Your heat turned up,
You better turn your damper down."

Ring-tailed Tom is the stuff.
He's a natural-born crack shot.
He finds a new target
Every night
And he sure does practice a lot.

The agents who booked us were distressed that we wouldn't do more popular songs in our program, songs other than folk, and that we wouldn't accept a concert if the schedule didn't allow us time to check out the sound and the lights.

In a restaurant, waiting to order, on a plane waiting for takeoff, places like that, suddenly I'd be engulfed in self-dread. I'd sit in the panic, show nothing, and wait for the food. I would, literally, sweat the thing out. It never happened on stage. There, I was present and real, in the midst of our creative attention. And although the hit record and all of this action provided a level of distraction, as well as a kind of security, I still knew that my life was at risk, but life on the road with the group trundled on.

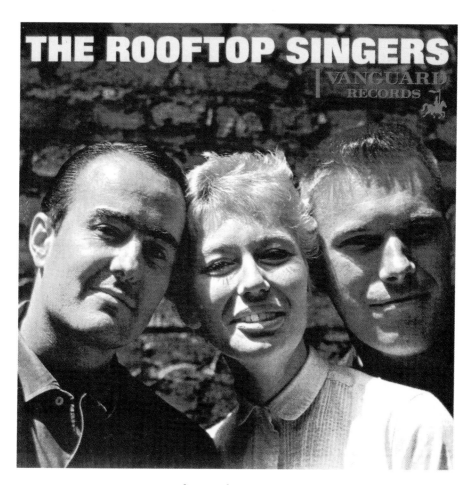

The Rooftop Singers
Me, Lynne, and Bill

Bill, Lynne, and me

40

"Good morning, good morning, good morning to thee,
O, where are you going, my pretty lady? . . ."

Steve's Ville

On the road, Lynne and I fell more and more into being like children, suddenly free from the bonds of some hidden unpleasantness out of our pasts. We would fill our mouths with bubble gum, for example, while Bill was filling the station wagon with gas or going to the bathroom. Then, quickly, we would decorated the inside of the car between the front and back seats with long swags of gum and laugh ourselves silly when he got back into the car and saw what we'd done. Bill was a "neat freak," you see, always picking small pieces of lint off his clothes. I always envied the neatness with which he kept his apartment, however. But the gum bit was funny. One night, when we got to a motel and all four doors of the station wagon were open (in the process of unloading), Lynne and I started slamming and opening the doors to the beat of some rock thing that came on the car radio. What a cool instrument, we thought. *"The station wagon, man, the station wagon."* Bill shook his head, smiling. Lynne and I were beside ourselves. Bill and Lynne would get into arguments like whether one or two Ferris wheels were on a Ferris-wheel thing we had passed ten miles back, or whether Lynne could chew twelve packs of gum at one time. It was all hanging loose.

At the Hillbilly Homecoming in Maryville, Tennessee, someone had apparently not read our contract. A big fuss erupted because our contract stated in clear black and white that admission could not be restricted or segregated. How they signed the contract without catching that was a mystery, but there was the big question as to whether we would be doing the show or heading back home. Because we were the main attraction, they finally relented, I guess. I think they figured blacks wouldn't come anyway. What we cared about was that they could if they wanted to.

Having Peck Morrison onstage, the black bass player who was with us this trip, was no problem for them, but he had to stay in some other place than the motel they'd put us in. Peck had traveled in the South in mixed jazz groups, so he knew upfront what the scene was. An automobile dealership sponsored the event, and they lent Peck a new Oldsmobile to drive. We got to making a joke about keeping the motor running, just in case people rushed the stage and we had to get out of town in a hurry. I guess things have changed in the South, but I never go there without feeling I've got to look over my shoulder. Every time I see a cross in the South—and there are some—I see it burning on somebody's lawn. Nothing breeds a self-righteous anger to the point of a lynching better than some kind of religion, it seems.

In rural Kentucky, somewhere down South, the three of us were headed for a college town, and we had been driving too long. Being the best driver and with the best stamina, Bill always drove. But even he'd had it, this trip. Miles and miles went by after we had decided to stop wherever we could, with no sign of motels. They simply weren't there or were closed, weeded over, ideas that had faded away. In the middle of nowhere came a sign: STEVE'S VILLE. We figured we had better take this or we'd end up sleeping on the side of the road.

We checked in, got our keys at the office, which was downhill from the units, and then drove up the hill to the two units we'd booked. We saw no other cars, but the place didn't look bad, just kind of rough at the edges. As soon as Bill and I had unlocked the door, got into our room, and put our stuff on the beds, we heard a knock on the single-panel door between the two rooms. The door rattled in the doorjamb. It was Lynne with her typical cackle: "What's your room like?," she asked.

The rooms were like animal pens, no rugs, cement floors with a drain in the middle. I had the impression they hosed the place out when they cleaned it. Plenty of wire hangers were in the closets, and the closets, of course, had no doors. Linoleum had been glued to the walls instead of the floor, and the screens on the windows had holes.

The towels, you could see through. Steve's Ville became the low-water mark. Anything that was marginal from then on, we would call Steve's Ville.

Wherever Lynne went, she wore a skirt, a blouse, and high-heeled shoes. She could run in those things, if perchance we were late for a plane. She never, ever wore dungarees, and I never saw her in sneakers, but she was the most good-natured, gracious, and down-to-earth person I'd ever met. And she was unflappable. Rather than being bummed out by places like Steve's Ville, she got a kick out of them.

We played one high school, which may not have been too far from Steve's Ville, maybe. The concert took place in their assembly hall. I remember the spotlight flickered, almost like it was lit by a huge, magnified candle. The kids screamed from the minute we got on the stage until the concert was finished. It was like being the Beatles or something. We couldn't make introductions to songs, no one could hear what we said; nor did they care. We had no sense that they'd actually heard any song. It was some other sort of event, which by the end it left us shaking our heads in a daze.

In late fall, we were booked at the Dallas Convention Center. We were in a motel owned by Doris Day. All the rooms had motifs—and way too much pink. It was an architectural joke. After the concert, we got Chinese food and took it to Lynne's room. Bill and I took our instruments back to our room and then went back to Lynne's. She had everything nicely laid out. When Bill and I got back to our room after we ate, once again we got that elated feeling and stayed up all night gabbing away.

I remember going into the john and feeling I was pissing forever and like it was my life I was pissing away. Bill had been recently reading about LSD, amphetamines, and the other stuff that was going around, and realized she had slipped us one of those things, whatever it was, yet again. It had never crossed our minds that, on the road, she would have whatever it was she had spiked our drinks with the first time.

I hadn't told Lynne what happened to me the first time and what life had been like since then. Had she admitted, outright, that she had done it, maybe I would have. Because she never admitted it outright,

I could not but wonder if she had actually done it. I had no hard-wired proof, as I saw it.

This time, we had a generic meeting on the issue of drugs. Bill played the heavy and told her: no drugs on the road! We should be totally clean at all times, nothing left in our rooms, or in a dressing room, or in our luggage, no joints, nothing. If any one of us got caught with anything, we would all be in deep shit. She said, "Okay," in her usual agreeable manner. She was so bright-eyed, playful, and clean-spirited in so many ways, however, it was not easy to tell what she actually meant when she said, "Okay."

But one ironclad rule was that we were to be in the dressing room a half hour before every show, just as in any professional Broadway production. It was quarter of eight, at a big concert in Toronto, which went on at eight, and no sign of Lynne. She walked in at ten of and quickly got ready, and we went out onstage. She had bought a bustle, a fake rear end, from Frederick's of Hollywood, and had been waiting a month to wear that damned thing. In itself, I didn't think it was particularly funny, nor did I think it looked good, but I could not help smiling at her glee in the prank. Between songs, though, I could see her lips quivering. Clearly, stoned out of her gourd. Life near the edge. Fragile.

I had no idea, at the time, what the balance of her insides were like, or what her life had been like on the road with jazz bands, I knew none of the stuff that Heidi eventually told me. In fact, it struck me that I didn't know what anyone's world was like on the inside, for the most part. I didn't ask enough questions. I sure hadn't known about mine. But, for the first time, I could see she was fragile, in spite of how much she gave out in a song.

When she started to sing, she was totally present and swinging her head off. But then, she looked scared. Strung out in some internal way. I could begin to catch on that a lot of her good natured behavior, although it made her easy to be with, was a cover for pain, and it struck me that being on the road might not be the right thing for her, even though singing was all she lived for, and even though she made the group what it was.

41

Weavers Reunion
15th Anniversary
Concerts

The Reunion concerts were booked for May 2 and 3, 1963, at Carnegie Hall, and they wanted to include everyone who had been with the group. In spite of my reasons for leaving them, I wanted to do this. The Weavers were too much a part of my heritage. Frank Hamilton had replaced me in the group, and although I'd thought the group would be better with him, personality clashes arose, apparently, and he hadn't stayed long. Groups are not easy. He'd been replaced by a non–banjo-player, Bernie Kraus. I didn't know of any recordings they'd made with Bernie, or how they were getting along, but we would all be in this concert together. Seven of us.

The difficult part turned out to be "San Francisco Bay Blues," which Frank and I chose as a duet.

Déjà vu, with Frank coming over to my mother's old place, to the same rooms where, ten years before, he had come for one night, stayed for a month, and then had to leave in a hurry.

There was never, ever enough time to rehearse anything, anywhere, as far as my sense of things was concerned. I felt the need to give songs the time to sink in and take hold, time to let improvisations evolve, until we found the best ones. I had always been more of a composer than an on-the-spot improviser, anyway, as I didn't trust that the best of what I could invent would come out in the moment.

Things always changed in performance, but I liked taking off from a place that was reasonably sure. Frank was more of a bird-in-flight person, wanting to get down the basic idea and create the rest of the work from the hip, like jazz people do. Nevertheless, working together harkened back to more innocent times, when I had just fallen in love with this music.

The high point in the concert, for me, and for reasons I could not have predicted, was "San Francisco Bay Blues."

On the May 2 performance, there was a good beat to the song by the time we laid out the intro and got into the words (people were already clapping along). We'd conceived it as if we were horn parts, like in a Dixieland band, not too tightly arranged. The first part came out pretty much as we'd thought. The instrumental was more like the flight of some bird—a cross between a crow, a duck, and a pelican (a crowduckan?), and even though I barely knew where we were, we were making it happen, as phrases miraculously evolved between us, and we were creating something that had not gone before. That's part of what I mean by a high point. Coming out of the instrumental, I began internally celebrating, because we were home free. A relief, to be sure! That is, until I sang the wrong words.

From that instant on, the song was no longer about getting the blues because your baby was gone and you were sorry for treating her mean. It was about two musicians who had fallen apart and were struggling to get back together: a life-and-death moment on stage.

Any rehearsal we'd done was superfluous now; it was a matter of trust. No time to think. We just did it. I was scared shitless, hoping I'd somehow find a way out. When I managed to sing, "She said goodbye, made me wanna lay right down and die!," Frank chuckled and threw in the line, "Well, you better learn the words first!" And this got a laugh. The audience was laughing with us, not at us, and that got us back. It was an improvisation, the essence of jazz. And then, when we finally got home and the rhythm got down, everyone began clapping to the beat.

Perhaps, more than any other song in the concert, this screwed-up performance was what life-affirming drama portrays: setting out, getting lost, getting separated, and then, with a big moment of trust, managing to get back together—otherwise known as spontaneous creative existence, the essence of what life is about.

The song is not well constructed and not that compelling by it-self. It was the drama of the struggle we lived through that gave it its juice. Michelangelo's *David* is no more than a naked man about to throw a stone at a giant. What's the big deal? It's in *how* he sculpted it, not *that* he sculpted it that made all the difference.

The big lesson, for me, came from a different direction, however. We were all down at Vanguard listening to the May 2 and 3 perfor-mances of songs, choosing which ones were best to be put on a forth-coming record. I didn't make any mistakes on the May 3 performance of "San Francisco Bay Blues," and that was the version I wanted. Not a doubt in my mind. I saw the first one as flawed, and I'd made the flaw. I felt I'd be embarrassed forever, if that one went out. This was my work, and I had the right to make that decision.

Frank wasn't there for these sessions, but every single person in that room said I was wrong. And each one was adamant.

I was conflicted, nonplused, and surprised. Everyone was spon-taneously aligned against me. I had been ready to fight tooth and nail to throw that thing out. At the same time, I felt that they had to be right about something that I couldn't hear. I did not understand any of what I've just said, at the moment, about what the performance was about. All I could hear was: *mistake!* End of story.

Part of me thought I was selling out artistic values under group pressure by even wondering if they were right.

While I held onto the idea that if I went along, then changed my mind back, I could call Maynard and wheedle the "good" version onto the record, later on, I acquiesced and let the flawed version stand. And, it would take months after the record's release before I'd begin understanding what they had heard and I didn't. And years before I'd finally get it: that a performance doesn't have to be perfect, any more than a person. The imperfect is often more perfect than perfect could ever have been.

Years later, Frank wrote me a note about what we had done: "It was a jazz snowflake, going to happen just that one time." It remains as a footprint of where we had been, and why it was worth being there.

Bernie Kraus, me, Frank, Ronnie, Lee, Fred, and Pete

Ronnie and Frank Hamilton
(Photo: Joe Alper)

42

"Fare you well, oh, honey,
Fare you well . . ."

Ford Mustang

When Ford introduced the Mustang, the Ford Company hired the Rooftop Singers to tour with Herbie Mann and his band, and a bunch of other acts, for three weeks. The tour went down South, out West, and ended up back up in Syracuse, New York. No commercials were in the show, but wherever we performed, a Ford Mustang was there.

In Texas, the company had mistakenly booked two concerts in two different places for the same night, thirty or so miles away from each other. When we got there, they figured it out that we would start our segment of a concert at one venue while Herbie Mann would start his at the other, then we would switch venues, while other acts would do the same thing. They flew us to the second venue in two Piper Cubs, us in one plane, our instruments in another. Some of the other acts were transported by bus, because there was more time, somehow, or not enough planes. The audiences at both venues had to wait for their shows to continue.

We're sitting on the tarmac waiting for our dinky little plane to take off, wondering how many acts had died in small plane crashes. It was one of those things where "the show must go on," and you trust that they know what they're doing and go with the flow. People drive bumper to bumper on the L.A. freeways going sixty miles per hour, trusting people will know what they're doing. I figured this was a hell of a lot safer.

An American Airlines 707 was scheduled for takeoff. Our pilot wanted the 707 to hold. Over the Piper Cub's radio, we heard the communications between the control tower and the 707.

Control tower: "Would you hold?"

"Hold for what?" said the 707.

"The Rooftop Singers," said the control tower. "They have a concert to make."

"Oh, the Rooftop Singers, 'Walk Right In.' Sure, let 'em go," said the 707.

Show biz, I guess. The entire absurdity gave us a night's worth of shaking our heads.

Lynne had left Skip, gotten her own place on the upper west side, and hired a live-in housekeeper to take care of Heidi when she went on the road. When she had us up to rehearse, I will never forget the look on her face. It was a face of self-ownership. Her whole spirit seemed freer than we ever saw it. It was probably the first time in her life she had ever been fully in charge of her world, with no one to lord anything over her.

Her independence was not to last long, probably for a whole lot of reasons. One of them was the tax system, which did not allow her to deduct the expense of the live-in housekeeper. This meant she couldn't afford to live on her own and be on the road. Had she been willing to call the housekeeper a "secretary," as far as the IRS was concerned, that would have worked. She wouldn't do that.

She moved back in with Skip, and that's when her drug use began showing up on the road and her days with the group became numbered. Our last performance together was in an amusement park. It was in June 1964. The park wasn't amusing. She gave us both kisses, and that was the last time we ever saw her alive.

Lynne had come from the world of jazz, but she sang folk songs as songs, and with more feeling, space, and authentic musicianship than any other singer around, save Edith Piaf, Billie Holiday, Texas Gladden, or any one of those original people who came out of the Ozarks.

At first, it seemed it could work without Lynne, once we found a replacement. But our essence was gone. Lynne had been a sprite who spirited the corners of our sound. She had brought an authentic joy to our music, the kind of thing that makes you feel you're glad to have lived to hear that. And, as a performer, when she gave you a look while singing some song, or threw in a line from in back of the group, her total aliveness was present, and your insides were got. She wore her heart on her sleeve, and when she left, the creative synergy of the group disappeared.

Although we kept going—did a tour of Australia with Judy Collins, Bud & Travis, and my hero, Josh White—not only did Lynne's leaving kill our inner momentum, but the singer-songwriter movement had started with Dylan. Folk music, as we had known it, was on the way out. And there were the Beatles. Then drugs and drums without swing would take over the industry, and even jazz began to fade out. Once you got stoned, anything swung. Donald Duck could be hip.

We could have done covers of songs such as "Blowin' in the Wind," but it wasn't our kind of thing, any more than "I'm Just Here to Get My Baby Out of Jail" or "Stardust" was. I thought Dylan's asking "How many roads must a man walk down before you call him a man?" was an eloquent question, as regards prejudice, and he did it with poetic potency. But, I wasn't sure the answer could ever be found in the wind, as it were. Prejudice's horrors were sown in the wind. It was a well-intentioned idea, but the feelings it evoked seemed like a salve that could make a dark and festering wound feel good for the moment, while the infection ran deep and would lie ever more hidden as time plodded on.

Whatever the case, we could never do music because it was trendy or popular. We had recorded Duke Ellington's "It Don't Mean a Thing," which was as far from folk as it gets and one of the best things we ever did, but it was more like bringing that into folk rather than expanding our options. Dylan, along with many others—including Paul Simon, Joni Mitchell, Don McLean, and James Taylor—were showing us that we had to write our own songs if we were to survive.

I had been seeing Joni's psychologist until I met a songwriter, Pat Street, at the Limelight, a coffeehouse bar, not far from the Christopher Street stop on the IRT subway. Pat and I began writing songs for the group, among other things, and I no longer felt that I needed chitchats with a comforting psychologist. I now had another woman in my life to cover old frailties.

Our songs often turned out to be wrong for the Rooftop Singers and right for elsewhere in the world. The group's contract with Vanguard was ending, as well, and we were in search of a label. Of all companies, Atlantic showed interest—the label of Otis Redding, Ray Charles, and the Modern Jazz Quartet. It didn't make sense, but an interest was there. We got Johanan Vigoda, a hot music lawyer, to handle a deal.

Vigoda sat on the edge of his desk in a rumpled beige suit, wrinkled white shirt, and loose-hanging tie, eating yogurt and wheat germ out of the yogurt container. Between eager mouthfuls, he shouted: "What are you doing, dealing with those guys? Artists are *schmucks!* . . . Artists are *schmucks!*" Then he kept gobbling the yogurt. He knew the business up sideways and back, and he could be tough because he knew how things were. With the Tarriers, once, I had seen him rip into a roomful of music publishing executives with his outspoken manner and reduce them to blithering idiots.

He wondered, as well, what they wanted us for at Atlantic, but he got us a deal, along with an advance. We had let go Lynne's replacement, Pat Street joined the group, and now we signed with Atlantic. Yet, the question remained: "What did they want us for?"

43

"Way down in New Orleans, got that lion's club . . ."

The Abyss and the Arrogant Doctor

Ahmet Ertegun, the president of Atlantic—born in Istanbul in 1923, dark-complexion, bald, black-rimmed glasses—wore a goatee and was chauffeured around in a Rolls Royce. As cool as they get. He wore well-tailored suits, but I didn't think he was trying to impress anybody, or be someone he wasn't.

The idea of being on a hip label like Atlantic felt as if we were, perhaps, coming up in the world. Ertegun came right to the point. If the Rooftop Singers recorded 1940s Andrews Sisters–type songs—"Chattanooga Choo-Choo," "Boogie Woogie Bugle Boy of Company B," songs from that era—we could make hits with our sound.

Right on the mark! Creative idea! And it fit for a contrast to the angst of the times, the war in Viet Nam being not the least of our problems. It wasn't, however, about making hit records, *per se,* as we sat in our skins. For us, it was about making hits that came from our musical blood, whatever that was. Although the songs of the '40s were part of the American psyche and what I had heard on the air as a kid, they were not what I felt I could get under my fingers. They may have been where I was from, but not where I was now.

Ertegun ended up putting us with a folk-rock producer, Felix Pappalardi, who couldn't get who we were; or we couldn't get with who he was. Viet Nam was still raging, and the existence of the draft drove me crazy. If ever there was an abrogation of inalienable rights—the whole point of the country, the draft was it. "My Life Is My Own" was a song Pat and I wrote protesting the draft, and Atlantic released it. I'm not sure any radio station played it, but with the power of Atlantic, somebody must have. Nobody bought it, for sure.

The group's destiny seemed destined to remain as it had begun, with its introduction of the twelve-string guitar to popular music, and a nod to the genius of Leadbelly. By 1968, bookings had slowed, Bill was writing plays, Pat and I were eager to do our own thing, it was time to move on.

Life is a breathless ordeal, in all of its wonder. You really don't know what's around the next corner. You may think that you do, but it seldom comes out as you dream it. For me, it would twist in the wind in hurricane seasons and I'd never know when they were coming, or from which direction. I had a friend, an English professor. He and his wife and two boys had moved to a college out west—he'd known my father and liked him a lot, and that made him family; he was suddenly killed in a tornado, along with one of his sons. Left another hole in my sense of existence. Life as it happens. So, there came a covenant I would make with this life; you could call it The Journey Within. I could say that I had to go in, that even I fought it at first, but once I got used to the values involved, I found it compelling, more vital than anything else I was dreaming about or hoping would happen.

Had I found a religion, a politic, a salvation of sorts, a group of people I could have meditated with, marched with, blown things up with, if I'd had a child, anything other than just being me, I might have felt more secure. But I couldn't join things that seemed like a place to hide deprivations or the ills of a somewhat impoverished soul. I needed it real, as music had been.

Pat and I were doing everything possible to promote our material. We even plugged in, at one point, went electric. With Scott McKenzie, Susan Manchester, and Bill Svanøe, we recorded "No Reason to Cry" for Vanguard. They released and promoted the hell out of it. For publicity shots, we wore Lone Ranger masks and named the group Project X. It was a typical teenybopper, loved-and-lost lyric, with the twist that there was no point in crying, as this "lost love" was a jerk. The chorus went, "My cryin' is over. My cryin' is over. My cryin' is over, got no reason to cry." After nothing happened, Maynard said, "We took a bath on this one."

Pat's and my romance was not matching up to the romance in most of the songs we were writing, however, an unpleasant surprise to us both. The complex incompleteness of a love can sneak up over time, in spite of your dreams.

> I got somethin' on my mind
> Somethin' good that's hard to find.
> Somethin' you don't happen on every day.
> Tell you what I'm thinkin' of.
> You're the one I'll always love.
> Maybe that's what's makin' me feel this way.

We wrote what we believed in and hoped for rather than complaining about what wasn't happening, or figuring out what was wrong, or making the choice to move on. This left me, again, at loose ends, shall we say.

At the same time, an ad in the *Village Voice* began bringing me students who wanted to learn the guitar or the banjo, and the process of teaching gave me some solace and a sense of my deeper creative self, which I needed. No two people could learn the same way, or had the same patterns or fears; I had to be inventive, creative and vigilant. When the last student of a day walked out of the apartment, however, and I was alone, the shadowy abyss would be waiting. I learned not to go there, and to think of who the next woman might be: someone to patch up the hollows. It was no way to live.

Short, bug-eyed, arrogant, sturdily built, with kinky brown hair, tougher than nails, Lonnie Leonard, M.D., could drill holes through your brain with his eyes. Some people's eyes flit away all the time, or they never make contact; Leonard's never let go. All that was clear by the end of our first session.

He drove a big red Honda motorcycle, as well as a tan-colored Cadillac. I don't remember if he'd been a scrapper when he was a kid, if that ever came out, but I think it did. He kept a knife in his car, just under the left side of the seat, in case of an attack, and if he was with a woman, he walked in the streets with a spike in his fist. He saw the city as seriously dangerous and was fully prepared not to let it get him or whomever he walked with. Before I learned what he felt about the city, however, or anything else, I could tell that this guy could get into a fight if he felt he had to. In the navy, he had been a flight surgeon. Upon quitting the navy, he went into psychiatry.

His office/apartment, in one of the projects downtown, was way the hell east, at 21st and First Avenue, and a pain in the ass to get to. He'd had a decorator furnish the place in contemporary-sterile, with modern comfortable couches, at least, though the paintings on the walls were quite uninspired. You could tell what they were, but the artists hadn't been to the temple.

But, bullshit the man, you could not. It was like he could see through your face to the back of your skull. Nothing got by him. I saw him as arrogant, even though he often would say, "If you find it different than I'm telling it, you let me know. Because I need to know where I'm wrong." I would want to find out if he was straight-on about that.

Beneath a deceptively soft-spoken style, tough emotions lay under his skin, with an underlying sense that we were, after all, dealing with life-and-death issues. Okay, that I respected.

I'm letting you in on a few things about this creepy, complex human being because he represented a turning point. A new way to deal with my inner being. Of all the imperfect people I'd ever meet, everything stopped with this guy and took on a different direction.

The third time I went to his office, he queried: "Are you a good introspector? Do you know who you are and what's going on?"

"Yes." I replied. I had been sharp since I was a child, always able to tell whether people were phonies or not. And I didn't remember ever having been wrong. Further, I had been singing songs about inner feelings most of my life.

"Do you have any depression around?," he asked.

I had to think about that, but my answer was "No." My problem with the abyss and my acute loss of self-value had not been about being depressed, as I saw it. It had been about the invasion of inexplicable terror.

"You are not a good introspector, and you have a lot of depression," he said, as if to say, "End of that story."

"The nerve of this asshole!" I thought. I knew who I was in terms of those things. "Who in hell did he think he was, after no more than three sessions?!" I would not be coming back.

I didn't have the balls to cancel the session right there. I made another appointment, knowing full well I would call during the week and cancel him out. More than one way of skinning a cat.

Several times, I picked up the phone with the idea he wouldn't answer and I'd leave a straight message. "Something came up." Not quite a lie, if not the whole truth. I kept thinking, however, "Is that who I want to be?" I ought to be able to answer in kind, be as straight as he would, if I were to live up to who I sort of figured I was.

I hadn't liked how he'd looked, what he'd said, how he'd said it, where he lived, but I needed somebody—that much I knew. Although I decided to make the next session, I was forearmed, and I would be ready to challenge the bastard at any misstep.

Sitting in front of his desk and watching his face was like being a suspect, like when my uncles had interrogated me about how I got along with my mother. Except that I didn't feel judged by the guy. It was an issue of the state of my own inner judgment coming to grips with what life had been like since the last time I was here. Sitting across from his face in that hot seat was this idea that, "Here, you don't lie, you don't cover up, you don't hide." If you feel like a jerk, or a loser, or downright depressed, it's going to come out anyway, so be tough enough to let it be known. Fearless. And often I didn't know where I was or had been, until I walked in and sat in that seat.

That I didn't know shit about what I did with my mind, and that I was depressed most of the time, didn't take long to find out. Nevertheless, I kept waiting to catch him.

44

"But forgetting what I say,
You can dream you're a Chevrolet . . ."

The Possible
Dream Song

A child sat crying. Endlessly crying. It was the way he was crying that got me. In front of Leonard's apartment building, I was sitting on a bench looking into a community playground, a thirty-by-thirty–foot sand-covered area. It was all I could do to keep from crying myself. When I went up for my session I shared this, attempting to show how fearlessly in touch with my feelings I was. Leonard's response: "Why did you feel like you had to hold back?"

"Well, there were women around," I said, "and I didn't want to appear unmanly."

"Do you actually think," he said, "that if a woman saw you crying over the plight of a child, she would think you unmanly?"

I knew the answer to that. Far more important, however, was that I hadn't thought about the issue, yet I had picked up a way of thinking about it that had me afraid to be who I was!

End of that story and the beginning of the rest of my life.

I was filled with these sorts of things, an anthill of erroneous attitudes and misunderstandings about life that cut off my balls, separated me from the heart of my soul, and advertised to my own sense of self that I did not have the courage to be who I was. It's one thing to let out the feelings that resonate to a song, then send them out from a stage to an audience, where permission is given. Quite another to do that in everyday life. And to stand up behind it. I could be angry, of course, but tears were a weakness, I thought. From here on, life began to be about gaining the strength to be who I actually was, or

wanted to be. Not like a show-off, a bully, or a whiner, but just playing it straight. The covenant began to take shape.

Pat and I remained good friends, although no longer living together, and we finally finished taping our own album for Vanguard.
Meanwhile, I was putting together a banjo instruction book. One mid
afternoon I'm sitting on my bed, I've got pages, tablature and drawings all over the place, and the phone rings. This is the winter of '75.
"Hello!" I'm impatient. This guy says his name is Lorenzo Music, and
he wants me to come to Hollywood, be in a folk group and part of a
television series.

"Sure, Charlie." I couldn't take seriously someone who claimed
his last name was Music, and who kept his voice so low on the phone
I could barely hear it. I mean, hip is one thing, inaudible another. Half
annoyed at being interrupted, I told him I was busy for at least the
next month on this book. He said he'd call back. After I'd hung up the
phone, having been full of myself, I wondered if he wasn't for real.
Did I just throw away stardom? The days in that month rattled past,
and no call from the West. I nearly forgot it.

And then came the call. At that point, Vanguard was adding strings
to Pat's and my album, *The Possible Dream*. The title song, a calypso.

You can dream the possible dream,
Baby, if you try, if you try.
You can dream the possible dream,
If you try, if you try.
And I bet you there's a way
You can start to get it today.
Don't be shy, don't be shy.

You can dream the possible dream,
Baby, don't be shy, don't be shy.
You can dream the possible dream,
Don't be shy, don't be shy.
If it's something you believe,
Even somethin' hard to achieve,
If you try, if you try.

But forgettin' what I say,
You can dream you're a Chevrolet.
You can dream you are a spy,
You can dream you're a pecan pie.

But rememb'rin' what I say,
You can learn the banjo to play,
You can even learn the guitar, too,
You can learn to tie your shoe.
You can learn to lose some weight,
You can ask the man for a date,
You can learn anything you could be,
In this whole reality.

Lorenzo and Henrietta Music, Bob Gibson, and I would make up a quartet, if I passed the audition. There would be other actors and writers, but we all would take part in the writing, and we'd all get to act in the skits. With Grant Tinker at the helm, MTM would produce and syndicate the series, to be called "The Lorenzo & Henrietta Music Show." I got more prepared than I'd ever been in my life before I took off for L.A.

Joni had married Bill, they had moved to L.A., and our friendships remained. We had been a good part of each other's lives for at least twenty years. This meant I had a great place to stay when I got to the coast. Joni was a successful director and had the top acting class in L.A. Bill was writing and selling screenplays. I envisioned that if I got this series and moved to L.A. (one way or other), I'd get into the movies. A possible dream, for damn sure. If Pat's and my record took off, I'd be in a fix, but I couldn't wait to find out about that. Off to L.A.

45

*"When you were a child, child,
Did you want to be listened to? . . ."*

The Teachers

The block of years between the Rooftop Singers' folding in 1968 and this trip (1976) to L.A. (and, hopefully, stardom) began with a painfully boring job in an "art" studio that made replicas of Avon packaging. I needed to bring in some money and the ad in the paper mentioned the words *art studio*. When packaging is designed, manufactured, then folded around the product, it's never quite perfect enough to photograph for advertisements. "Art" studios like this one constructed photo-perfect replicas: to-a-sixty-fourth-of-an-inch perfect. That is a hard-to-read ruler I had to work with! Whatever skills I'd picked up from my father, as a painter, were completely irrelevant here. The job was disgruntling—to-a-sixty-fourth-of-an-inch disgruntling.

I'd find myself in the streets on gray days fantasizing I was a secret agent—James Bond, more or less—my raincoat and umbrella-gun. Walking along, as I swung the umbrella, I'd shoot at unfriendly cabs, driven by spies, and, of course, many cabs were driven by spies in those days. I even thought this was funny, though I wondered if I wasn't losing it. In contrast to these sorts of games, the underlying question that pervaded my actual life, particularly since therapy had started was *"Did I want to live my own life or somebody else's?"* And maybe that's always the question.

Why it hadn't dawned on me to put an ad in the *Voice* and teach the guitar, before taking this job, I haven't the vaguest idea. In looking back, I may have been too depressed to be creative about shifting my life. But the ad would change things.

The first student I had was a criminal lawyer who wouldn't come to my apartment, but lived not far out of the way on my way home from the packaging studio. He wanted to learn the banjo. I'd teach him to play some plucking pattern and then write it down, so he could see what it looked like on paper and practice it later. All through the lessons, however, he'd get these calls. Somebody's kid had been picked up for car theft or murder; could they get this or that judge for some trial; how long could they hold someone in jail? His phone conversations were always intense, telling people what to do and not do, raucously calming them down, while constantly smoking these little Te-Amo cigars. I began smoking those things. Then he would come back to the table, pick up his banjo and sit, looking out from his face.

"Erik!," he'd suddenly shout, looking straight at me. "When am I gonna learn the banjo?!" Week after week, he'd say that. Only he wasn't joking, it was like he couldn't see the connection between interrupting the lessons all the time and not learning the stuff. Finally, I had quit the art studio and didn't want to come to his place, as it was no longer on the way home. He did all he could to get me to keep coming over, but I had to move on. I had learned about criminal law, about the clockwork of justice, and how intense it all is.

But the interplay with the people who came to my apartment for lessons became an integral part of existence; it wasn't just something I was doing to get by. I developed a passion for relieving the fear that most people had around music. The more time I spent, the more that old saying that, "Those who can, do, and those who can't, teach," struck me as ludicrous.

The process of convincing adult human beings that they're not born already knowing the stuff, and learning when to keep quiet—letting them take their own time, as they must—has a lot more to do with a passion for making things clear to a person than it does with knowing the subject, I found. The most brilliant musicians can have no idea whatsoever about how to teach what they know; and if they want to put down a student, for whatever their unconscious reasons, they have the power to do that in all kinds of ways. Stories from my students on that theme abounded. Now that I was working on my own underground psyche, these sorts of stories garnered my interest as never before.

In one session, Dr. Leonard said I was repressed. I would nail him, this time! I had been there awhile, and I knew I was open with all sorts of people. Not everyone, of course, there are people you're close to and people you aren't, but I made the decision to interview every student with whom I was easy and free, and build a statistic on how transparent and open I *actually* was. Maybe not in his office, but out in the world. I would bring him their names. It was going to be interesting to see if he would be true to his word about needing to know when he was wrong. The runt bastard.

Susan Warner was the first one I chose. We couldn't get through a lesson without laughing at something, and we easily shared our views about the pretentious pomposity of various people in folk music, as well as our takes on the state of the world. I knew she got who I was, and felt I got her.

"You're quite hard to get to know," she said. "It's like you have a bubble around you that is hard to break through."

I was dumbstruck. There was no way to argue with that. And I didn't need to interview others. I had chosen Warner because I was more sure of her than anyone else.

That was the last time I tried to prove Leonard wrong. From then on, I came off my high horse and made up my mind just to listen and learn what I could. And I made it my task to express who I was from then on, be as open as possible to anyone possible. It would be straightforward feelings, no need to sell something, just get myself out there. Something as simple as, "I like your handwriting" or "I just want you to know, I like talking to you." Little things of importance that expressed who I actually was in a natural, unritualistic way.

Along these new lines, I chose Susan Holt. She was another student with whom talking was easy. The river that ran through our exchanges, although I hadn't known the details, had made us good friends. It should not have been a big deal to say: "I'd like you to know I like talking to you."

She was across the room getting ready to leave. I was leaning against the edge of the doorjamb that led into my studio, getting ready to speak. My heart began pounding, my throat became tight, I had trouble breathing, my mouth was bone dry. I began feeling a touch of the abyss that had been such a threatening part of my life in that room. I forced out the words because that was the job; I wanted to be who I actually was. I heard the words in the room, thin and high, at the top of my range, with no feeling behind them.

She came back with, "I like talking to you, too."

Simple as that. I had nearly passed out.

"That's how it goes," said Leonard when I told him. "You get the words out, and then, the next time, you lay in the feelings. It takes practice."

Over twenty years later, while researching these times, I found out what lay underneath Susan's side of our lessons:

> I was young and didn't know how to deal with my husband, who was indifferent to my needs and who was not complimenting me for my contributions to the family, especially those of my helping to fix up our house, as well as working for his business. The only way I was able to describe it to our marriage counselor, at the time, was that I felt like a statue that was slowly being chiseled away at, and that now there was only a small piece of stone left. My lessons with you were an oasis in a storm of arguments, accusations, and a marriage that was becoming devoid of any loving feelings. What I was begging for at home, I was receiving from our lessons, and with no strings attached. Those moments have stayed with me for twenty-six years.

> After one evening lesson, you walked me to my car and we continued to talk. All of a sudden, it was 3 in the morning. "Oh my gosh!" I thought, "What will my husband think?" Of course, he thought we were having a sexual relationship. I explained that this could not be further from the truth, that you were not exactly Mr. Warmth, which was true, and that we had never even touched each other, except to shake hands.

> I remember discovering how our politics differed. I was mostly a liberal, and you were mostly some kind of conservative. Yet, our feelings about respecting other people's rights and being as courteous as possible to others were at the core of our belief systems. I remember vividly that one thing we both had experienced, and was one of our mutual peeves, was being with people who would proclaim they were concerned with all of mankind, but when they would come to your home, they would show no concern about their cigarette ashes falling on your new carpet.

Another woman refused ever to sing in my presence. I explained why this made it impossible to teach her how to play songs that I didn't know. Yet, time after time, she kept asking did I know this or that song, which I didn't. But, because she was the only one like that, I'd always forget, and ask her to sing me a verse. Out of the blue, this one time, she sang me a line from a song. She had one of the most beautiful voices I'd ever heard, beyond any of the contemporary well-known female singers of folk songs. It was naturally sexy, which made it unique, it was deep, and it flowed with a natural grace that only a gift can provide.

"Hey!" I exclaimed, jumping back in my seat. "You're the one who won't sing, for Godsake! Why?"

When she was a little girl, one of her teachers had said she was tone-deaf and told her not to sing with the class. Mortified, she had never sung since within anyone's earshot.

What she didn't know was that the tonal key the teacher was using wasn't right for the size of her vocal cords. In that key, no one like her could have sung with the class. She wasn't tone-deaf at all. But shaming a child, if you are an elder, is easy to do; and shaming a child in front of her peers works even better. It actually works pretty well with adults, on occasion. Once you know you can shame someone, your foot's on their neck. All you need do is to push.

I wondered how many times, and in how many ways, and over how many issues that kind of process takes place. Because it hurts, it sticks in the quiet of memory, and it gets carried forward. The hiding and fear become a part of one's life.

Child, Child

When you were a child, child,
Did you want to be listened to?
When you are a child, child,
When you were a child?

When you were a child, child,
Did you want to be hugged awhile?
When you were a child, child,
When you were a child?

CHORUS:
And Johnny, did they ever tell you
you were important?
Bonnie, did they ever tell you,
when you were a child:
What you thought and what you wanted
Should be fought for all undaunted,
Did anybody ever tell you . . .
When you were a child?

BRIDGE:
And people could take the time
To learn how to do it,
But it isn't just reading a book,
To somehow get through it.
'Cause a child doesn't know what to say
And it's so easy to be led astray,
Where their love could be strong,
Somethin' goes wrong . . . or they just fade away.

Out of these years, my view of the human condition evolved (along with my political slant, if you will), and I came to believe we are not interchangeable units. I saw that we all live alone, which is why authentic relationship, friendship, and functional families are so damned important. These years amounted to more than getting to see how complex we all are; I got to see how different we are from each other. We learn differently. I could teach no two students the same way. Hidden secrets of unearned shame and disorientation lock people away from their talents and core sense of being. Then they build up defenses.

I was riding the bus across town on Fourteenth Street and saw a woman lying dead in the street, having been hit by a truck. I'd never seen that before. But I had a sense that New York was wearing me down. With my trip to L.A. coming up, I was dreaming of Hollywood, stardom, a new sense of hope. It was time to move out of the doldrums, get out of New York, and go west, seeking fortune and fame. And as Joni had often explained, "The reason for becoming a star is not for the fortune or fame. It's so you can choose the best parts."

46

"I went to the animal fair,
The birds and the beasts were there . . ."

Hollywood
(From the Casting to the Arbitration) and a "Woman" on Trial

Santa Barbara, California. Two hours north of L.A. Early morning. I jogged down the line of the railroad tracks overlooking the ocean at the Miramar Hotel, and would be back before breakfast. There must have been a nude beach below the tracks, out a ways, because I saw a completely tanned woman, stark naked, walking along on the beach in the morning. It was like coming across a deer in the woods, only a hell of a lot better. "That's how life should be lived," I thought, as I watched her. Something so unashamed about this dark-haired creature. I began liking southern California.

Lorenzo and Henrietta Music, Bob Gibson, and I were stuck by the ocean up here for two weeks, working on songs and seeing if we could create a quartet of some kind. That's how the audition was held. A fine way to start off in Hollywood, I thought. By the end of the first week, Lorenzo informed Gibson and me that we were on board. At the end of the two weeks, I flew back to New York, sublet my apartment, then came back and stayed with Joni and Bill up on Mulholland Drive. This was serendipitous, as Joni was having problems with her life, and my years of therapy had put me in a place to be of some value to her, just as she'd been to me when I'd lost it.

"The Lorenzo & Henrietta Music Show" would be an hour of T.V. a night. There would be skits, Lorenzo and Henrietta would interview the rich and the famous, the quartet would sing, and a friend of the Musics would be making things out of wood. (On prime-time television? I didn't get that.) We were all contracted for twenty-three weeks, with additional options so that they could keep the show going—we all hoped, forever.

Our set was built in one of the sound stages at the Burbank studios, a huge barn of a place. I had my own parking space, with my name on a sign. The back lot had sets of old New York streets with 1940s automobiles parked at the curbs. When I saw a fake street of New York, even though I knew it was all a facade, I caught it as real, as if I were a camera. Farther out was a set of an adobe Mexican village.

We ate lunch in the commissary along with other actors working on the lot, dressed in their makeup and costumes. Someone eating lunch in a cardinal's outfit, or a covey of actresses dressed as Native Americans—I saw them as a cardinal and Indians. The only thing missing at lunch were the words "Camera! Action!" On closer perusal, the Indians' Caucasian features, although disconcerting, did not stop the experience from being a creative turn-on. The only turn-off was the Lorenzo & Henrietta Music Show.

Lorenzo did not have enough time to head up the writers, rehearse the skits as well as be in the quartet, and create five hours of T.V. per week. As a quartet, we were awful. No schedule was ever stuck to, and the show slipped apart at the seams. Joni stopped by and pointed out that the director didn't even know how to call out the shots in the booth when we taped. In a month and a half, it all folded.

The lawyers at MTM told us we could sue for payment on the remainder of our contracts and we would probably win, but it would take many months. Right then, they would settle for fifty cents on the dollar. It was over. Grant Tinker *et al.* were not going to honor their word if they could possibly help it. Natural Hollywood. All of us had to find our way back to our original lives and move on.

Still looking for stardom, I enrolled in Joni's acting class, began doing scenes and monologues and singing songs in the class. She insisted, however, that I sing whole verses of songs to specific human beings, and not look away.

Entrusting my insides to someone right there, face to face, as it were, was emotionally out on the edge. Standing in front of a concert-hall audience was playtime compared to the pressure of this. A large audience is an anonymous whole, and although you connect with in-dividual people, your eyes slip away, and you try to reach everyone. And everyone is, in a way, no one specific at all. They're all at a dis-tance and safe.

I began understanding what telling the truth was really about on a stage. It's a lot more than furrowing the brow, being earnest, and pulling up familiar emotional energy—emotional masturbating, as Joni called it. It is more about telling it like it actually is, from the core, moment to moment—not quoting yourself. You might laugh, for ex-ample, where you thought you'd be sad, or be sad where you thought you'd be angry. Whatever is there, you allow. You get real. You un-plug the pipes, step away from concerns over making a fool of your-self; the moment will guide you. It's about one simple pattern, the thing I had gone to folk music about in the first place, and what ther-apy wanted, and the covenant I was seeking to honor: a process of being authentic. Acting is not a pretending, as it turns out. It's finding true parts of yourself that relate to the moment at hand, and letting those parts fly.

One day, as an actor, however, when I'd finished a monologue, Joni said, "You're getting good enough now so it's time to get eight-by-ten glossies, go get an agent, and start looking for work."

"Doing what!?" Out of nowhere, it seemed, that question came into my conscious awareness. Her statement was like one of those super-bright lights the cops shine in your car late at night at a road-block. I hadn't connected the dots. You don't just find yourself in a movie, you work your way up. If some theatrical agent thinks that your glossy looks right, you get sent out for readings, and you might get a small part in whatever film, or a walk-on in whatever sitcom. If you got a running part in any sitcom whatever, you'd thank your lucky stars. And that made me want to throw up.

Never, to that point, had I seen a sitcom that I'd want to have any-thing to do with or that inspired me to do what the actors were doing. My dream was to be in a movie, on the big screen, that said something important, good versus evil, and the good guys win out: *Casablanca, The Maltese Falcon, Separate Tables, Bridge on the River Kwai.* Stories of human survival and courage.

I had found the process of acting rewarding, what little I'd done on "The Lorenzo & Henrietta Music Show," but when I had seen my-self in a skit through a monitor, I hadn't liked how I looked, walked, sounded, or spoke. If I were a casting director, I thought, I wouldn't have cast me in anything.

"Time to get eight-by-ten glossies and an agent?" The minute I heard that, the dots came together, and my heart silently went out of the quest. I looked at Joni and nodded, knowing I'd probably get glossies but would never get around to sending them out a whole lot.

In the meantime, I'd found a new partner, Marissa, a kind and supportive human being, a Child Welfare and Attendance Specialist in the Burbank Unified School System. Her endless stories of life in the schools confirmed ever more acutely my convictions about parents as well as the school systems they palm their kids off on. I wasn't sure which were worse, the parents or the schools, by and large. It seemed all rather hopelessly grim, the closer I looked. It didn't seem grim to her, though, she was good, did her job well, loved the energy of difficult kids. She had a great spirit.

Then life took a turn, as it so often does, and I'd get to look a bit deeper into what Hollywood often is like, under its skin—maybe more than just Hollywood. Joni got the job of directing a movie and got me hired as a Creative Assistant to the Director.

A movie begins with the casting, and I was right there for the start of it all.

This actor took a hard-boiled egg and a restaurant salt shaker out of his raincoat pocket, licked the shell, sprinkled salt on it, and began eating the egg, shell and all, as he tried saying the lines of a scene. The shell cracked as he ate, making a mess on the front of his raincoat and on the floor, bits of egg yolk and whites everywhere. He talked with his mouth full. You know, being a tough guy; he was auditioning for the part of a mobster, an enforcer. Somebody else got that part.

The movie, *The Check Is in the Mail*, written by Bob Kaufman, starred Brian Dennehy and Anne Archer. It was about a family man, a pharmacist who gets fed up with "the system" and decides to leave it, while continuing to live in his suburban neighborhood. He tries digging a well, for example, in his back yard so he won't have to deal with the city water supply, mistakenly punctures a water main, so forth and so on.

The two things I'd heard about Kaufman were that he had dumped a pail of garbage in a bathtub while his wife was taking a bath, simply to see her reaction; and he had written *Love at First Bite*, a take-off on the Dracula legend. George Hamilton and Susan Saint James starred in that one. Thus, he had Hollywood currency as a writer. I found him to be an adroit, outrageous, stream-of-consciousness talker, who always had the stub of a cigar in his mouth. He had a wide, roundish face, intense darting eyes, thinning brown hair combed over one side of his head to the other. This one day, on location, he wanted to stroll, as he ranted and raved.

"Joni is such a great director," he raved. "If she wasn't a woman, she would be world famous." I didn't mention that she already was. I just tagged along, as "The Listener." I felt this was part of my job.

Shaking his head, looking intensely down at the ground as he plodded along, entertaining he was, except for the smell of his soppy cigar now and then.

Kaufman proudly told Joni he had run into the producers in Hawaii, that he'd wanted a hundred thousand dollar payday, and told them he had a script, which he hadn't. In fact, he didn't even like them, called them "The Coyotes," and thought they were sleazy. Kaufman was like a con man, very smart, very quick. He and is wife drove a white, rented Rolls Royce; I was sent to get something out of it, once. When the door closed it sounded much like a Chevy.

In the middle of the shoot (at somebody's house in the Hollywood hills), two guys in dark suits walked into our trailer one afternoon. Something about low-level accountants, theatrical agents, and CIA people lets you know, instantly, that they are not actors or part of the film crew. Actors would be more believable. These were completion bond guarantors. These guys are supposed to protect the investors' money, seeing to it that the movie comes in under budget. The head honcho of the duo told Joni she was shooting too much film. She told him she didn't think so because she had looked into the issue, and knew from the editor how much film she was using and that it was a lot less than other Bob Kaufman films usually used.

"I have an idea!" said the head honcho. "Why don't you just shoot the takes that are going to work?"

"What a good idea!" Joni exclaimed. "Why don't you just come right on the set and tell me which ones those are going to be?"

He backed out of the trailer, along with his buddy. We never saw them again.

Kaufman (who was also producing) suddenly left the picture for some other project in Europe and was gone. When he came back, he wouldn't speak to Joni, not on a phone or anywhere else. His reason?

"He couldn't speak to her because he couldn't say 'fuck you' to her, because she was a woman." That was the message she got. What in hell did that mean? There was no one on earth to whom this guy couldn't say "fuck you." And what was his problem? No communication whatever, no reasons given. I never did trust guys who put garbage in their wives' baths, sucked on cigar stubs, and ranted and raved.

Joni had taken a cut in her fee so that she could put together a director's cut of the film to be seen in a preview, in front of a paying audience. That's how directors can prove their work works. When push came to shove, the producers did not want to pay for the preview. To cut costs, they put her in a post-production house that was used for porno films. It had only seven tape heads, whereas a feature film needs twenty-three.

She had to go to arbitration at the Director's Guild for her rights under her contract. Such people as Frank Morris and John Badham came and testified on her behalf. Morris was a film editor who had been nominated for an Academy Award and had won an Emmy for editing. John Badham was the director of *Blue Thunder,* starring Roy Scheider.

As we waited for the arbitration to begin, the arbitrator and the producer began discussing the country club to which they both belonged. A good-old-boy thing was going between them that could have swallowed a southern politician. I have no proof that the arbitration went against Joni because of that bonding, or that Joni, being a woman, did not belong to The Club, but the hairs on the back of my neck stood on end as I sat in that room, and I am convinced that that's what went down, as they chatted about their last golf games. I'd seen other things, too, as the shoot went along, stuff I took for granted as part of the job when you deal with people. Brian Dennehy, for example, I didn't think he would have given Joni the crap that he did, had she been a man. Then again, I'd heard he had been a Marine, fought in Viet Nam or Korea, maybe that was his problem.

In any event, I hadn't seen how women, as a general rule, were treated unjustly. I had carelessly thought all the hoopla on that was cooked up by women who didn't have lives of their own or were unlucky in love. Those rose-colored glasses were now blasted away, big time.

Anger, frustration, and regret were the feelings with which I left that arbitration. Not only was Joni a friend and one of the few people I'd ever known whose integrity was as true as the ocean, but it was my job in this context, I thought, to fight for her at some level. If your friend is being railroaded, you say something. Should I have stood up in that arbiter's court and yelled, "Bullshit!"? That crossed my mind. It would have felt good, but I was not representation, or the judge of appeals, or the Incredulous Angel of the Innocent. I was just a small cog below decks, as it were. Until now. Is this how one's destiny works? As in, never give up?

At the wrap party, the producer asked Joni to dance. While they were dancing, he told her that they had been stealing raw film stock off of the truck and selling it back to the film company, charging it off to the film, and then blaming her. He thought it was funny. Nothing personal, really.

Waiting all night for the lighting crew to light a small section of street for a drive-by shot, or the setting up of extra vegetables and fruits to be dropped from a net in the ceiling of a grocery store, so that an automobile crash through the front of the store would look good on film—all the details and mechanics that go into the magic of movies could not have inspired me more. I harbored the idea of making these kinds of paintings one day. I wouldn't write my first screenplay until fifteen years later, however. Not only would it be a Western, but it would dramatize how women have so often been treated and thought of and feared. The script got to the finalist stage at the Sundance Film Lab, though it did not get produced. More than anything else (and this was the lesson): writing that script was the most compelling adventure I've ever had. It used more of my being than anything else ever had. And, in this world of possible dreams, it still lives, as it waits in the wings.

Many years later, by the way, when Dennehy ran into Joni in Santa Fe, New Mexico, he did make amends. For me, that makes him a man of high order.

For a couple of years, I became a volunteer counselor at the Southern California Counseling Center. My years teaching music as well as my own therapy predestined a passionate interest in this. I seemed to be getting results, and felt I was good at the work. It's all part of the same basic journey, a working at getting it real.

As life had gone on in L.A., by and large, I was unsettled. The idea of living the rest of my life in North Hollywood unsettled me further. As well, in New York, you always knew who the crazy ones were. In L.A., you seldom could tell. I felt I needed to go. Marissa and I had an apartment on Moorpark, North Hollywood, not far from Vitello's, a great place that made pizza as good as New York.

Leaving Marissa, however, held a deep sadness that none of my other partings contained. All partings of good will, where people have tried to be lovers, are endlessly sad. I heard one family therapist say that people never completely divorce. On the whole, I experienced a desolate feeling of still needing to find more of what I was about. At least throw out the old clothes I was wearing.

47

*"It was on a Wednesday night, the moon was shining bright,
They robbed the Glendale train . . ."*

The McAlester Kid

Folk music—the original stuff that came out of the hollows, bayous, mountains, prisons, railroads and farmlands of the South—speaks to the heart of the human condition in unique and eloquent ways. This raw mix of nineteenth-century culture filtered up to the North through such collectors as Carl Sandburg, and John and Alan Lomax, and through such singers as Josh White, Burl Ives, Leadbelly, John Jacob Niles, Pete Seeger, and the Weavers. It exploded into a national phenomenon with the Kingston Trio, and that explosion created a loam for what D.J.s would eventually call "folk," a form of American pop culture driven by singer-songwriters who wrote out of New York, Chicago, and L.A. apartments. This new music transmuted into something all of its own. It became intellectual, philosophical, political, and romantic, often more from the head than the gut. "Both Sides Now," "Bridge over Troubled Water," "Turn, Turn, Turn," "Blowin' in the Wind," "Green, Green," "I'll Never Find Another You," "Don't Think Twice, That's All Right," "Parsley, Sage, Rosemary, and Thyme," "The Times They Are a-Changin'," "American Pie."

The musical threads of the original music, however, with their straight-on minimal statements from the guts of this life, only got stronger over the years, as the music called Country evolved. Its use of everyday language turned on its end, hooking the senses, became the literary mark of the country songwriter, which has such a simple and eloquent genius that it goes by, often times, hardly noticed, like life itself:

"I've always been crazy but it's kept me from going insane."
—Waylon Jennings

She got the gold mine. I got the shaft.
—Jerry Reed

I'm a man of means by no means, king of the road.
—Roger Miller

If I were the man she wanted,
I would not be the man that I am.
—Lyle Lovett

Because you're mine,
I walk the line.
—Johnny Cash

Not all music sends people in a different direction, however, than where they were headed, as urban folk did. Of interest is the journey that folk music led people on, how the course of lives changed, as even the music itself. I've gone to the street, to a member of the audience, my friend, Ada Brown, to illustrate this. I call her the McAlester Kid because she took off from McAlester, Oklahoma, and through this American music, found balance and wisdom.

There was a place called Teen Town in McAlester, where teenagers would go and they would play records and dance. Typical rock-and-roll stuff, fairly vanilla at the time. The other music we had was one of those million-decibel-scream-across-the-airwaves stations, with those ranting-and-raving disc jockeys playing the same sort of stuff.

We were on a trip to Oklahoma City for a church function with one of the priests and we went to a coffeehouse called the Buddhi. This place was exotic and appealed to me totally. There was an air of mystery there. People dressed differently, had mannerisms that were foreign. I heard a different character in folk music. Joan Baez, Judy Collins, Peter, Paul & Mary.

But then, when I heard Dylan, my first year in college, *Highway 61 Revisited,* I liked the radical aspect. I recognized him as a departure from Baez, Collins, and Peter, Paul & Mary.

The tone in McAlester had always been even. You did things that were right. It was gentle, honest, and pleasant. But it was also controlled and modulated. There was nothing about Dylan that was modulated. At one point, I felt like my first twenty years, I wasn't living life, like the books in grade school about growing up in Any Town,

USA, where everybody does the same things. Dylan would talk about being lost in the rain in Juarez, and all of this pathos.

There was a sense of the individual I got from Dylan. He had a lack of respect for authority I liked. He said, "To live outside the law, you must be honest." It was against the law to smoke pot, or take acid, and you had a sense of living outside the law, if you did. Yet, there was a camaraderie there, and a trust. It felt like a theme we were living: here we all were, these outlaws, living outside the law, but we're honest. If one of us was being dishonest, we would say, "Hey! Wait a minute; let's be straight, here. What's happening?" So one of us should go to jail for one joint while people in the government were stealing the wealth of the whole country, one way or another?

At that point, I began to recognize the corruption within the political system, how slimy it was, with all the pretenses of being honorable. In Texas back then, you could spend thirty years in jail for possession of one joint. We may have been doing things that were illegal, but they weren't dishonest. And they weren't hurting anybody. There was an implication that you could easily live within the laws and not be of moral character. And the proof of all that has been coming out ever since, with Viet Nam, Watergate, Oliver North, the federal government in relation to deficit spending, and the banking system. It goes on and on and on.

And the people in McAlester had no interest in seeing all this. It was interesting, going back to see my parents and saying, "Please, look what's happening to you. You're slipping into the Dobie Gillis mindset, watching the sitcoms on T.V., buying all the processed food, becoming like the rest of Middle America." And my not wanting them to become part of this amorphous group of unthinking people, while the country was being stolen right out from under their eyes.

Then the psychedelic era of the Beatles came along, and by the end of that next year, I was starting to take psychedelics. I shifted into acid rock and the music coming out of the San Francisco scene: the Grateful Dead, Jimmy Hendrix, the Doors, Jefferson Airplane, typical psychedelic music. A lot of that message was about experiencing stuff, inner journeys, and about introspection, as well. It just wasn't very well-thought-out introspection.

Then I began roaming around, hanging out down in Mexico, trying out different situations, seeing what was going on, how the rest of the world was living. I was doing everything I could to "do my own thing." That was the phrase: not just to accept secondhand values handed down, without looking at them with my own kind of measuring stick. A lot of the values that were handed to me were actually quite valid, but I needed to make them my own.

If it were Dylan or the blues, at this point in life, it would be what I felt like listening to in that moment, either one. I could no longer listen to Peter, Paul &Mary and that folk music stuff. It would be dated for me. It was a beacon to me then, but it can't be that now. I think if I had to hear "Puff the Magic Dragon" one more time, I would want to throw up.

Book V

Political Quagmire

48

"How happy I am when I crawl into bed,
A rattlesnake hisses a tune at my head . . ."

Startled Journey

What I first understood about the culture of Communism was that somebody else would run everything. That the government would, ultimately, make all decisions about what to invent, manufacture, and sell, including what music to record and play on the air. But who would they be, these deciders? I mean, somebody "official" would have to decide. What kind of people would those jobs attract? (People who aren't doing a thing, or teaching it, tend to enjoy power over those who are.) I imagined it all as a divine right of bureaucracy, with everyone looking over his or her shoulder. People's feet on your neck. I began having nightmares about having to perform for some huge committee in order to gain their approval to record in some state-owned studio, if it all came to pass. I'd always wake up from the dream before I'd have to sing (in a dark theater full of 2,000 officials), glad I was in bed in a New York apartment, free to follow my musical dreams, no matter how anyone else understood them.

My father had not been a political person (he was more of a cynic); my mother hadn't been into politics, either; and neither had I. Until, suddenly, I was, and found myself in the Weavers—one of the most political groups that ever walked on the face of the earth. Kind of funny, I think. Perhaps I'd been blinded by a myopic perspective, not having seen all of this from the start, but I had little interest in left or right-wing understandings of things. Those weren't the lenses I wore. But as I walked into political thought, government bureaucrats running our lives struck me as totally ludicrous and against everything I'd come to believe without even knowing I'd come to believe it.

As for the actual politics of the individual Weavers, I knew little about them. We had never had a political discussion. I saw Lee as persnickety, drinking more than he should. Freddie seemed hyper; Ronnie, the salt of the earth. And their music was about eloquent struggles in all of mankind: "McPherson's Lament," "Darling Corey," "The Greenland Whale Fisheries," "Run Come See," "Last Night I Had the Strangest Dream." They didn't think blacks should be discriminated against. Seeger, whom I had replaced, had recorded union songs with the Almanac Singers. On his own, he was known to be left, but so what? Social security is left. There was the Working Men's Party as early as 1829 in New York. In the near-recent past (the '40s), the United States had seen a Marxist movement, a labor movement, a Communist Party advised by the Soviet Union. But the cloth of that movement was perilously woven, and many had left it when the horrors of Stalin were exposed in the "secret" Khruschev report to the Twentieth Congress of the Soviet Union, 1956.

As for me, I wasn't there in the flux of that entire landscape; I was in upstate New York sailing a boat on a lake, or in Baltimore, Maryland, hoping one of my uncles would buy me a Martin guitar, or at Washington Square.

My conflict began with the fact that the Weavers—as an icon, as a name, out of a past I wasn't a part of—stood for an underground Marxist agenda. People would acknowledge me from a distance at parties, for example, knowing I was a Weaver, and wink, like the people in the French underground winked at each other in the movie *Casablanca:* "Bravely and quietly, we know who we are." But, I wasn't a "we." I wasn't aligned with any political group; in fact, I would end up in a political no-man's-land, believing there were crooks of one kind or other on all ends of the political spectrum. I did not feel comfortable aligning my name with anyone's platform or slogans; I had never felt comfortable wearing a uniform, even in the Boy Scouts—although I did like the idea of badges for a while. Never got very far with the Scouts, I'd lived too long in the woods with my father, and we were like Indians more than like homesteaders. (Never did meet an artist who put stock much in badges.)

Seeing Michelangelo's *David*, reading *Atlas Shrugged* by Ayn Rand, and having my marriage to Joni falling apart were three major events that coalesced in my psyche to prompt my leaving the great group for political as well as musical reasons. The message I got from Rand had an effect I could not have expected to get from a book (I wasn't much of a reader and never had been). But Rand's writing, as I read it, said that I had a right to my life and that I should be true to it. Rather mundane, having been raised in this country, perhaps, but as unwieldy as life began feeling, I found it attractive. It didn't solve any marital problems, of course, or stand me up to the image I saw in the *David*. But it was a thing to hang on to, a new path to follow, and it got me to think about the idea of actual freedom, and motives of human behavior, the matrix of political thinking.

Having a political conscience made leaving the group a bit easier, maybe, but I still didn't have a whole lot of certainty about where I should stand, just that I wanted to stand.

As the years drifted on, and the closer I listened, the ideas behind political movements did not seem to fit how humanity is in the streets. The expounded ideas had little to do with what took place after elections—quite the opposite, really. What I had expected the adult world to be like, when I was a child, was not panning out. I found myself shaking my head a whole lot and living at an appropriate level of shock, I would say.

49

"And I thought they'd left me all alone,
A long, long way from home . . ."

I'd Give My Life

Things can come back to haunt you. The great, the good, and the ugly: errors of judgment, records you wished you'd not made, performances you wished you'd not given, one or two that you liked; things you wished you'd not said, and, then, those where you nailed it. Not all haunts are bad ones. The songs and the women. The ones that I'd loved. The ones I had hoped would love me; those who were far from soulmates but helped me get through the night. If you're lucky, a surprise can come out of the past and fall into conscious awareness, letting you know that life is worth living.

Out of the blue, Joni began taking piano. This was in the mid-1990s, in Santa Fe, New Mexico. Out of our shared consternations and battles of life, along with a similar ethical standard, it was inevitable that Joni and Bill and I would end up in the same town. I had moved to Santa Fe in 1986, thinking I'd paint. Orangey earth, buildings made of adobe, rounded and soft, blue sky, purples and pinks in the shadows. I wanted to do the same thing with painting that I'd wanted in music: to offer a reason for living. When I discovered that I couldn't create thirty acceptable paintings per year, which is what artists do when they get with a gallery, I gave up the idea and kept most of the work. Later, I became ever so grateful for that. The work now reminds me of the inner places I went to in order to get where the paintings came from.

Joni and Bill were still happily married, and I lived twelve minutes away. While Bill was off playing golf on occasion, Joni and I would meet for a lunch or for tea and discuss the continuing battles of life. Now, added to this, was her experience of suddenly becoming a musician.

252

The details that make up the magic of music go mostly unnoticed by people who don't learn an instrument. Half notes and whole notes, three/four and four/four, sixteenth and eighth notes, notes that are dotted, compelling chord structures, syncopation: they all come together as a homogeneous whole and they're just what it is. Music. Whether it swings or it doesn't, rocks or just flows mellifluously, has to do with how it's all done. In the process of folk music, you learn these inner workings by the seat of your pants, simply by doing it, trial and error, year after year. But in taking piano and learning to read from a page, it happens right now. It's a process of counting stuff out right away, until it gets into your fingers. And then, after you've dealt with the cogs and the gears of the thing, a new world is there, and you can hear music you've heard all your life like you've never heard it before.

Joni began hearing things in the music of the Tarriers, Weavers, and Rooftop Singers that were blowing her mind. She began flipping out over this or that syncopation or dotted eighth note, so to speak, the odd phrase here and there that matched up with the words. She would insist on playing some C.D. in the car as we were on our way to wherever, wanting me to hear this or that nuance she'd found.

I didn't need this. I'd heard all that stuff. Above all, I did not want to hear the mistakes, or where I didn't live up to some expectation I'd had.

Not wanting to kill her experience, however, I suffered the listening. On Bishop's Lodge Road, headed downtown, as I stared out the window of the car, I accepted the twists in my stomach and drifted as far as I could from it all, while doing my best to acknowledge what she wanted me to hear. Riding along, outside of the car, as it were, and because I hadn't actually heard most of this music in years, I was surprised by a lot of it. I hadn't remembered how this or that song was laid down, how much effort and care had gone into the work, and how a missed note or a beat here and there made little difference to the overall feel of some piece. It's about giving the breath of hope to the sinews of life, after all, those invisible threads that, when struck, generate feelings of worth. It's not about numbers and math and being metronome-perfect. As I sat looking at cacti, piñon, and juniper trees, a song I had done with the Weavers came on. I was far enough outside the car, by this time, that I heard it as if from a distance, as if I had been transported back to when I was a kid, and as if I'd never heard this before. In that subconscious, uncritical moment, a thought drifted up out of nowhere (I could even feel my lips move to the words in my head): "I'd give my life to sing in a group like that."

Book VI

Reflection and Triumph

50

"Early in the morning, when it looked like rain . . ."

Train Ride

Gray wisps of a predawn sky accompanied the train as it entered New Jersey from the tunnels of New York. Even though I was hungry at five in the morning, I'd resisted the doughnuts in Pennsylvania Station. A morning's achievement. I was early, as I did not want to miss this train, and the station was pretty much empty. This gave me time to find a Robert Parker mystery at one of the newsstands.

Old curiosities about what sort of rooms lay hidden in the dimly lit tunnels leading out of the city, gave me a sense of being back home. As the train made its way out of the station, the blue lights that float in the darkness down there, along with the dirty old white ones and the occasional red one, triggered old feelings. My adolescence took place in New York, and I'd taken this train many times. A round-faced vendor, hair plastered back, would get on the train at Thirtieth Street Station, Philadelphia, and get off at Philadelphia Station; he would shout, "Almond Joys! Hershey Bars! Magazines!" as he came up the aisle. You could hear the song of his hawking the entire length of a car.

Conductors had their own way of hawking: "Wilmington, Delaware! All out fer Wilmington!" At the end of our ride would be: "Baltimer, Maryland! All out fer Baltimer."

I'd be traveling with my mother to visit my uncles and paint manufacturing. Those were the World War II years; I was nine, ten, eleven. The coaches were packed with soldiers and duffel bags, people sitting on suitcases, stuffy and hot. Everyone smoked. At the movies, in those days, you got a cartoon and a newsreel saying how many ships had been sunk, with footage of battles at sea. Most of my sense of the war came from the songs. "Coming In on a Wing and a Prayer," "Over There," "Roger Young," "Anchors Aweigh."

At the moment, rain had moved in and away from the New Jersey coast, and the landscape on my side of the train was misty and still, reminding me of hunting with my father in upstate New York. The gray began showing orange and red on the ocean side of the train, and the yellow November grasses, on my side, warmed with an air of good will.

I thought of Canandaigua contrasted with Baltimore, Maryland. How I'd loved the lake and its town, as a kid. It was so still one winter morning that the reflection of dock pilings, snow-covered stones by the shore, and the hills of the lake were in perfect reflection. Not a ripple. You see something like that once in a lifetime. I began sifting through other odd things, like the smell of the Coy Street Hardware—wooden cubbyhole drawers for bulk screws, kerosene barrels, pickaxes, wire and brooms.

I was back in the milieu of an East Coast thing, feeling train-safe and free to roam through a lifetime of thoughts. The foremost of which was the previous night's concert at Carnegie Hall, once again, as a Weaver. November 29, 2003.

The idea had crossed my mind that this would be my last hurrah as far as performing at Carnegie Hall. I hadn't expected to be there again, anyway. In fact, I had been working on letting go of my musical past. I had discovered a definition of what I was doing in life that had to do with the value of creative thought, in and of itself. Music was only a part of it. I had realized that art, as a principle, saved more lives than road paint; and I had found more of myself in the process of writing than ever I had in the process of music.

I had picked up an old book from my past, *The Art Spirit* by Robert Henri, on painting. He wrote something that summed up the whole thing, sort of an answer I'd needed for most of my life, and I wondered how I could have missed it when I'd first read his book. Paraphrased, it is that the object behind every true work of art is not the work itself. Rather, it is the attainment of a state of being: a more-than-ordinary moment of existence. The result, the artwork, is but a by-product of that state of mind, a footprint of that place from which the artist has found to create his or her art. It is more than the dishes from yesterday's breakfast. It is something more important, more essential than the subject the artist has painted (or sung about), something related to the creative nature of human survival.

But letting my involvement with music drift off seemed like that artist in the movie *Titanic*, played by Leonardo DiCaprio, who sank into the North Atlantic, having frozen to death, forever away from his love, his art, and his woman. It was an uncomfortable idea. I wouldn't be able to say, "I'm a musician," for example. I'd have to say, "I once was."

Lynne entered my mind. I'd always held the dream that one day I'd run into her somewhere, and we'd begin laughing again. Through Lynne's daughter, Heidi, I'd recently learned that Lynne killed herself in '79. Shot herself in the head. Among other things, she'd had lupus. Even after I knew she was gone, I couldn't get the idea of running into her out of my mind.

As I stared out at the New Jersey landscape, the entire Carnegie concert experience with all of its moments, from when I first got the call until the singing of Leadbelly's "Good Night, Irene," was a blurred happenstance, a series of disparate parts, which had settled uneasily. One moment or other came floating back, but it was like my whole life was flashing before me in pieces and bits. I began taking notes on the front and back pages and margins of the Robert Parker book I had bought.

The idea of being part of this concert had come out of nowhere, with less than a month to prepare, and there would be only three days of rehearsal. Not good. I did not want to fly to New York and I did not want to stop writing this book. I'd promised myself not to stop until it was done, and I'd broken that promise to record a C.D., go to Japan, and write a screenplay. "No more!" I had said. On top of it all, I was in the middle of selling my Santa Fe house and moving to North Carolina. Joni and Bill had moved there to teach. They were my family, and the New Mexico bark beetle seemed to be killing the trees. It felt like the right time to leave.

The show would be Arlo Guthrie's annual Thanksgiving Carnegie concert, as well as a tribute to Harold Leventhal. Harold had handled the Tarriers at one point and as many as thirty-two folk acts over the decades, never short-changing or screwing one person. A tribute to Harold was in order.

A documentary would be made of the entire event, and they wanted the Weavers to close the show. Harold had begun his career with the group, and the Weavers had inspired the entire folk thing. Not only would my expenses be taken care of, but I'd have enough extra money to buy a new couch when I got back to North Carolina.

Besides Arlo and us on the show, however, would be Leon Bibb (with guitarist), Theo Bikel (with pianist), Peter, Paul & Mary (and band), Sarah Lee Guthrie (Arlo's daughter), Tao Rodriguez-Seeger (Pete's grandson), and others. That many folk singers was, in my mind, a problem. In the old days, folk extravaganzas tended to turn into train wrecks, even at Carnegie Hall.

Although only a few of Woody Guthrie's songs were occasionally sung at the Square, his here-today-gone-tomorrow hobo-like existence had had its effect on the folk world. The idea of rambling around with no roots, sleeping on couches or in cars, making music of life's tough stories, free in the world with no obligations—this was an attractive life style. Woody had the genius to carry this off, however; his playing and singing came out of his purpose in life. He wrote his songs to the old folk tunes, and his style was as compelling to some as Leadbelly's had been to me, even though Woody had more of a made-up personality. Jack Elliott, for example, devoted his entire life to being like Woody. He even added the word "Ramblin' " to his name and left his wife and his child at home as he crisscrossed the country with performance and song, as Woody had done. In the documentary *The Ballad of Ramblin' Jack,* made by his daughter, we see her desperately trying to have an exchange with her father, for once! Only, he couldn't get there. He couldn't make it back—off in his head being Woody, unable or afraid to let go.

Dylan was also taken with Woody, of course, and rode off on his own lonesome road, picking up more on Guthrie's poetic concerns about social injustice than Elliott did. Dylan seemed driven more by the words, as an artist, and less by the music, but he went on to define his own unique style, a rhythm-and-rhyme style of writing, like an early white rap, I suppose, a cross between Dylan Thomas and Elizabethan balladry, maybe. Woodyesque, to be sure, but Dylan's style would resonate creatively with a generation of people who felt alienated from the plastic mendacity of American life without substance. "He went against the grain; he sang songs you couldn't hum; his personal appearance, the opposite of slick," related a friend who had hung out at the Square when she was thirteen. "I'd sit with his lyrics and listen to some song over and over, until I knew what they said. He didn't sing in a group. A lone voice. Like I felt alone."

But most in the urban folk world of my day were unable to live like Guthrie or write like Bob Dylan. Instead, they seemed to develop a lackadaisical manner toward the art of performing, as if that made them hip. It was like an unwritten syndrome that said, "Who cares about being in tune or on time?" It became a lack of responsibility refined to a musical life style. This phantomlike syndrome evolved, and people began using the word "folk" jokingly, as a four-letter word, as in, "Let's folk this up."

When I first heard that phrase, I wanted to vomit. I knew that this syndrome existed, but I saw the music as noble, unique, even heroic. And even though folk had transmuted to something quite different since my days at Washington Square, the idea of this phantomlike process appearing at Carnegie Hall for this upcoming concert gave me the willies.

After emailing Freddie that I couldn't make the event, he got on the phone and convinced me I could, as far as the logistics of selling my house, anyway. I did not actually have to be present for the sale of the house, he told me, or for the movers. The fact of his personal interest began changing my mind, but I'd need a week before I could get my head around this and say yes. Among other emotional things, I needed to sit down and see if I could still sing "Wimoweh." As soon as I hung up the phone, I dug out the banjo and got down to work.

"Intelligence" (E. Darling)
Oil on canvas, 30″ × 20″
Santa Fe, NM

"Archie's Place" (E. Darling)
Oil on canvas, 20" × 27½"
Santa Fe, NM

"Spanish Dancers"
Mono print, 14½″ × 19½″
E. Darling: Studies at Tom
Riker's studio, Espanola, NM

"The Girls"
Mono print, 14½″ × 20¾″
E. Darling: Studies at Tom
Riker's studio, Espanola, NM

"Game"
Mono print, 14½″ × 20¾″
E. Darling: Studies at Tom
Riker's studio, Espanola, NM

"Tree"
Watercolor, 10″ × 13¾″
Canandaigua, NY

"Treasure"
Oil on canvas, 12″ × 19″
Santa Fe, NM

51

"Roses love sunshine, violets love dew,
Angels in heaven know I love you . . ."

Lost Love and Found

Right before I left Santa Fe, I made up with a woman I'd recently split with, and we met for lunch. We had fallen in love rather quickly a few months before, and she had moved into my house within weeks, lock, stock and barrel. We'd had as much fun as I'd ever had with a person. I'd shove an odd thing under the bathroom door when she was brushing her teeth, she would laugh silently, and I'd think she'd not seen it. Because I'd heard no response, I was ready to shove something else under there, and then she'd whisk the door open and startle the hell out of me. We'd both laugh ourselves silly.

But things got confused and regretful between us, and within a month of her fitting her stuff into my place—a bureau, bookcases, an antique French chifforobe—she moved them all back to her place, which had not been re-rented. It was as if the arc of a five-year relationship compressed itself into a Twilight Zone space of a matter of weeks. I saw things about me, however, that I'd never seen, stuff that still needed turning around. Which I did. But the timing was off, and it all threw me back on my heels. Life had been endlessly like that, it seemed, yet I did feel I was learning—and that, maybe, it takes a long time.

When we met this last time, she owned her side of our discord, as I did mine, and told me that she'd run away. Our laughter returned. In the parking lot of the restaurant, we kissed and hugged deeply. All the rancor had been lifted between us. When I'd got the call to be a Weaver once more and finally decided to do it, it was with a similar feeling. My old political differences with them seemed unimportant, irrelevant to a life force that was beyond the usual political postures.

I felt that our country (our culture) was sick, and that the Weavers represented a pull away from that sickness.

It seemed that when huge corporations, as well as religion, get into bed with the government, bastards are born; then they suck on the breasts of Big Mamma government, which, of course, helps them survive. In 2003, it was as if another Dark Ages were creeping up on us, even creeping up on the world. I kept being reminded of a Mark Twain quote I had used in a collage I had called "Stars and Stripes":

> "Our country, right or wrong" . . . The nation has sold its honor for a phrase. It has swung itself loose from its safe anchorage and is drifting, its helm is in pirate hands.

Then, during one of the interview segments Jim Brown was filming (which never got into the film), I talked about how a lot of people's lives seemed to be invested in acquisitiveness, or in more money than anyone needs, and to no purpose other than more. Too many people wrap their emptiness around automobiles, hair styles, sunglasses, video games, drugs, and quick fixes, to the distraction of anything relevant, human, and sane.

Suddenly, Pete said, "Amen! I agree with everything you just said." In that instant, I could feel where our points of view meshed, and that even though I probably would not agree with his solutions, there was a place where we saw the same things and knew they were seriously wrong.

52

"This is not thirty-eight, but it's old ninety-seven,
You must put her into Canton on time."

In Search of Excellence

Our rehearsals were held in Peter Yarrow's Sixty-seventh Street studio apartment, he being out of town with Peter, Paul & Mary at the moment, and gracious enough to lend us the place. It was a tall, airy room, two stories high, with huge windows that looked toward the street where my mother's apartment had been. I was the first to arrive, 9:40 a.m. for a 10 o'clock start, Monday, November 24, 2003. I had walked the five blocks from the hotel and that anchored me fully back into the city.

Freddie was the next to arrive, at least forty years since I'd seen him. Although impatience was still part of his style, the moment I saw him, I understood it had never been about failings of mine, it's just how he was. He held nothing against me at all. And at that point, I could allow him to be who he needed to be, without using whatever that was to run myself down.

I felt like an equal, a buddy, a veteran of wars we'd been through. He had a new Martin, and his playing was as cool as it ever had been: simple, intelligent, direct, and on time. He had a way of spacing his notes that gave the Weavers their sound.

When Ronnie walked in with her familiar big smile, I was aghast. Her hair had turned white! Well, mine had, as well, but she walked with a cane, and I'd had no sense in my head that these guys would ever grow old or be frail. They were like movie stars, in my mind, and since I hadn't seen them in decades, part of me assumed they were as they'd always been. Pete's voice was nearly gone and he used some kind of hearing aid, but his spirit and power were totally present. Eric Weissberg walked in with his usual ear-to-ear grin. I had suggested he be a new Weaver, play and sing bass parts. Everyone went for it. He had been part of the bluegrass contingent in my days at Washington Square, like everyone else, a fan of the Weavers, had taken my place in the Tarriers, played on Pat's and my record, and he liked Chinese food.

The attention to detail, the getting little things right, and the listening and watching each other that prepares a performance are a reaching for excellence, even though that's not the word I would normally use. Each person wants it just right, according to how he or she thinks it should go. And if each person gets there, you've got a moment of excellence. That encompasses a struggle, a big give-and-take, a lot of diplomacy, and disgruntled remarks; but you hang in there and hammer it out. Your standard of how it should go shifts here and there, as you work in the context of who people are at the moment. You prepare to go to the center of where everyone's at, find some agreement down there, and bring back a musical sense that this life is a good place to be.

You can't rewrite it, either. You've got the one chance. Once you walk out on that stage, there it is, and you really can't fake it. There's an ecstasy to that, of course, unless you're repeating yourself, which the Weavers never did. Like Ray Charles, they were never quite slick.

Sound check and camera rehearsal on Saturday afternoon, the day of the concert, seemed to go well. We set the mikes in an arc so that we had the eye contact we desperately needed, especially with only three days of rehearsal. The sound in the monitors got set so that we could hear ourselves sing, along with our instruments.

Clearly, nobody was in charge, however, holding the whole thing together—in theater, they call it a stage manager. The phantom folk process was near; I could feel it crawling around in the wings. I'd e-mailed that somebody needed to be in charge, but I knew it was none of my business. Often I felt as if I lived in a parallel universe when it came to these sorts of things. Stuff that seemed obvious to me wasn't to anyone else. I had learned to let such things go after speaking my piece.

When the concert began sometime after 8 p.m., the picnickers and groupies, family and friends who had jammed up the dressing-room area took off for their seats. I grabbed a couch right away and lay down, keeping track of the concert through the speakers backstage. Two hours to wait, give or take. As some intros took as long as two of our songs, I *knew* it was coming. We would have to cut songs. At first, it was one; then, as we stood in the wings, someone told us to cut yet another. Freddie was furious. "Okay, cut only one," came the word. Although we knew it wasn't our concert, this didn't feel good.

One of the Carnegie people in charge of the hall couldn't believe it when he looked at the backstage monitor and saw the film's cameramen on the stage, between the audience and the performers. He was throwing a fit, making noises like he wanted to stop the show, even though thousands of dollars had been paid for the right to film there. Didn't he know how you make films? Had he not seen the camera rehearsals? I stood silent and mused. The phantom was near, and the folk devil was laughing.

Arlo's "City of New Orleans" still rings in my mind as the high point of the evening. I always feel good when somebody does something well.

When the doors to the stage opened as Arlo began introducing us, mentioning each of our names, a standing ovation exploded. This was the Weavers' hometown, after all. Since the 1950s, the days of Town Hall, whole families had followed the group and had gone to their concerts every year. Arlo, however, being out of touch with the details, didn't know that our mikes and the table we needed hadn't been set. It would be like a Marx Brothers scene, if we went out on stage before those things were done. We stood in the wings as the ovation lost steam. It may have been me that shouted for somebody to get off their asses and get the mikes set and our table out there. In any event, the stagehands woke up and got the stuff done.

When we finally walked out, it could not have been clearer that the mikes were all skewed, the sightlines were gone, and the mike heights were wrong. Amateurville. When we began singing, the sound in the monitors had nothing to do with what we had heard at the sound check. I could not hear the banjo or Freddie or Weissberg, on bass. When you can't hear a banjo, something is truly bizarre. The folk phantom had landed.

But your job is to sing for that audience. Any technical problems, you put them aside. No anger, frustration, or judgments allowed. You gather your resources, forget about magic, and get the job done, giving all that you've got. And when you go home, you live with it, hoping it went well enough for the people who devoted their money and time to come hear you.

Freddie had said on the phone, regarding how little rehearsal we'd have, that the Weavers had done some great concerts, some good ones, some only fair, but never a bad one. This one may not have been bad, the spirit was there, but it was as close as it gets. The audience gave us their love, their hearts, and their loyalty. But this was no way to leave.

Our part of the concert had a stillborn aura about it. After the concert, we didn't speak to each other, say any goodbyes, or look anyone straight in the eye. And for us to have been only fair was a tough one to swallow. You never feel good after that, no matter how much they loved you. It's never about being loved, in the first place, it's about getting it right, and then we shall see. This would have been a good concert to forget, but it's hard to forget the last one at Carnegie Hall.

But it didn't end there. Thank God it didn't end there.

53

"Risselty-rosselty, hey bombossity,
Knickety-knackety, retrical-quality
Willaby wallaby, now, now, now . . ."

Never Give Up

The film of the concert, entitled *Isn't This a Time,* was edited into a documentary artwork. Ill-fated songs and our delayed entrance were edited out; interviews were added and skillfully edited into the music; and it was scheduled to make its debut on September 17, 2004, at the Toronto Film Festival. Michael Cohl, the producer, a professional cat, with a low-key but elegant style, wanted the Weavers to come up and sing a few songs at the Elgin Theater, following the movie's debut.

This time, it was with a tight ship, captain and crew all as one, one for all. Michael Cohl provided the soundmen that handled the Rolling Stones' sound. We had two more complete days of rehearsal, a 1500-seat movie house packed to the rafters, and the film critic Roger Ebert, a fan of the Weavers, introduced us. We sang "When the Saints Go Marching In," "In My Mother's House," "Wimoweh," and "Good Night, Irene."

And we nailed it, this time!

I sang "Wimoweh" better than I'd ever sung it. We used to sing it in G, years ago, but I had lowered the key to F sharp to get the right mixed-falsetto that the high wail needs. The hollers happen on the tonic of the key (in this case, F sharp), but for one little note, I hit a whole tone above it, G sharp (a ninth). It was like reaching for hope, or survival, or destiny. And it felt like I got there. At the end of the show, Pete said, "Congratulations on hitting that G sharp." Pete always knows where everything's at, and what the notes are. It would have been nice, I suppose, to have made it this way at Carnegie Hall, but, in a way, it was sweeter. We performed on the apron in front of the curtain. The press was invited, flash bulbs went off as we sang. I could hear the whole group in the monitors—the bass, the two banjos, and Freddie's guitar—I could feel everyone's effort, apart and together, in time, and on time. It was like being in the movies. This was the moment I'd hoped for when I'd left Santa Fe. I just hadn't conceived of it with flash bulbs and press, and in Canada, a less violent place than the States.

Back at the Fairmont Royal York Hotel, an old-world building with elevator landings big enough for practicing tennis, Cohl threw a big party. At the end, I hugged Freddie goodbye. We had one of those exchanges you only can have when you've finally won in a creative battle. I kissed Ronnie goodbye, and her sense of good will, as it always had been, was a world of its own. I wanted to carry these moments as long as I could, and avoided the thought in the back of my mind, that we'd probably never see each other again.

The hotel was feeling too large and the hallways plain empty as I headed back to my room. I couldn't find Pete at the party, but I'll never forget the sense of his effort as we made it all work in those moments of truth. These people cared about life in a way that was truly electric, but without any electric guitars. It was a triumphant farewell and goodbye to an era of my life. It had been filled with the steeling of myself to this music, and to a hope of survival through that. I steel myself now, away from the world, to these combinations of words that hold on to the world in a way that experience doesn't.

As for the movie, if you've read this book and have not seen the film, chances are, the phantom won out.

On that train out of New York and into New Jersey, not only had I been unsettled by how we had done at Carnegie Hall, but I was headed for North Carolina, to a land where I'd never expected to live. I'd thought out the move, but nothing is ever quite as it seems until you get there and actually live it. Angst is a peculiar emotion, and once it is there, it seems to seek out other reasons for being. It was 2003 and the country lived under the threat of another attack by religious fanatics willing to die for their God and the idea of ending up with seventy-two virgins in heaven. I wondered if the world might not be brought to its knees by religious belief, the desire for virgins, along with the fear of what women are about.

Whatever the case, it struck me, as it had in the past, that something quite different could happen from what we've been doing. We don't have the information we need, and we don't have a whole lot of time. What we need may be out there, in pieces, blowing around in the wind, as Dylan might say, but it's not in a form or a place where it does much good.

Near the town of Rosetta on the delta of the Nile, in Egypt, in 1799, a French officer of engineers found a tablet of black basalt. Cut into this stone was a trilingual inscription, and it turned out to be the key to interpreting the Egyptian hieroglyphics. I think we need such a "stone" to decipher the human condition, an experiential guide for the civilized soul. I think we are missing the study of day-to-day human relations. Clearly, we don't know how to marry: the divorce rate isn't high, the marriage rate is low. Our culture is violent. Each day, on average, three women are murdered by their spouses or boyfriends, according to U.S. Bureau of Justice statistics, Special Report, October 2001. We do not know how to love, as a general rule. Any information we may have acquired, as a people—that which is commonly "known" about what relationship is, and what raising a child is about, is way out of sync with the human condition and what needs to be learned. The socialization of children at home and in school is such that it's a miracle they didn't start shooting each other a long time ago.

The land is awash in one terribly unethical event after another, from the depths of religion to the seat of the nation. The one thing I feel that we need, above all, is a University for Becoming More Fully Human: a college for parenting, a school for relationship, an institution devoted to finding the tools that can actually handle the problems of prejudice, suicide and, in general, the human relationship. We need to go to ground and repair the mess we are in.

Am I on a soap box? Well, maybe. It's how I've come to feel.

As a people, we have had our great moments, our heroes from all walks of life, sung and unsung, along with our crooks and our unfathomable idiots. Democracy empowers the foolish as well as the noble. From the bottom to the top. We have no reason whatever to strut, however, as some of us do.

At times, as a boy, I'd be put on the Lehigh Valley Railroad at night, headed to upstate New York to return to my father from visiting my mother. Taking a sleeping car, then, I would arrive the next morning just before dawn.

An old black guy, a night porter, worked on this line. I remember his cap and the heavy neat clothes he wore. If you left your shoes out, below your bunk, on the floor of the train, this guy would shine them by morning; not many traveling people wore sneakers in those days. All the people who worked on the railroad seemed to be neat. They seemed to do their work well and knew how to walk down the aisle when the train was in motion. It got so this guy would recognize me and me him, and we'd always smile at each other. I suppose that at ten or eleven, traveling alone, I wasn't hard to remember. Lying in the bunk at night with the shade up, watching the lights of a station pass by, snow coming down, automobiles with their lights on, was like a Norman Rockwell illustration, only hard-edged and cold, while I was safe on the train.

Leaving the coach through the steam in the morning, stepping down metal stairs to a snow-covered ground, my father would be there as I stepped off the train with my suitcase. It was always so good to see him each time, good to be thought of, cared about, picked up, and driven seven miles to our home by the lake. I didn't realize, then, how much we wanted to be present for each other's lives, how much I loved him. True love probably comes as one ages.

"Wheats" (E. Darling)
Oil on canvas, 14" × 17"
Canandaigua, NY

"Berby Hollow" (E. Darling)
Watercolor, 10" × 14"
Canandaigua, NY

Afterword

A few teachers, close friends, acquaintances, writers, none of them perfect, some whom I thought might be, but were far from it, made all the difference. The one thing they all had in common was a warrior passion for protecting the soul, a passion for common-sense decency, and for changing old patterns of thought and behavior. I see these people as warriorlike because of their passion. They were men, they were women, sensitive for themselves as well as for others.

I will turn, now, to honor the support they gave me by putting their code into words, a Soul Warrior Code, by bringing together the scattered ideas that still help me get by and inspire the journey. As Virginia Satir wrote:

> I want to join you without invading,
> Appreciate you without being judgmental,
> Love you without clutching,
> Invite you without demanding,
> Leave you without guilt,
> Criticize you without blaming,
> And help you without insulting.
> If I can have the same from you,
> Then we can truly meet and enrich each other.

Or, as Goethe said:

> No matter how close two people may be, there will always be infinite differences. And a wonderful growing up side-by-side can occur, if they learn to love those differences, so that each can see the other whole against the sky. A good marriage is where each is the protector of the other's solitude.

About the C.D.

The selection of songs and their order on the compact disk that accompanies this book speak to their resonant experience rather than to chronology, or when they were recorded. Also, I've included two versions of songs here and there, to show how changes took place.

"True Religion," for example, the first track, was recorded early in my musical life, while I was with Vanguard. It is followed by "The Dit Dit Song," an original composition recorded in Santa Fe, New Mexico in 2002. The latter implies the "true religion" or system of moral values I eventually came to, which has to do with "you'd feel so fine, if I could hear you loud and strong." The idea being that if we speak from the core of our beings, and then listen to one another, as a way of life, much would be known that lies hidden. Authentic life sequences could take place, and some level of sanity could then begin.

1. True Religion
   E. Darling. Based on traditional music. Man Alive Music, BMI.

2. The Dit Dit Song
   E. Darling/P. Street. Man Alive Music, BMI.
   Recorded in Santa Fe, NM; engineer: Scott Cadenasso; bass: Jon Gagan; drums: Ray Anthony.

3. I Love My Love
   E. Darling. Conceived from traditional sources. Man Alive Music, BMI.

   Back to my years with Vanguard, and an unusual theme for a blues: the love of one woman who hasn't left you.

4. Walk Right In Blues
    E. Darling, B. Svanøe, Gus Cannon, Hosea Woods. Peer Music.
        In truth, I was never satisfied with the song when we had the
    hit. I had tried endlessly to come up with something to give a re-
    lease, and a bit more to say. In the end, we just used instrumen-
    tals. But, for me, it got boring. For over sixty other artists who
    recorded the song, of course, it was fine. Finally, over thirty years
    later, my quest ended when I managed to come up with a bridge.
        No one I know has liked this addition as much as I have, except
    for the magnificent Hitoshi Komuro, the pioneering Japanese singer/
    songwriter who made acoustic folk music come alive in Japan. He
    understood, and he admired my willingness to do something new
    with a song that was already accepted. The nature of art, as I see it,
    is that it breathes over time; you see and feel different things in the
    prism, unless you keep quoting yourself over and over again.

5. The Cuckoo
    E. Darling. Created from traditional sources. Man Alive Music, BMI.
        When I first heard the banjo, it haunted my brain. Once I could
    play it, that's all I wanted to play, along with its songs. "I often have
    wondered what makes women love men. Then looked back and
    wondered what makes men love them." There isn't an obvious an-
    swer, or even what love really is. Such open spaces are the lure of
    the folk song. They often leave you alone as they draw you to them.

6. Bright Morning Stars
    Traditional Civil War awakening song. Recorded by Chris
    Stamey, Modern Recording, Chapel Hill, NC. Bass: Chris
    Stamey; drums: Logan Matheny.
        Of a still morning (the War Between the States rages on), and
    I imagine two women alone on a desolate Arkansas mountain,
    their parents are praying, their brothers are dying, "and day is
    breaking in my soul," an awakening to the idea of a personal life,
    in spite of all else, and a private connection to sanity. There is no
    soul like one's own, and someone to share it with.

7. Shady Grove
    E. Darling. Created from traditional source.
        There's nothing on earth like the mountain modal banjo, with
    its sense of the lonely, complete and at home within itself. Life is
    a thing we do live alone. This is why friends are so precious.

8. Woody
   circa 1955–56, New York.

9. Woody
   circa 2002, Santa Fe.
   E. Darling. Created from traditional sources, new words and melody added.
   Man Alive Music, BMI.

   Track 8 is the first song I fell in love with. Over time, some songs you drop, as you've sung them enough. This one I kept. And, as I changed over time, the song spoke to me differently. The second version speaks to that change. It can take quite a while to resolve things that gnaw at the back of your mind. And why not? I'm not sure there's a hurry for this sort of thing.

10. Child, Child
    E. Darling/P. Street, Man Alive Music, BMI.
    Recorded in Santa Fe, NM; engineer: Scott Cadenasso.

    How we hear children, if we do much at all, and *how* we have families and schools has more to do than anything else with the violence we have and with the so many hearts that get broken or bent as they find out what it's actually like in the world, contrary to how it was sold. They don't have the tools to adjust. Along with the fact that common-sense decency no longer is in general practice, the idea of a sane, peaceful world to live in hasn't evolved. People scream "peace" but with no substantive way to get there. It's about how people live in their souls, and how children are raised. Their needs are not met, and they become stuck at some level of anger or lethargy. For the most part, we haven't learned how to be married or how to hear children or school them. And the question remains, "When you were a child, child, did you want to be listened to?"

11. Jumpin' Judy (circa 1955)

12. Moanin' Dove (circa 1955)
    E. Darling. Traditional songs.

    From my sense of the scene, the endless alienation that black people have managed to endure, as expressed in their music, has such a compelling simplicity that I am always stopped cold by its sound.

13. Train Time
    E. Darling. Based on traditional sources, Man Alive Music, BMI.

    I grew up in the days of the train. The conductors had watches on chains, and the people who worked for the railroad kept themselves neat. A thing existed about pride in one's work, and about being on time. Robert Mitchum rode the boxcars to Hollywood. There was "Casey Jones," "Railroad Bill," and "The Rock Island Line." I marveled at how human beings had made those huge engines out of something you took from a rock.The enduring romance around trains and train stations doesn't translate to planes and airports. And when music stops being in time and you stop tapping your foot, you become just a little bit deader. "Time" is a great teacher—and rhythm, a life giver.

14. Santa Claus Is Comin'
    E. Darling. Man Alive Music, BMI.
    Recorded by Chris Stamey, Modern Recording, Chapel Hill, NC.
    Bass: Chris Stamey; drums: Logan Matheny.

    The greatest gifts we receive are those that we never unwrap from a box, that people don't buy, but that come from their understanding and caring. It may be receiving the right words when we need them or, as the song says, "could be a new love, or a brand new start."

15. Boll Weevil
    E. Darling. Based on traditional sources. Man Alive Music, BMI.
    Recorded in Santa Fe, NM in 2002 by Scott Cadenasso.
    Bass: Jon Gagan; percussion: Ryan Anthony.

    This is one of the classic folk songs, collected by Carl Sandburg as well as Alan Lomax. Just about every singer of folk songs in the old days had a version of this. For me, this recording came together, somehow, and I never sang anything better.

    This song has depths that I never got as a kid in Manhattan. It can take many years to get to the core of some songs, to get under the skin of what drew you to them, in the first place.

16. God Knows She Ain't No Angel
    E. Darling/Tom Riker.
    Recorded in Santa Fe, NM, 1995 by Scott Cadenasso.

    In Santa Fe, the Anglos, Hispanics, and Native Americans do not get along very well, for cultural, historical and present-day reasons. Yet, if you look, you always find people you like. And that's what this song is about.

17. Don't Go Mad
    E. Darling. Man Alive Music, BMI.
    Recorded in Santa Fe, NM, 2002 by Scott Cadenasso.
    Bass: Jon Gagan; percussion: Ryan Anthony.
    9/11 changed everything. It seemed to make clear, in my mind, how mad we've been going, for thousands of years, and how so many people are crazy at some level or other: alone, in groups, or as nations. Maybe this madness is part of our nature, I thought, and my turn will come. So I wrote: "Don't go mad, until you got to."

18. I Know Where I'm Going
    Traditional Irish song.
    When you get with a group, and you get with who those other people are, and they get with you, if you all manage to listen, the sum is more than the sum of its parts. You become part of each other and you become different, the music is different, and you couldn't do it alone, even after you've been there. It is a world of its own, this being together. If you let it run free, you work out a system of timing and hearing that's truly exquisite.We were the Tarriers. I was a Tarrier. And I was not like myself, and yet more like myself than I'd ever been. I played the banjo, sang harmony. Alan Arkin sang most of the leads, and invented the coolest guitar lines and harmonic structures. Bob Carey sang some of the leads. As time went along, the group became looser and freer, more playful, more improvisational, as I think you will hear in some of the music that follows.

19. Shadrack
    Traditional song.

20. The Banana Boat Song (Studio)
    A. Arkin, R. Carey, E. Darling. E. B. Marks Music, BMI.
    This one was tight.

21. The Banana Boat Song (Live)
    By now we had loosened things up and began to make creative adjustments that made the arrangements come alive.

22. Rock Island Line (Studio)
    This one was tight.

23. Rock Island Line (Live)

Again, by the time we got here, we were making new grooves every night, dancing within the old structures.

24. Aunt Rhody's Christmas.

E. Darling. Man Alive Music, BMI.

Recorded by Chris Stamey, Modern Recording, Chapel Hill, NC.

Bass: Chris Stamey; Wurlitzer: Chris Stamey; drums: Logan Matheny.

The inept and tragic misuse of young, trusting American warriors in Iraq drew these words to this song. It had to be here.

Tracks 4, 10, 16, 18, 19, 20, 21, 22, 23 by agreement with Wind River/ Folk Era Records.

Discography of Erik Darling

As a Member of Groups:

Folksay Trio, *American Folksay*, Stinson Vol. II.

The Tarriers, Glory Records PG 1200 (reissued Folk Era Records).

Les Tarriers à' l'Olympia Panoramique, President Records KU-23, Paris, France (reissued Folk Era Records).

The Tarriers, Columbia Records FP 1103, France.

The Tarriers, *Hard Travelin'*, United Artists UAL 4033.

Songswappers, *Bantu African Folk Songs*, Folkways.

The Folksingers, *Run Come Hear*, Elektra #157.

Erik Darling & Border Town, *Border Town at Midnight*, Folk Era FE 1417 D.

The Weavers at Home, Vanguard.

The Weavers, *Traveling On*, Vanguard VSD 2022.

The Weavers Almanac, Vanguard, 79100-2.

The Weavers at Carnegie Hall, Vol. II, Vanguard 79075-2.

Weavers Reunion at Carnegie Hall '63, Vanguard 2150-2.

Weavers Reunion at Carnegie Hall, Vol. II, Vanguard 79161-2.

The Weavers, *Wasn't That a Time*, Vanguard 147/50-2.

The Rooftop Singers, "Walk Right In," single, Vanguard '62 (used in the movie *Forrest Gump*).

Rooftop Singers, *Walk Right In*, L.P., Vanguard VRS 9123.

Rooftop Singers, *Good Time*, Vanguard VRS 9134.

Rooftop Singers, *Rainy River*, Vanguard VRS 9190.

Rooftop Singers, *Best of Rooftop Singers*, Vanguard 79457-2.

Rooftop Singers, *Best of the Vanguard Years*, 79749-2.

Rooftop Singers, "My Life Is My Own," single, Atlantic.
Darling & Street, *The Possible Dream*, Vanguard VSD 79363.

Solo L.P.s:

Erik Darling, Elektra #154.
True Religion, Vanguard VRS 9099.
Train Time, Vanguard.
True Religion (& Train Time), Japan, King Records.
True Religion & Train Time, Folk Era.
Child, Child, Wind River WR4013CD
Revenge of the Christmas Tree, Man Alive Records 101.

As Banjo or Guitar Accompanist:

Ed McCurdy, *Blood, Booze & Bones*, Elektra 108.
Ed McCurdy, *Songs of the Old West*, Elektra 112.
Ed McCurdy, *When Dalliance Was in Flower and Maidens Lost Their Heads*, Vol. I & II.
Ed McCurdy, *A Ballad Singer's Choice*, Tradition.
The Ralph Hunter Choir, *The Wild Wild West*, RCA Victor.
Rambling' Jack Elliot; Judy Collins; Jean Ritchie; Malvina Reynolds; the Chad Mitchell Trio; Oscar Brand; Johnnie Ray; the Kossoy Sisters ("I'll Fly Away," used in the movie, *Oh Brother Where Art Thou?*).

Index

Page numbers in italics represent photographs.

A

Al (Erik Darling's uncle), 14–15
Algart, Les, 53
Allen, Woody, 22
Almanac Singers, 250
America cruise ship performance, 111
Anders, Merry, 100
Angelou, Maya, 100
Anxiety attack, 196–200
Apollo Theater performance, 97, *104*
Archer, Anne, 238
Arkin, Adam, *85–86*, 89, 111
Arkin, Alan, ix, 78–79, 83, *85, 86*, 89–92, *96*, 107, 111, 118–119, 285
Arkin, Jeremy, 78, *86*, 89, 107, 111
Arlo Guthrie's annual Thanksgiving Carnegie concert, 259–261, 270–272
Isn't This a Time, film of, 273–274

B

Baez, Joan, 163, 165, 244
The Ballad of Ramblin' Jack, 260
Baltimore Paint and Color Works, 13–14
"The Banana Boat Song," ix, 77, 78, 79, 89, 93, 97–102, 285
"Barbary Allen," 35
Bard College performance, 37–40
Basie, Count, 18, 53, 54

The Art Spirit (Henri), 258
Asheville Folk Song Festival, Bascom Lamar Lunsford's, 31
Ash Grove Coffeehouse, 165
Assemblage point, 62–65
Atlantic Records, 219–221
Atlas Shrugged (Rand), 148, 250
"Aunt Rhody's Christmas," 286
Avon, 229
Axton, Hoyt, 176

Beatles, 219
Beersheba performance,
146–148
Beethoven, 7, 34, 61
Belafonte, Harry, 17, 97
Bennett, Tony, 91
Berle, Milton, 32
Berry, Chuck, ix
Bibb, Leon, 259
Bikel, Theo, 259
Billboard Hot 100 chart, 201
Biondo, Victor, 182
Birdland, 18
The Bitter End, 22, 165,
166, 202
Blacklist, 127, 165–166
Blacky, 173, *173*
Bleecker Street, 22
Blues, 21, 34, 167
"Boll Weevil," 284
Bond, James, 229
Border Town, Erik
Darling &, 287
Boston performance, 92–93
Bowery, 18, 46, 47
Boy's Town, 57, 59
Brand, Oscar, 17, 44, 75, *82*
"Bright Morning Stars," 282
Brown, Ada (McAlester Kid),
244–246
Brown, Jim, 268
Brown, Les, 164
Brownsville, Texas perfor-
mance, 57
Bud and Travis, 177
Buddhi Coffeehouse, 165, 176,
177, 181, 244
Buffalo, NY performance,
90–91
Burbank Unified School Sys-
tem, 238

C

Café Wha, 22
Calypso, 21, 97–98, 118,
191, 227
Calypso Heat Wave, 100
Campari on ice, 148, 151, 157
Canal Street, 196
Canandaigua, NY, 258, *266,*
277–278
Canandaigua Lake, 3, 5, *9, 10,*
158, 173, 187
Cannon, Gus, 177
Carbone, Peter, 22–25, 49
Carey, Bob, 77, *77*–79, 83, *85,*
89–90, 92, 100–101,
107–108, 111, 115, *121,*
123, 128, 285
Carey, Harry (wife of Bob),
107, 111, 115
Caricature, 22
Carlton, Carl, 77–78, 79, 89
Carnegie Hall
Arlo Guthrie's annual
Thanksgiving Carnegie
concert, 259–261,
270–274
first concert, 128–129
reunion concert (1963),
211–213, *215*
Carson, Johnny, 202
"Casey Jones," 92–93
Cash, Johnny, 244
Cash Box chart, 89
Castaneda, Carlos, 62
Catskill Mountains perfor-
mance, 78–79,
83–84, 128
Chad Mitchell Trio, 76
Chain gang, 19
Chalmers, Keith, 50, 53
Charles, Ray, 197, 219, 270

Charters, Samuel B., 177
"Chaucoun," 100
The Check Is in the Mail, 238–241
Chicago Civic Opera House, 52
"Child, Child," 233–234, 283
Child, Child (LP), 288
Chinatown, 11, 17, 47, 196
"Cindy, Oh Cindy," 88, 89
City Auditorium, 50
Clarence Williams jazz trio, 93
Cohl, Michael, 273, 274
Cole, Nat "King," 91, 107–108
Coleman, Ornette, 182
Collins, Al "Jazzbo," 76, 77
Collins, Judy, 75, 163,
    165–166, 219, 244
Color codes, 101
Columbia Concerts Manage-
    ment, 50
Columbia Records, 78, 89, 191
Communism, 249
Communist Party, 250
Compact disk information,
    281–286
Cooper, Clarence, 119, *121*
Corsack, Herb, 201, 202
Cosby, Bill, 22
Count Basie band, 18, 53, 54
The Country Blues (Charters), 177
Coy Street Hardware, 258
Cripscule (crepuscule), 6–7
"The Cuckoo," 282

D
Dallas Convention Center per-
    formance, 209
Darling, David Thurston
    (Dave), 3–6, *9–10,*
    172–174
Darling, Erik, *56, 77, 81–82,*
    85–86, 95–96, 103–104,

    121–122, 135–136,
    205–206
  as actor, 234–235
    The Check Is in the Mail,
    238–241
    "The Lorenzo & Henrietta
    Music Show," 228,
    235–238
  anxiety attack, 196–200
  as banjo and guitar accompa-
    nist, 75–76, 288
  banjo instruction book, 227
  childhood of
    brother of, 5
    with father, 3–8, *10*
    with mother, 11–12
  Lonnie Leonard, M.D. ses-
    sions, x, 223–225, 226,
    230–232, 235
  marriage to Joni (Las Vegas
    ceremony), 106–107
  paintings by
    "Archie's Place," *264*
    "Berby Hollow," *277*
    "The City Morose," *159*
    "Game," *265*
    "The Girls," *265*
    "Intelligence," *263*
    "North of Lake Como," *160*
    "Spanish Dancers," *265*
    "Treasure," *266*
    "Tree," *266*
    "Wheats," *277*
  political views, 249–250,
    267–268
  solo career
    LPs, 76, 181–182, 191, 288
    performances, 176–178
  as teacher, 223, 229–233
  train ride, reflective,
    257–261, 274

Darling, Erik (*cont.*)
uncles of, 13–15
as volunteer counselor,
241–242
see also Darling & Street;
Rooftop Singers; Tarri-
ers; Weavers
Darling, Joan Kugell, 75, 89,
98, 101, *105,* 106–107,
111–112, 114, 128–129,
137–138, 140–146, 148,
151–156, 161, 162,
172–174, 196, 198,
199, 228 , 234–241,
252–253, 259
Darling & Street, 221–223, 281,
283, 288
"My Life Is My Own," 221
The Possible Dream, 226–228
promotion of, 222
The *David,* 158, 161–163,
250, 251
Da Vinci, Leonardo, 43
Davis, Karl, 195
"Day O," 76, 97
DDT, 3
Dean Martin and Jerry
Lewis, 184
Decca Records, 78, 192
De Gaulle, Charles, 116
Dennehy, Brian, 238, 240, 241
Denver, Colorado performance,
176, 177
Desmond, Johnny, 100
Deux Chevaux cars, 114
DiCaprio, Leonardo, 258–259
"The Dit Dit Song," 281
D'Lugoff, Art, 22, 84,
89–90, 118
"Don't Go Mad," 285
Doors, 245

Dorsey, Tommy, 53
Dr. Zhivago, 5
Drifters, 202
"Drill, Ye Tarriers, Drill," 78
Dryden, 69, 70, 71
Duke of Iron, 97–98, *104*
Duomo, Il, 152
Dvorak, 34
Dyer-Bennett, Richard, 20,
62–63, 88
Dylan, Bob, x, 23, 163, 165,
219, 244–245, 246,
260, 275

E
Ebert, Roger, 273
Ed Sullivan Show, 97, 99
Edward, King, 98
Egyptian hieroglyphics, 275
Ein Gev, Israel, 139–140
Eisenhower, Dwight D., 116
El Cortez casino, 101, 105
Elektra Records, 35, 75, 76
Elgin Theater, 273
Elizabethan ballads, 21, 260
Ellington, Duke, 219
Elliott, Jack, 20–21, 30, 75–76,
260, 288
Empire State Building, 16
Epic Records, 78
Epiphany, 115, 165
Erik Darling (LP), 288
Ertegun, Ahmet, 221
Etruscan mimes, 19
Exodus Coffeehouse, 165,
176, 177

F
Faier, Billy, 23, 24, 29, 49
Fairmont Royal York Hotel, 274
Fasching, 117

Felton's Lounge, 24
15th anniversary concert
    (1963), 211–213, *215*
"Fireball Mail," 51
Fisher, Eddie, 89
Florence travels, 157, 161–162
Folklore Center, 23
Folksay Trio, 77, *77*, 287
The Folksingers, 287
Folksong Festival, Oscar Brand's,
    17, 44
Folkways Records, 19
Ford Company performance,
    217–218
Fourth of July parade, 118
France performance, 6–7, *9,*
    111–116, 118–119, 287
Freedom Rides, 187
French Riviera, 148, 152

G
Gare du Nord, 112
Gate of Horn Coffeehouse, 165
Gene and Francesca, 75
Geraci, Mickey, *27*
Geraci, Tommy, *27–28*, 38, 39,
    76, 169, 183, 190
Gerde's Folk City Coffeehouse,
    165, 202
Germany performance,
    116–117
Gibson, Bob, 32, 76, 174,
    228, 235
Gilbert, Ronnie, 63, *67–68*
Gladden, Texas, 218
Glasgow performance, 167–168
Glory Records, 84, 87–90, 93
"God Knows She Ain't No
    Angel," 284–285
Goethe, 279
"The Golden Vanity," 167

Gooding, Cynthia, 75
Goodman, Benny, 184
Gordon, Max, 93
Gordon Jenkins' orchestra, 63
Gordon's London Dry Gin, 175
Graham, Martha, 51
Grateful Dead, 245
Green, Freddie, 18, 53–54
Greenhouse, Dick, 31
Grey, Joel, 100
Guthrie, Arlo. *See* Arlo
    Guthrie's annual
    Thanksgiving Carnegie
    concert
Guthrie, Sarah Lee, 259
Guthrie, Woody, x, 17, 20, 21,
    29, 44, 62

H
Hamilton, Frank, 23, 30–32,
    211–213, *215–216*
Hamilton, George, 238
Hamilton, Ronnie, *216*
Hamlet, 84, 167
Haring, Lee, 75
"Haul Away Joe," 51
Hawes, Bess Lomax, 31, 34, 170
Hays, Lee, 63–64, *67–68*, 77,
    129–130, 132–133,
    135–136, 141–148, *144,
    149, 150*, 151–155, 168,
    215, 250
Heidi (Lynne Taylor's daugh-
    ter), 181, 183, 190, 210,
    218, 259
Hellerman, Fred, 63, *67–68*,
    127, *144*
Hendrix, Jimmy, 245
Henri, Robert, 258
"Henry Martin," 167
Herbie Mann band, 217–218

Herman, Sam, 51, 53–54, *55,* 57–61
Highway 61 Revisited, 244
Hillbilly Homecoming performance, 207–208
Hillel and Aviva, 75
Hi-Lo's, 100
Hinton, Sam, 39
Holiday, Billie, 218
Holt, Susan, 231–232
Homasote, 3
House, Son, x, 34
Human condition, 4, 99, 130, 234, 243, 275
Hunter, Mary, 49

I

"I Know Where I'm Going," 109, 285
"I Love My Love," 281
"I'm Just Here to Get My Baby Out of Jail," 195–196
Inquisition, 176, 177
Isn't This a Time (film), 273–274
Israel, 137, 139, 141
  see also Tel Aviv
Israeli airspace, 137
Israelis, 141
Italian Riviera, 148
Italy
  "The City Morose," *159*
  The *David,* 158, 161–163, 250, 251
  "North of Lake Como," *160*
  travel experiences in, 151–158
Ives, Burl, 18, 20

J

James, Harry, 164
Jefferson Airplane, 245

Jenkins, Gordon, 63
Jennings, Waylon, 243
"The Jewel Box Review," 99
Jose Quintero's Circle, 77
Journey Within, 222
Julia, 69–71
"Jumpin' Judy," 283
Jung, Carl, 19

K

Kameron, Pete, 78, 79, 137–138, 141
Katzman, Sam, 100
Kaufman, Bob, 238–239
Khruschev report, 250
Kibbutz, 139
King, Martin Luther, 187
King Lear, 167
Kingston Trio, ix, m 119, 163–166, 243
Kohler & Kohler, 53, 91
Komuro, Hitoshi, 282
Kraus, Bernie, 211, *215*
Kugell, Joan. *See* Darling, Joan Kugell

L

La Bonne Crêpe, 115
Labor movement, 250
Lake Como, 155–156, *160*
Las Vegas
  double your money, 105–106
  marriage ceremony to Joni, 106–107
  performance, 109–110
  prejudice in, 100–101
Laura (Erik Darling's aunt), 11
Ledbetter, Huddie (Leadbelly), 19–21, 34, 39, 43, 62, 169–171, 178, 183, 193,

197, 202, 222, 243,
    259, 260
Lehigh Valley Railroad,
    275–276
Leonard, Lonnie, M.D., x,
    223–225, 226,
    230–232, 235
"Les Tarriers, à le Nouvel
    Olympia Panoramique . . .
    votre Music Hall," 117
Leventhal, Harold, 138, 145,
    168, 259
Lewis, Jerry, 91, 184
Liberace, 109
Library of Congress record-
    ings, 19
Limelight Coffeehouse, 219
"The Lion Sleeps Tonight," 64
Little Italy, 11, 47, 48, 196
Lomax, Alan, 19, 30, 31,
    243, 284
Lomax, John, 19, 34, 170
Lone Ranger masks, 222
Lord and Taylor, 16
"Lord Randal," 168
The Lorenzo and Henrietta
    Music Show, 228,
    235–238
Love at First Bite, 238
Lovett, Lyle, 244
LSD, 209–210
Lunsford, Bascom Lamar, 31

M
Macambo performance,
    98, 105
Macbeth, 167
MacDougal Street, 22
Maggie Valley Gap, 30
Mambo bands, 18
Manchester, Susan, 222

Mann, Herbie, 217–218
Mann, Thomas, 157, 158
Mariachi bands, 57, 58, 62
Marijuana, 58, 59
Marissa, 238, 242
Martha Graham dancers, 51
Martin, Dean, 91, 184
Martin, Vince, 88–91, 92, 93,
    95, 118
Marxist movement, 250
Maryville, Tennessee, Hillbilly
    Homecoming, 207–208
Maslow, Abraham, x
Matamoras, 57, 59, 60
McAdams, David and
    Gloria, 111
McAlester Kid (Ada Brown),
    244–246
McCurdy, Ed, 18, 75, *81,
    93*, 288
McGhee, Brownie, 24, *28*, 167
McKechnie, Fred, 7
McKenzie, Scott, 222
McLean, Don, x, 163, 219
Medaglia d'Oro coffee, 3,
    48, 172
Merrill, Mac, 172
"Messieurs-dames," 113
Miller, Roger, 244
Milton Berle Show, 32
Mississippi State Penitentiary
    (Parchman Farm),
    187–190
Mitchell, Joni, 219
"Moanin' Dove," 283
Mocambo, 105
Modern Art museum, 11
Modern Jazz Quartet, 78, 219
Mollie (Erik Darling's mother),
    11–15, 19–20
Morrison, Peck, 208

Mosier, Volney, 11
Mott Street, 47–48
Mountain tunes, 21
"Mouse on a String," 42
Mozart, 34
MTM, 228, 236
Music, Henrietta, 228, 235–237
Music, Lorenzo, 227–228,
    235–237
"Musical Americana," 49–50
    auditions, 49
    bus, 52
    crew, 50
    itinerary, 52, 57
    Mexico, journey to, 57–61
    receptions/dinners, 53
    rehearsals, 51
    Sam Herman and, 53–54
    songs/acts, 51
Myles, Meg, 100
"My Life Is My Own," 221, 288

N
NAACP, 107
New Yorker, 93
New York University law build-
    ings, 22
Nonviolence training, 187
"No Reason to Cry," 222

O
Oklahoma City performances,
    176–178
Old Gold cigarettes, 7, 172
"Old Joe Clark," 51, 52
Olympia Theater, 112, 115,
    117–118
"Only If You Praise the
    Lord," 89
Ouspensky, P. D., 146, 148, 151

P
Paley, Tom, 21
Palladium, 18
Pappalardi, Felix, 221
Parchman Farm, Mississippi
    State Penitentiary,
    187–190
Parker, Robert, 257, 259
"Pay Me My Money Down,"
    88–89
Persona, 19, 20, 21, 23, 184
Peter, Paul & Mary, 163, 244,
    246, 259
Piaf, Edith, 115, 218
Pinball, hooked on, 92
Pinkus, Diana, 31
Pittsburgh, PA performances,
    91–92
Platters, ix
Plaza Hotel, 16
Poitier, Sidney, 87
Politics, 249–250, 267–268
The Possible Dream (LP),
    227–228
Prejudice, 6, 20, 101, 109,
    188, 219
President Records, 112
Presley, Elvis, ix
Price, Tony, 182
Project X, 222
Psychedelic music, 245

R
Rachlis, Bob, 31
The Ralph Hunter Choir, 288
Rand, Ayn, 148, 250–251
RCA Victor, 78, 97, 176, 288
Redding, Otis, 219
"Reds," 127, 165–166
Reed, Jerry, 244

Revenge of the Christmas Tree
    (LP), 288
Reynolds, Malvina, 288
Reynolds, Nick, 164–166
Rich, Buddy, 53, 184
Richard, Little, ix
Rienzi, 22, 71
Ripley, Leonard, 75–76
RKO Palace performance, *103*
Robbins, Jerome, 51
Robin Hood, 167
Rockefeller Center, 16
Rockefeller Plaza, 11
"The Rock Island Line," 39, 92,
    109, 170, 284, 285–286
Rodriguez-Seeger, Tao, 259
Rooftop Singers, *205*
    Atlantic Records deal,
        219–221
    first performances,
        202–203
    folding of, 222
    formation of, 181–184
    high school perfor-
        mance, 209
    Lynne Taylor
        departure from band,
            218–219
        drug use, 209–210
    Parchman Farm, 187–190
    rehearsals, 190, 194–196
    Steve's Ville, 207–210
    Tommy Geraci and, failed au-
        dition with, 191–193
Rose, Phil, 87–89, 118–119
Rosetta Stone, 275
Rosmini, Dick, 22–25, 29
Roulette, 98, 105–106
Rue de Montholon,
    113–114

S
Saint James, Susan, 238
St. Paul's Cathedral, 167
Samuelson, Dave, ix
Sam Wo's, 17
Sandburg, Carl, 19, 30,
    243, 284
Sands Casino, 108
"San Francisco Bay Blues,"
    211, 212
"Santa Claus Is Comin'", 284
Satir, Virginia, 279
Seafare Restaurant, 11
Sea of Galilee, 139
Seeger, Pete, x, 17, 19, 20, *27*,
    30–31, 63–64, *67–68*, 88,
    127–129, 132, 137–138,
    166, *215*, 243, 268–270,
    273–274
"Shadrack," 109, 285
"Shady Grove," 282
Shaw, Allan, 163
Show folk, 20, 98
Simon, Paul, 219
Skelton, Tom, 52
Smith, Kate, 63
Solomon, Maynard, 191–192
Songswappers, 287
Soul Warrior Code, 279
Sound system, 92, 101, 177
Southern California Counseling
    Center, 241–242
Soviet Union, 250
Spitzer, Robert S., M.D., x
Sprung, George, 16
Sprung, Roger, 16, 77, *77*
Square Theater, 77
Stalag 17, 189
Stalin, 250
"Stars and Stripes" (collage), 268

"State of Arkansas," 142–144

Steig, Mike, 23, 24

Steve's Ville, 207–210

Stinson Records, 77

Street, Pat, 219, 220, 281, 283
    see also Darling & Street

Sullivan, Louis Henri, 22

Sullivan, Maxine, 35

Sundance Film Lab, 241

Supper clubs, 90

Sutton, Ted, 30

Svanøe, Bill, 183, 187–191,
        188, 193, 195–196, 201,
        205–206, 207–208, 210,
        222, 228, 235, 252, 259

Symbol of *Man*, 162

T

Tacos, 58

Tarriers, *85, 96*, 111–119
    America cruise ship perfor-
        mance, 111
    auditions, 78–79
    with Clarence Cooper, *121*,
        123–124
    disbanding of, 79
    formation of, 76–78
    Fourth of July parade, 118
    France performance,
        111–116, 118–119
    Germany performance,
        116–117
    Glory Records, 84, 87–90, 93
    Les Tarriers (in Paris), *122*
    name origin, 78
    press party, 112
    as the Tunetellers, 76
    with Vince Martin, *95*
    Weavers, 133–150
        Beersheba performance,
            146–148

flooded bathtub experi-
    ence, 153–155
Florence, 157, 161–162
Glasgow performance,
    167–168
Italy, 151–157
Lake Como trip on
    scooter, 156
Milan, 152
Nice, 151–152
Pete Kameron and,
    137–138
public bathroom experi-
    ence, 156–157
Venice travels,
    157–158, *159*
    (*see also* Tel Aviv)

Taylor, Harty, 195

Taylor, James, 219

Taylor, Lynne, 183–184,
        185–186, 190–196,
        199, 201–202,
        205–206, 207–210,
        218–220, 259
    art of, 181

Tel Aviv, 137–150
    army concerts, 145
    breakfasts, 141
    dinner with Tel Aviv
        couple, 145
    Ein Gev performance (*Should
        I stop the concert*),
        139–140
    Erik Darling's sore throat, 137
    flat tire experience, 140–141
    heat, 138–139
    Lee Hays' physical pain,
        142–144
    P.D. Ouspensky writings, 146
    "State of Arkansas," 142–144
    Yarkon River, 138

Terry, Sonny, *28*, 167
Texaco Theater, 32
Thatcher, Nickie, 37–43, 61,
    62, 183
Theater Guild, 49
Thomas, Dylan, 260
Three Rivers Inn performance,
    98–99
Thunder, Johnny, 202
Tiffany's, 16
Tinker, Grant, 228, 236
Titanic, 258–259
"Tom Cat," 21, 202–203
"Tom Dooley," 24, 119,
    163, 164
The Tonight Show, 202
Toronto Film Festival, 273
Toronto performance, 210
Town Hall, 17, 62, 75, 128, 271
"Train Time," 284, 288
Train Time (LP), 288
Travers, Mary, 32
    see also Peter, Paul & Mary
Travis, Merle, 21
Troubadour Coffeehouse, 165
"True Religion," x, 281
True Religion (LP), 181–182,
    191, 288
Tunetellers, 76
Turpentine, 3, 4
Twain, Mark, 268
Twelve-string guitar, ix, 19,
    178, 183, 192, 202, 222

U
United Artists, 78, 119
U.S. Bureau of Justice statistics,
    Special Report (Oct.
    2001), 275
University for Becoming More
    Fully Human, 275

V
Vancouver, B.C. performance,
    176, 177
Vanguard Records, 191–192,
    201–202, 213, 219, 222,
    227, 281, 287–288
Venice travels, 157–158, *159*
Victoria, B.C. performance,
    176, 177
Viet Nam, 221, 240, 245
Vigoda, Johanan, 220
The Village, 22, 40, 46, 47, 77
Village Gate, 22, 128, 202
Village Vanguard, 17–18, 93,
    183–184
Village Voice, 223, 229
Vitello's, 242

W
"Walk Right In," ix, 177–178,
    192, 201–202, 218,
    282, 287
Warner, Susan, 231
Washington Square, x, 12,
    16–18, 20, 22, 77, *77*
Weavers, ix, x, 18, *67–68*,
    135–136
  on blacklist/labeled as
    "Reds," 127, 165–166
  Darling and
    conflicting political views,
      249–250, 267–268
    group's reception of,
      129–130
    Pete Seeger's reception of,
      128–129
    resignation from, 168
  human condition, songs re-
    flecting, 130–133
  Marxist agenda, 249–250
  reunion

Weavers (*cont.*)
Arlo Guthrie's annual
Thanksgiving Carnegie
concert, 259–261,
270–274
15th anniversary concert
(1963), 211–213, *215*
rehearsals, 269–270
see also Mediterranean
travels
Weissberg, Eric, 270, 271
Weshner, Skip, 181,
190–194, 218
White, Josh, x, 18, 20, 43, 44,
62, 93, 164, 219, 243
White Tower hamburgers, 24
Williams, Andy, 92
Williams, Clarence, 93

"Wimoweh," 64–65, 128–129,
147, 261, 273
WNYC, 17, 44
"Woman Lover Blues," 21
Women murdered by
spouses, 275
Woods, Hosie, 177
"Woody," 283
Working Men's Party, 250

Y
Yarkon River, 138
Yarrow, Peter, 269
see also Peter, Paul & Mary
Young, Izzy, 23

Z
Zaraya, Jeff, 192